The States and
Land-Use Control

R. Robert Linowes
Don T. Allensworth

The Praeger Special Studies program—
utilizing the most modern and efficient book
production techniques and a selective
worldwide distribution network—makes
available to the academic, government, and
business communities significant, timely
research in U.S. and international economic, social, and political development.

The States and Land-Use Control

Praeger Publishers   New York   Washington   London

PRAEGER SPECIAL STUDIES IN U.S. ECONOMIC, SOCIAL, AND POLITICAL ISSUES

Library of Congress Cataloging in Publication Data

Linowes, R. Robert
    The states and land-use control.

    (Praeger special studies in U. S. economic, social
and political issues)
    Includes bibliographical references index.
    1. Zoning—United States—States. 2. Regional
planning—United States—States. I. Allensworth,
Donald Trudeau, 1934-   joint author. II. Title.
HD260. L55   333. 7'0973   75-3624
ISBN 0-275-05210-9

PRAEGER PUBLISHERS
111 Fourth Avenue, New York, N.Y. 10003, U.S.A.

Published in the United States of America in 1975
by Praeger Publishers, Inc.

Printed in the United States of America

The authors bring a blending of perspectives together in this book ranging from zoning law and large-scale commercial development to city planning, political science, and university teaching. It is our purpose to point out some of the ways to effective state planning and land-use policy, both at the state level directly and at the local level as it is affected by state actions. The emphasis is on planning but not to the exclusion of zoning and other land-use regulations that give teeth to master plans. We would like to see local planning and zoning work better than they do, and we have suggested some avenues to this end in our recent book The Politics of Land Use: Planning, Zoning, and the Private Developer. We explain in the current book how the state can help make this a reality and in the process examine the politics of state government and the potential of the states generally in the comprehensive planning field.

The book deals with a relatively new concentration in American government, planning at the state level. It traces the history of state planning and land-use control and state involvement in regional, metropolitan, rural, and local planning and zoning, evaluates the degree of success associated with state activity in these areas, and suggests avenues for most fruitful exploration by the states in the future.

Although the study stresses planning, it is broader than that and considers state zoning, state land management activities, and other forms of state land-use control, regional planning and operating programs, metropolitan planning, and local planning, zoning, and subdivision regulation. It also demonstrates the interrelationship and interdependency between land-use controls and various public facilities and services such as sewers, water supply, highways, mass transit, parks, open space, air and water pollution control, conservation, airports, and others, and suggests means of making the links more productive of a coherent land-use and community development policy in this country.

The work has sought to draw upon the most recent ideas in the literature and the professions of city planning, political science, and law, and these ideas are related to some of the current and emerging practices in the states and assessed in this light.

The discussion also extends to state politics more broadly, with particular attention to the impact of the different state institutions, such as the legislature and courts, on state and local planning and land-use policy. It focuses on the influence of the different private and public interests that have a concern with state land-use policy.

The book should provide a base for congressional judgment on the future role of the states in the development of a planning strategy for the nation as a whole. Congress is presently considering legislation making the states the key planning units in the federal system, and this book should throw some light on the ways the states can be best used in this respect.

In general, the study has found that the states can be useful in structuring more broadly based planning in the country and that their most valuable input is in terms of stimulating regional and metropolitan planning and widening the perspectives of local planning and zoning agencies.

The central ideas in this book were presented to a general session of the 40th Annual National Planning Conference held in Chicago in May of 1974. The response caused us to place even greater emphasis than before on a combination of state planning strategies, including state zoning for specific purposes like floodplains and wetlands, comprehensive state planning for rural and urban areas alike, substate regional planning, and greatly improved state enabling legislation for local governments.

LIST OF TABLES

LIST OF FIGURES

The States and Land-Use Control

1

**INTRODUCTION—THE
STATE PLANNING
SYSTEM**

FRAMEWORK

Some framework for the study of public planning is necessary,
some conceptual means that allows us to understand the subject
theoretically as well as practically and that shows the interrelationship among the various parts and aspects of the planning process.
In recent years it has become increasingly common to study government in terms of a political system. This is known as the systems
approach, as applied to politics. A political system is only one system in a society—as there are economic systems, ecological systems, and so on—and is seen by some including sociologists as part
of the broader social system. But a political system is the most
"authoritative" (Easton) of all systems and, at least in the theoretical and legal senses, represents the highest and ultimate power
in a society. Thus it may not merely be part of a social system.
This is the political science view, and it is reasonable. Probably
the one who contributes the most to systems analysis in political
science is David Easton, and Ira Sharkansky has likely done the
most with the concept in public administration, a main concentration
of this book.[1] This chapter draws on the work of both but especially
Easton.

A political system contains a number of characteristics and
ingredients, with the government at the center; some term it—the
government—state. Other forces in the political system relate to
government or the state or particular aspects of it in some way or
another. They may do this in various ways—by pressuring government, making demands on it, or providing support for it. These
forces would include interest groups, political parties, and the
different bodies and officials in government itself in the case of one
aspect of government (one bureaucracy influences another; one

FIGURE 1

Simplified Version of the Political System

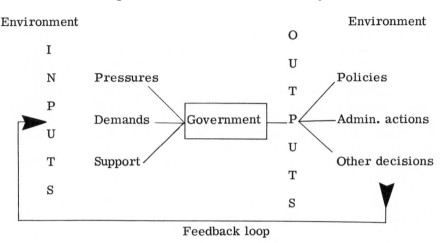

Feedback loop

Environment   Environment

congressional committee, another; one branch, another), and these forces can be termed "inputs" in the political system. The way it works is shown in Figure 1.

It is the inputs that shape government, its actions, and policies. These inputs come from the "environment" of politics. In this, which is the most simplified way of showing it, the inputs are brought to bear on government, and government reacts (conversion process) and turns the inputs into "outputs." The "government" in this sense would include all formal institutions such as administrative agencies, legislatures, and the courts that are normally considered part of it. The government is a neutral force as discussed for the moment, although in fact it is of course not, and in this sense it is nothing more or less than a registrant of pressures, demands, and support. These inputs determine government's actions, or outputs.

Now, as suggested, government can never be entirely neutral notwithstanding what some of the early group theorists like Bentley and the first legalistic studies of government came close to saying; to Bentley the base of government actions was "interests" and to the early legal scholars, "the people." In fact, the various groups in government such as administrators, members of legislative bodies, governors, and mayors play two roles in the process: They help "supply" inputs in a more or less independent sense, and these inputs may reflect their own interests or those of particular agencies, congressional committees, and others; they register the inputs provided by others. The different pressures, demands, and support may be reflected in the form of lobbying, the presentation of views in public hearings, the mobilization of the public for political actions, funding of elections, backing particular parties, and in other ways.

What the government does is depicted on the output side, with the outputs of the political system being the decisions of government. These represent the authoritative political decisions of a society acting through its government, and the decisions would include public policies, government administrative actions, government judicial decisions, its spending patterns, regulations, legislation and other rulings, acts, or pronouncements. The outputs may influence the inputs, through the feedback loop, by shaping the inputs and the various pressures on the government. These points are illustrated in more concrete form below.

The most broadly based political system in existence today is the nation-state, and this is so because it is sovereign, containing the ultimate power for the people and land under its jurisdiction, and represents the highest political power in a particular geographical area. It is possible to reserve the term political system for the nation-state and to consider other political systems within a particular nation-state to be subsystems, or political subsystems. The United States would then constitute a political system, and the states of Nebraska and New York political subsystems. This can be carried a step further, and since local governments are "part" of the states, they could be viewed as subsystems of state systems or subsystems; Los Angeles would be a subsystem of California.

A governing body, a court, or an administrative agency within any system or subsystem could also be seen as a political subsystem or political system. In the case of an administrative agency, this would be particularly appropriate if the agency had more or less independent status within the government as most local and some state planning agencies do. Thus we can talk of the political system of the planning agency, or more simply the planning system, which means the same. This is the way Sharkansky uses it in his introductory text on Public Administration.

There are some difficulties of doing this in this book, if the state planning agency is our focal point. The first difficulty is that the state planning agency has only recently become a force to be reckoned with in this country, and in many states, perhaps most of them, we could not even make this statement. State planning is in an embryonic form, and its "political system" is rather flimsy at this point. Second, the "planning agency" in the states has changed from one period to the next. In the colonial era, the state planning agency was the state legislature and perhaps the governor, combined,

FIGURE 2

The Political System of the Local Planning Commission

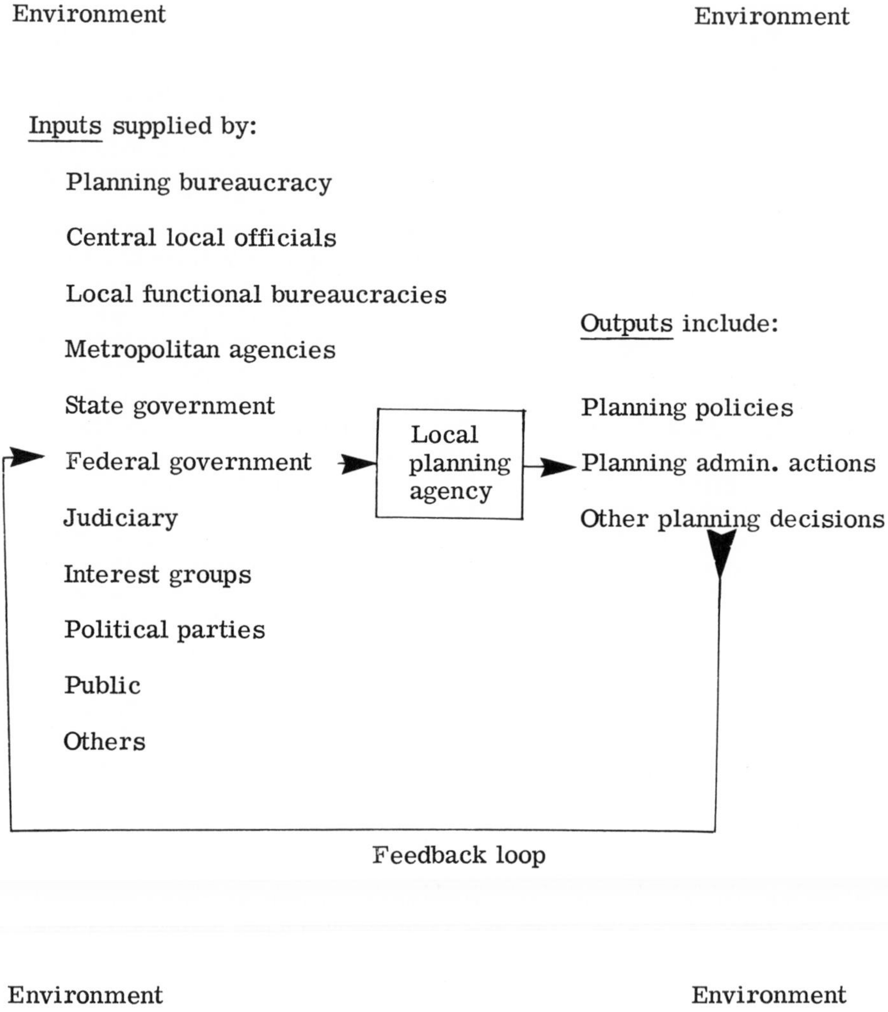

Environment   Environment

Inputs supplied by:

    Planning bureaucracy

    Central local officials

    Local functional bureaucracies

    Metropolitan agencies   Outputs include:

    State government   Planning policies

    Federal government   Local planning agency   Planning admin. actions

    Judiciary   Other planning decisions

    Interest groups

    Political parties

    Public

    Others

Feedback loop

Environment   Environment

Source: Don T. Allensworth, The Political Realities of Urban Planning (New York: Praeger Publishers, 1975), p. 70.

4

that is, or one of the two independent of the other. At that time there were no bureaucracies as we know them today and few administrative officials, with the legislative bodies perhaps performing both legislative and executive functions as well as a considerable fusion of activities. During the 1800s, there was a decline in the incidence of state planning, and what was done was promotional for the most part, only to a limited extent regulatory; it was commonly done by the state board of public works. This body funded canal, wagon roads, and later railroad projects as well as other public internal improvements, and the job was only in the loosest sense planning; it was better described as state support of development and the provision by state boards of public works of assistance (state land, money) to private entrepreneurs and companies to promote schemes of western expansion. This was done, of course, by public facilities and not war or open conflict, and this may be the most effective way.

Later, in the 1930s, state planning came into its own again, but this time under state "planning boards" set up in connection with New Deal legislation and administrative guidelines. These were eventually to weaken and lose most of their federal support, and they were replaced by "economic development" departments, which represented the postwar thrust in state planning. In fact, these were not planning agencies as we understand the term today, but, like the units in the 1800s, development and economic promotion organizations. They were designed to attract industry and business, to fund related public facilities, and to provide jobs, especially for the returning World War II veterans. Finally, in the last and current stage, all the states now have formal "planning agencies," and they have been largely, but not entirely, separated from economic development and other promotional activities; about a dozen states combine the two functions in the same department as shown in Chapter 2. As hinted, these agencies are not as "independent" as local planning agencies, and thus they do not lend themselves as well perhaps to systems analysis of the variety presented here. One of the authors (Allensworth) has usefully applied the systems concept to the local planning commission, the most powerful of the subnational planning agencies, in the recently published The Political Realities of Urban Planning (Praeger, 1975), and a figure adapted from that book is provided here (Figure 2).

LOCAL PLANNING SYSTEM

In this case, the planning commission is considered the equivalent of "government" above and is seen in the same neutral sense; it is merely a technical registrant of pressures from others including itself (seen as the planning bureaucracy in the figure). The influences then are the planning bureaucracy, including the professional staff and lay board which has its effects on actions of the agency. The planning bureaucracy influence may reflect its own interests (higher salaries for professional planners, for example; decisions favorable to the agency's administrators) or the interests of others such as citizens' groups or developers. Other groups providing inputs may include central local officials such as the mayor, board of aldermen, county executive, county council, city manager, county administrator, or others who may have certain fiscal or substantive controls and powers that affect the planning agency; local functional bureaucracies or other agencies such as the Department of Public Works, mass transit authority, sewer district, or roads agency which have programs directly impacting on the planning agency and its decisions; metropolitan agencies such as councils of governments or metropolitan planning commissions which have powers over the region as a whole and which may influence the local planning agency and its policies; state government whose agencies like the state roads administration or pollution control board may influence local planning; the federal government and its units such as Congress, a particular congressional committee, or the Department of Housing and Urban Development which provides planning, roads, sewer, water, or other funds to local government including the planning agency; the judiciary, meaning for the most part state courts which consider planning and zoning decisions of the local planning agency and other local bodies on appeal and render decisions on these matters (see Chapter 8); interest groups such as developers, builders, and neighborhood citizens' associations which seek to influence local planning commission policies; political parties including the Democratic, Republican, or purely local parties which may control local government and the planning commission; the public which cannot be discounted and yet whose influence will come in 99 percent of the cases through one of the above groups, especially central local officials such as the chief executive in the locality, the federal government, one or more interest groups, or one or both political parties; and other influences which would include the local press and news media, churches, research groups, and advisory committees.

On the output side, planning policies, administrative actions, and other decisions should be broadly construed, and they are not limited to plans or master plans per se. They also include many other matters that are affected by plans, that relate to plans, or that are connected to any other power or duty of a local planning commission. Land-use control policies and decisions in such areas as zoning and subdivision regulation are included as are certain key determinations made on mass transit, water, sewers, highways, pollution control, open space, property taxes, parks, urban renewal, housing, and many other functions.

This discussion of the local planning agency will be most helpful to the reader in conceptualizing the basics and interrelationships in Chapters 6, 7, and 8, especially the latter two. Chapter 7 covers local planning and the state relationship to it and deals mostly with local planning agencies and staffs directly or indirectly. Chapter 8 is concerned with court decisions, and it is the decisions that are at one point or another made by the local planning agency that are of greatest concern here; these include direct planning decision (master plan), zoning (most important, where the local planning commission's decision is advisory), subdivision control, and official map decisions, with all but zoning being final administratively on the part of the local planning agency. Chapter 6 deals with regional planning or substate planning for the most part, and this is essentially ''local'' as opposed to state. The organizational form at this level closely resembles that in the local planning commission and local government, and often local planning units are directly represented on the regional bodies; the policies of the latter may reflect those of the local units.

STATE PLANNING AGENCY AND THE SYSTEMS CONCEPT

Yet the advantages of using systems analysis at the state level outweigh the problems. Dealing with the problems first, the state planning agencies are now beginning to take form, and many have sufficient power to be recognized as serious contenders in their political systems, with close ties to key legislative committees, the governor, federal funding agencies and committees, and private groups whose support they may well need. Second, it does not appear that there will be a drastic change in organizational form in state planning for some time, representing a departure from the past. The state planning agency is typically a separate department of state government or a division of the governor's office, and the secretary may be in the governor's cabinet and nearly always is consulted by if he is not part of the state's ruling officialdom. Most state planning agencies have boards that are attached to them and that make certain decisions such as the adoption and revision of state plans, but these bodies are not usually as independent as local planning boards that commonly have both administrative and policy powers over the planning staff. At the local level, this is the way the state enabling legislation typically made it as will be seen in Chapter 7.

For simplification purposes, we shall take the current state planning agency in discussing state planning in the context of its ''political system,'' although what is said here would apply as well to the earlier forms of planning policy making and administration such as the colonial legislatures and governors, boards of public

FIGURE 3

The Political System of the State Planning Agency

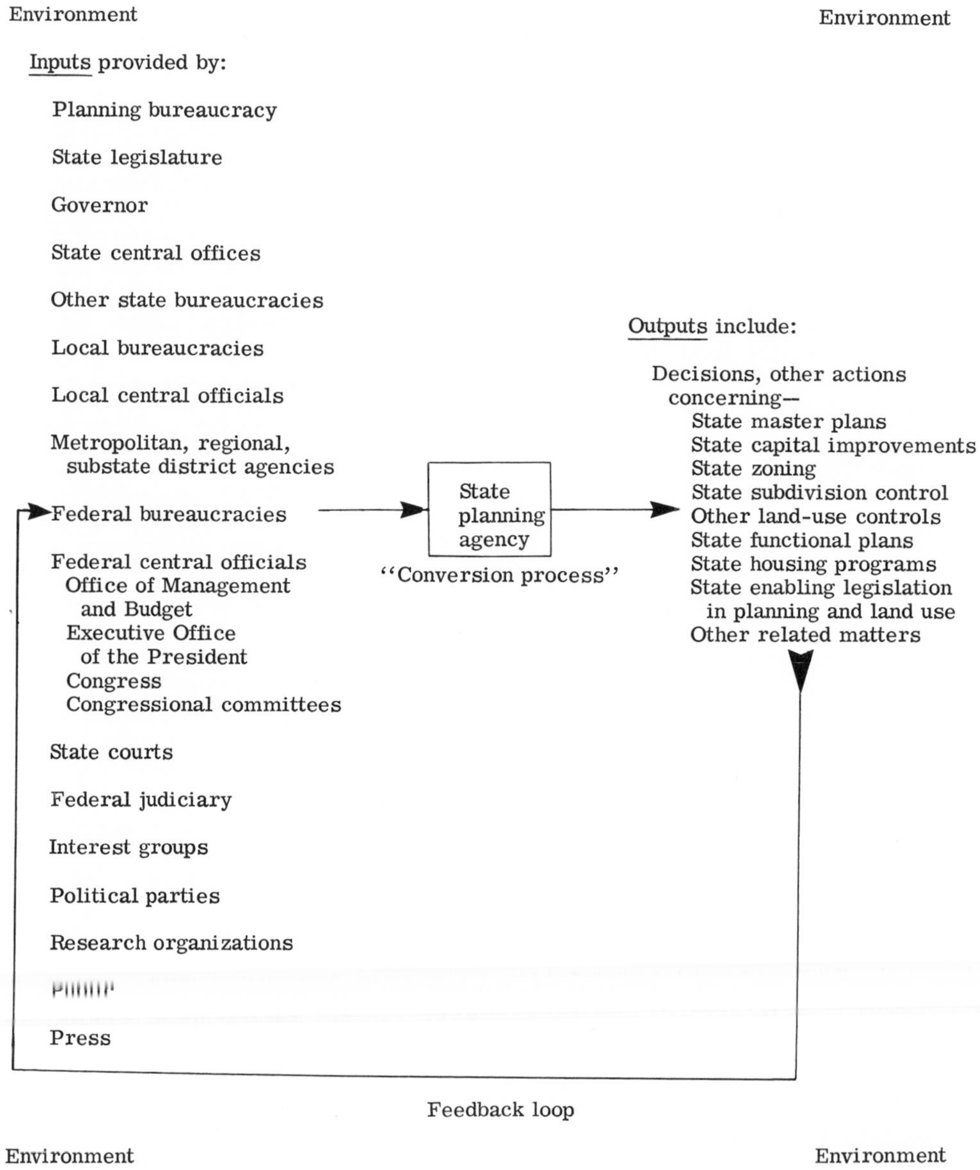

Environment   Environment

Inputs provided by:

  Planning bureaucracy

  State legislature

  Governor

  State central offices

  Other state bureaucracies

  Local bureaucracies

  Local central officials

  Metropolitan, regional,
    substate district agencies

  Federal bureaucracies

  Federal central officials
    Office of Management
     and Budget
    Executive Office
     of the President
    Congress
    Congressional committees

  State courts

  Federal judiciary

  Interest groups

  Political parties

  Research organizations

  Public

  Press

State
planning
agency

"Conversion process"

Outputs include:

Decisions, other actions
  concerning—
    State master plans
    State capital improvements
    State zoning
    State subdivision control
    Other land-use controls
    State functional plans
    State housing programs
    State enabling legislation
     in planning and land use
    Other related matters

Feedback loop

Environment   Environment

8

works, state planning boards, and state economic development departments. The political system of the state planning agency is depicted
in Figure 3. It might be noted that most state planning agencies do
not have the powers local planning agencies do; so their impact on
planning policy, actual land use, and on development may be less.
With appropriate changes and modifications, the model advanced
here applies to metropolitan, substate district, regional, rural, and
interstate planning agencies, also covered in this book (see Chapter
6).

The political system of the state planning agency includes inputs
from a variety of sources, and these include resources, demands,
support, claims, and the like, the process involving the agency itself,
the "conversion" process, or the registering part of it, where inputs
are "converted," and outputs. The feedback loop shows how the outputs of the agency may have an effect on inputs and how they may
actually become inputs. For instance, a state planning agency may
make a decision that shifts important planning powers from local
government to the state, or support legislation to this end, and this
may strengthen the inputs (interest groups that depended on and
supported a local planning agency may now depend on and support the
state agency) favorable to the agency and decrease the pressure from
local planning agencies on the state planning agency (perhaps the
local agencies were lobbying in the state agency against this decision).

It might also be mentioned that Sharkansky's notion of "within-
puts" or the forces in the agency itself that influence decisions of
that agency—such as values of the administrators, economic or
political interests of staff members and officials, and the particular
structure of the planning agency—forces that are not neutral and that
serve to shape decisions in one way or another, are treated on the
"input" side in our model. They are, in short, part of the first
category of inputs, those supplied by the planning bureaucracy,
which include all those things like the personal interests of agency
executives, political aspirations of agency personnel, enhancement
interests of the organization apart from the pressures put on it
from the "outside" by legislators and interest groups, and the like.
Thus "planning agency" in the middle and "planning bureaucracy"
on the input side are identical in one sense (they refer to the planning unit in state government, its employees, its rules, and organization), but are used differently in the diagram. Planning agency in
the middle is neutral, and planning bureaucracy on the left represents the live political dynamics of the agency.

Thus the planning bureaucracy has an influence in the political
system of the planning agency, and its influence may well be independent of that of other forces; in fact, that this is true is exactly
why it is placed on the input side, as otherwise it would merely
register the pressures, support, resources, and demands of others

and convert them, one for one, into outputs. It is correct, for example, to observe that professional planners want more power and money, and they will be in competition with other bureaucracies, other interests in the state, and other professionals in state and local government (especially local planners) for these things. They will want them (power and money) even if there are no interest groups or parties supporting them (state planners) in this regard, and thus they are not merely acting as agents of some powerful outside group. Planning administrators in state agencies have their own professional values, and these will likely influence their decisions, that is, independent of other influences; their professional values, backed up by professional organizations, may lead them for instance to support "critical areas" controls for the states or expanded budgets for particular planning programs like research on new zoning techniques.

State planners will also work for a planning agency that is independent in structure to some extent from forces they consider adverse to state planning, and this may include a competing field or bureaucracy (economic development), the governor, the governor's personal staff, another central staff such as the budget division or capital improvements section or some other body such as the state legislature, a particular legislative committee or a state controlling or capital approval board. This is the sort of thing we had in mind here.

The state legislature also influences the state planning agency and its decisions. For example, it provides the agency with its basic law and legislative authority. It may determine its organizational structure, and it provides it with funds and budget obligational powers. It can expand or cut back on the agency's powers or transfer them to another bureaucracy, and obviously it is important to the whole matrix of influences and actions surrounding the planning unit. It can give the agency certain land-use powers such as zoning or subdivision controls, or it can assign these to other state agencies; it can give the agency no power, some power, or great powers of review over other state agencies' capital programs, budgets, and land-use projects. Of course, given the realities of state legislatures (limited sessions, high turnover), it may be the planning agency that influences the legislature more than the other way around, and it could be the source of major pressure on the body to enact this or that planning legislation.

The governor has a clear impact and serves as a source of support and pressure on the planning agency. The governor typically appoints the planning chief and perhaps one or more of his assistants, may name the planning agency as the A-95 review organization (a federal regulation discussed later in the book), may put the agency in his cabinet (some governors have this power, without advance legislative authorization, that is), allocate all or only a portion of appropriated funds to the agency, may cut back agency budget requests or raise them, and generally provide the agency central backing or deny it this support. The chief executive could influence the agency in a variety of other ways, including lobbying in the public or legislature for it.

Central offices in the state such as the capital budget division, the finance department, or the management section, all commonly directly under the governor, may also influence the planning agency and its rulings. The capital budget division may share planning powers with the agency; the finance department may set up loose or rigid procedures on expenditures of the agency (the loose procedures provide it more discretion and are desired by the agency); and the management section may do studies facilitating administrative tasks and in general stimulate organizational changes which can be beneficial or seen as even detrimental to the agency (by present incumbents). In any event, the influence is there.

Other state bureaucracies will have their impact. These include the state highway department whose roads planning section may do the most important and far-reaching transportation planning in the state and whose highway plans may be rubber-stamped if reviewed at all by the central planning agency; the state pollution control department which may be a new environmental conservation agency or the traditional health board and which may set many important land-use, development, conservation, environmental, sewerage, solid waste, and other policies of importance to the state planning agency and its plans and constrain it considerably in these regards; the state natural resources department which makes much of the states' water, park, forestry, fish and wildlife, and open-space policies and which therefore directly influences planning policy and perhaps curtails options of the state planning agency; and the state housing and community development department which has authority over state programs in low- and moderate-income housing, urban renewal, community redevelopment, and other areas of significant interest to state central planners. Of course, these agencies may widen the options of state planners and make their job easier, especially where a governor has encouraged a spirit of cooperation among the different state bureaucracies, and we do not mean to say that options are always curtailed with outside pressure.

Local bureaucracies such as sewer authorities, water districts, city and county highway departments, local health agencies, municipal planning commissions, urban renewal and housing units, and mass transit organizations have their impact as well. They may be organized into statewide groups (associations of county planning officials, for example) that lobby for this or that decision in state planning agencies or in state legislatures that affects the state planning bureaucracy. As an example, a statewide planning officials group (local planning agencies) worked against legislation in one state that would have expanded the state planning agency's powers over "critical areas" in the state and cut back on local planning agencies' powers in these areas; this is discussed in detail in Chapter 5 (case study).

Local central officials may influence state planning policy too. These would include mayors, county executives, and city and county governing bodies; in some states these groups are organized state-wide (mayors are organized in New York, and suburban county exec-utives in Maryland, for instance), and they may put the pressure on state planning agencies favorable to the local government point of view, or to particular local governments such as the suburbs or big cities, or to particular local agencies such as planning commissions. As an example, county executives from the suburbs of one Eastern state lined up against a state bill that would have expanded the plan-ning powers of the state planning agency and cut into their own.

Metropolitan and regional planning and other bodies such as substate districts with planning and economic development powers are included. They may provide support for state planning agencies or serve as a source of pressure on them, seeking, for example, to get state planners to incorporate their (metropolitan, regional, sub-district) plans into the state plan. They may lobby in the state plan-ning agency for special projects such as an interstate highway or a regional sewage treatment plant at a particular location; the idea is that they want the state planners to put such projects on state plans and thus provide the projects with greater legitimacy (even then the plans are advisory). The state planning agency may be getting one set of pressures from a metropolitan body and another from a con-stituent local government, a situation that has characterized both Cleveland and Washington, D.C., on interstate highways (I-290 in Cleveland, I-95 in Washington, with the central city opposed and the suburbs and metropolitan agency dominated by the suburbs in favor).[2]

Federal agencies such as the Department of Housing and Urban Development, which funds state planning, and the Department of Transportation, which funds state highways and other state trans-portation projects, have their say as well. The federal transportation agency, for example, may overrule state highway or other transpor-tation plans and is frequently pressured to do so by local groups. This influence, of course, comes largely from the funding powers of federal agencies, and while the funding may go for a state department other than planning, it may well affect state plans. In no case does the federal government merely turn over the grants and allow the state to use them as it pleases, although the 1972 federal revenue sharing legislation comes close to this (we are not talking about this money, which is small by comparison to the federal grants for particular functions like highways and sewers).

Other federal interests may influence state planning policy, and these include central groups such as the Office of Management and Budget (OMB), whose recent A-95 Circular provided for the establishment of state planning and development clearinghouses to review federal grant proposals, and the clearinghouses may be state planning agencies (the governor does the designating); the Executive Office of the President including the Domestic Council which advises the chief executive on intergovernmental policy among other matters affecting state planning and which is headed by Nelson Rockefeller in the Ford administration; and Congress or particular legislative committees which fund programs administered or reviewed by state planning agencies including the ''701'' federal planning assistance effort that provides money directly to state planning units.

State courts also serve as inputs on state planning agencies and policy. They are more important than the federal judiciary, which may also consider state zoning, land-use and planning cases; the federal courts less frequently get involved in these matters as will be shown in Chapter 8. The courts hear appeals from aggrieved parties in the area of state planning, and these parties may include landowners whose property values are lowered by state planning regulations or decisions, or local governments who feel that their legal and constitutional rights are violated by state planning policies. Examples of both are cited and discussed at length in Chapter 8, and these are the two interests most likely to press state planning and land-use questions in the courts.

Interest groups in the traditional sense are also involved, and these would include state builders' associations (many states have them, and they include developers as well as builders per se), citizens, environmental and conservation groups such as the state unit of the Sierra Club, organized labor especially the building and construction trades, state chambers of commerce, state manufacturing associations, and organized local governments, officials and bureaucracies like the state leagues of cities, state associations of counties and townships, and state organizations of mayors, housing officials, county executives, sewer districts, water departments and authorities, and others which have their influence. All these organizations have interests or concerns affected by state planning and land-use decisions, and they watch state planners closely. The groups are typically manned by professionals, and most of their lobbying is probably done in state administrations and not the legislature except perhaps in the states with full-time legislators.

Interest groups are discussed throughout the book but particularly in Chapters 2, 5, and 9. As can be seen, they include both newer types of groups like environmentalists' and citizens' associations as well as the traditional variety like business and labor organizations; they include both public-spirited and private-motivated interests, and thus cannot all be labeled as undesirable or of questionable legitimacy. Interest groups also include organized governments, and this again takes us out of the traditional mold. In fact, the interest groups representing local governments may be the most important influence over certain kinds of state land-use and planning policy.

Parties typically run the states, including both the legislatures and the executives, although with varying degrees of effectiveness and influence. Generally the party counts for little in one-party states and is more important in highly competitive states like Ohio and Pennsylvania. Yet parties, even where they are important, are influenced by interest groups and, of course, influence these groups as well. The role of parties in the planning area may be minimal, and this is because of its highly technical nature perhaps, a point discussed more in Chapter 9. It seems that parties tend to defer to bureaucracies and interest groups in such areas.

Research and advisory organizations like the Advisory Commission on Intergovernmental Relations (ACIR) obviously have their impact on state planning agencies although they are often overlooked. The ACIR is clearly one of the most important of these, and it recently published a six-volume survey, which is bound to have its effects on state planning; the report focuses particular attention on substate regionalism, a real concern of state planners and an integral part of the state planning picture.[3] Technically the ACIR is a federal agency, but its intergovernmental representation and operational independence in the federal bureaucracy take it outside this frame for all practical purposes.

Other groups like the National Association of Regional Councils (NARC) serve in a similar capacity and conduct official studies of the effectiveness of certain kinds of regional planning in the states and do other research which affects state planning; NARC represents councils of governments and is technically an interest group (and could be treated in that category), working for legislation and administrative regulations in Washington favorable to regional councils as they are called. The National Association of Counties, the International City Management Association, the National League of Cities, and the U.S. Conference of Mayors also sponsor research on planning in the states, although again they are interest groups and in both capacities (interest group and research) affect state planning, state planning agencies, and state planning decisions. Similarly, the state government interest groups like the Council of State Governments, the National Governors' Conference, the National Legislative Conference (state legislators), the American Association of State Highway and Transportation Officials, and the Council of State Planning Agencies, all Washington lobbies, do research and studies in or affecting state planning and have their impact in this manner. Some conservative and liberal organizations have similar effects and also serve in a dual capacity, and both are commonly represented in legislative and administrative hearings on state planning held in Washington.[4]

The public is an influence on state planning agencies, and again, as with the local planning commissions, this influence may be felt most directly through one of the others on the input side of the ledger such as the governor, mayor, Executive Office of the President, Congress, parties, or particular interest groups. The press cannot be discounted, and this includes especially the press in the state capital and in the larger cities of the states. The newspapers' importance is discussed in this book, and they may give visibility to issues that otherwise may be minor; in fact, they can virtually "make" an issue all other factors being equal, as the experience in Philadelphia with comments of the chief justice of the Pennsylvania Supreme Court suggests (see Chapter 8).

Now we turn to the outputs. The state planning agency, a neutral mechanism it will be recalled, "converts" the inputs into outputs and in the process makes planning policy. It may do this more than is commonly expected since state bureaucracies generally have more power over policy than their counterparts in local and federal governments. This is so because of infrequent meetings of many state legislatures and the typical "board" or "commission" method of running state bureaucracies, where interest groups and others sit on collective bodies and make what amounts to both legislative and administrative policy (see Chapter 9). While the "board" method of administration is less common in planning than some other state functions like health and natural resources, it is used in a number of states in planning and probably means greater administrative (as opposed to legislative or gubernatorial) influence over policy. This is one reason why the state planning agency was chosen to depict state planning powers and processes in this chapter and why the state legislature, a particular committee of it, or the governor was not; also the ongoing activity in state planning can be better traced through the administrative aspects. It is easier and more realistic to focus on this.

The kind of policy outputs in the states does not include the wide range typical of local planning commissions, but it does cover much ground. It covers everything treated in this book. For example, state planning agencies may have direct or advisory powers over state master plans, state capital improvements, state zoning including comprehensive or specialized forms, state subdivision control, other state land-use regulations, state functional plans, state housing programs, state enabling legislation in planning and land use, and other related matters such as proposed federal or local projects impacting on development. They may consider many policies or proposals affecting local, regional, metropolitan, rural, subdistrict, and interstate planning agencies, and this puts them in a wide planning network. They may have some authority over state strip mining regulations, power plant siting regulations, state flood plain controls, and zoning around state buildings and institutions. As this suggests, once the basic legislation is provided, their powers and authority become administrative considerations, and it is the administrative decisions that seem to count the most in the states; at least the remainder of the book points in this direction. Of course in a narrow sense, planning policy is made by the state legislature and not the planning bureaucracy, but for our purposes the planning agency also makes policy as well as administers it and probably is the strongest single force in the legislature when purely planning matters are involved. The "influence" of the legislature, governor, and the courts naturally cannot be overlooked, and this influence may be decisive at any given time.

Nearly all the decision-making powers of the state planning agency are advisory, and the actual programs and regulatory authority are found in other agencies such as the state highway department (roads planning) or state public utility commission (power plant siting). Furthermore, unlike their counterparts in local government, state planning agencies typically have no power like local subdivision regulations, which are nearly always the exclusive function of the local planning commission; at the local level, subdivision decisions of planners are usually subject only to appeal to the courts and not the governing body, for example, although there are exceptions to this.

If this model is applied to other planning agencies discussed in this book, such as metropolitan or rural planning commissions, the state planning agency obviously becomes an input or source of pressure, support, or other influence on this body. The other influences remain the same by and large, although the degree will vary by level and type of planning organization involved. For example, the state highway department will be a source of influence on a metropolitan planning agency just as it is on the state planning agency, but it may exert less or more pressure on it depending on the issue, the time involved, or the importance of the project being considered. State highway interests may be represented on state planning boards, and they are formally represented on all metropolitan transportation planning bodies, which are increasingly part of a metropolitan planning agency. The pressure the highway agency exerts will also depend on the powers of the planning unit involved, whether they are advisory or final, and this varies by state and by the planning agency in any given state.

THE STATES AND THE OPENING OF THE WEST

This is not the topic of this book, and this is why we are covering it here and not later in the text. But it did come out in some of our research, and in many respects it fits into some contemporary ideas

about development and government power. It would appear that the
states were more important in opening the West than is commonly
supposed. This does not mean they did much planning in this regard
for they did not, but they were nevertheless key instruments in pushing back the frontier and encouraging the westward expansion. Our
investigation of the literature shows the importance of the states in
promoting, encouraging, and facilitating development in the nineteenth
century or, in economic terms, the truly formative years of the
nation's history. Perhaps private initiative was less important than
social Darwinism would have it in building the country and perhaps
the states, somewhat invisible as they are, more so. And perhaps
also this was known all along.

As noted, the states did little in the way of planning the westward
expansion and opening frontiers and more in promoting it, and certainly comprehensive planning as we now know it was not involved.
This is the reason we spend so little time on the state influence in
the 1800s since their involvement in land use during the period was
not really planning and not even regulation for the most part, the
two concentrations of the book. In the chapter on history, Chapter 2,
we do not deliberately ignore this aspect of state "planning," but
focus more on what we consider to be true planning. In its purest
form, the states did no planning in this age, and planning was not a
concern of the states again until the 1920s when they enacted enabling
legislation in planning and zoning for localities and the 1930s when
they undertook direct planning programs themselves. In the words
of one scholar, "After the death of colonial town planning, it was
almost as if the word 'planning' had disappeared from the American
civic lexicon."[5]

The layout of communities was no longer the business of government or the concern of public policy, and much development was
directly attributable to speculation and the profit motive. When government did get involved, it often reflected the needs of the marketplace and embodied its central tenets. As an example, the Indiana
legislature overrode community action in 1816 providing for carefully planned development and substituted a "plan" wanted by the
developers. The law authorized the replatting of land in the town on
the basis of the "gridiron" pattern, with conventional square and
rectangular layout, the designation of each lot for development and
no regard for topographical differences from lot to lot; this meant
no planned open space, which differed from the town's own plan. It
would be a mistake to assume that local governments did much in
planning at the time, and their involvement was generally limited
to deed recordings and platting in cities.

The real contribution of the states in the 1800s was to development; this was the goal, not planning. During the years between the
establishment of the new government and the mid-1800s, all levels
of government including the states were sponsors of joint stock

companies which undertook specific water transportation and canal
and wagon road projects, and the companies not only constructed the
facilities but maintained and improved them as well and controlled
their administration. Of course, canals and roads set development
patterns, and the state participation made this level a key determi-
nant of future land uses including both residential and commercial.
The idea is that development follows the public improvements as
today it does superhighways, mass transit corridors, sewer lines,
and water systems. The improvements stimulated development and
expansion and added to the profits of an ever-larger body of landowners and speculators.

State involvement in these projects may have been through a
special commission such as the state board of public works, which
represented the state on the stock companies; this board, in fact,
may have been the decisive voice in the firms, and the whole arrangement suggests considerable government assistance to those pushing
back the frontier. State "surveyors" did some planning of internal
improvements in the early decades of the century, but this was not
comprehensive planning and represented more "functional" planning
as we call it now, something like highway or mass transit planning.

Again in the last half of the nineteenth century, the role of the
state was promotional. There was an even greater emphasis on
internal improvements, and of course railroads were involved. Both
the states and national government provided land grants to private
companies to develop railroads. Public money was also available for
railroad construction and for rivers and harbors, local government
buildings and institutions, conservation projects, and other types of
public improvements. Also during the latter half of the century,
some states got into land reclamation, as a result of lumbering and
mining activities, an interest that has been rejuvenated in recent
years as we show in Chapter 5.[6]

This chapter adds an important dimension to the book because it
demonstrates how complex planning is. In a sense it seems simple,
and its fundamentals are. But we are dealing with a subject that is
operating in a real-world setting, where interests and not ideals
seem to be the governing force. This means that there are serious
limitations to viewing planning in theoretical terms. It is significantly constrained by the pressures and realities in the environment
in which it operates, and it will, to a large extent, take on the characteristics of the environment. Thus when we expect to see "planning" as it is taught in the beginning texts and we yet find business
domination or the use of government powers to promote development,
we are disappointed. Perhaps it is good at the start to make this
point, for it will prepare us better for a realization of the potentials
of planning. They are there and it is up to us to tap them, but in a
way they can be used. The book covers both "politics" and "planning,"
and this represents the spirit of the work, a combination of the

practical and the ideal, of the good and the workable, of the desirable and the possible.

NOTES

1. See David Easton, A Framework for Political Analysis (Englewood Cliffs, N.J.: Prentice-Hall, 1965). See also Easton's A Systems Analysis of Political Life (New York: John Wiley and Sons, 1965), and his earlier work, The Political System: An Inquiry into the State of Political Science (original publication—New York: Alfred A. Knopf, 1953), and now in second edition (same publisher, 1972). See Ira Sharkansky, Public Administration: Policy-Making in Government Agencies, 2nd ed. (Chicago: Markham Publishing Co., 1972), especially Chap. 1.

2. Advisory Commission on Intergovernmental Relations, Regional Decision Making: New Strategies for Substate Districts (Washington, D.C.: Government Printing Office, 1973), pp. 83-87. This is Vol. I of the commission's six-volume series on Substate Regionalism and the Federal System.

3. All six volumes are part of the series entitled Substate Regionalism and the Federal System, and all are published by the U.S. Government Printing Office in Washington, D.C. Vol. I is Regional Decision Making: New Strategies for Substate Districts (1973); Vol. II Regional Governance: Promise and Performance (1973); Vol. III The Challenge of Local Governmental Reorganization (1974); Vol. IV Government Functions and Processes: Local and Areawide (1974); Vol. V A Look to the North: Canadian Regional Experience (1974); and Vol. VI Hearings on Substate Regionalism (1974).

4. Conservative groups like the Liberty Lobby were well represented before Congress in 1974 when it considered state planning legislation. See Subcommittee on the Environment, Committee on Interior and Insular Affairs, House of Representatives, Hearings on Land-Use Planning Act of 1974 H.R.10294 (Washington, D.C.: Government Printing Office, 1974). See also Advisory Commission on Intergovernmental Relations, Hearings on Substate Regionalism (Washington, D.C.: Government Printing Office, 1974).

5. James G. Coke, "Antecedents of Local Planning," in William I. Goodman and Eric C. Freund (eds.), Principles and Practice of Urban Planning (Washington, D.C.: International City Management Association, 1968), p. 15.

6. The best source of information on state involvement in land use and development in the 1800s is the intergovernmental relations literature. See especially Daniel J. Elazar, "Federal-State Collaboration in the Nineteenth-Century United States," in Aaron Wildavsky

(ed.), American Federalism in Perspective (Boston: Little, Brown, 1967), pp. 190-222. See also Elazar's The American Partnership (Chicago: University of Chicago Press, 1962); Martin Grodzins, The American System (Chicago: Rand McNally, 1966), Chap. 2; William H. Riker, Federalism (Boston: Little, Brown, 1964), Chap. 3; and W. Brooke Graves, American Intergovernmental Relations (New York: Scribners, 1964).

2

Governor Tom McCall and other supporters of national land-use policy talk as though planning is something new to this country, and the state chiefs have recently put out a booklet describing planning as an "innovation" in state government.[1] But the facts suggest otherwise. Planning is not new, and neither is state planning. In fact, the history of state planning is virtually as long as the history of planning in the United States, and both can be traced to the early days of the new nation. This chapter starts by taking a look at the history of state planning, from the early times up through and including state planning during the depression; it then turns to contemporary state planning and land-use control and to the indirect involvement of the states in planning and zoning, namely, their role in authorizing and setting the ground rules for local planning and land-use control.

EARLY STATE PLANNING

City planning can be traced back to the early colonial days, to such towns as Williamsburg, Philadelphia, Savannah, and Annapolis, and state planning specifically has its roots in the enactments of the Maryland and Virginia legislatures in the 1600s.[2] The Virginia Act of 1662, for example, provided for the rebuilding of Jamestown and the development of four other towns. The measure specified the method of town financing, including provisions for land subdivision in the new towns. Ultimately, this legislation was repealed, and the permanent history of new town enactments in Virginia began in 1679 when action of the General Assembly and governor required each county to acquire 50 acres of land and lay out a new town. Sites were secured under this legislation and surveyed into streets and lots, and plots reserved for buildings and other improvements.

21

Similarly, the Maryland governor in 1668 designated 13 locations for towns, although this proclamation as in Virginia was later repealed by the colonial legislature. In both colonies, it was planters and traders who sought the repeal; they did so because the planning legislation set ports of entry and thus threatened a vast network of commercial relationships they had established with foreign groups. In the very early stages then, we can see how private interests impacted on planning measures, here in the context of what later was to become state legislatures, and this also is a tradition that continues to this day. Planning and land-use controls, in fact, are among the most "political" of all public policies, typically determining whose property will rise or fall in value and what groups will be the chief beneficiaries of governmental subsidies or regulatory policy.

In the eighteenth century, planning legislation was more specialized in impact, and in Maryland and Virginia it dealt with particular new towns and not new towns in general as before. This legislation provided for the formation of specific towns, prescribed how they were to be laid out, and called for the reservation of space for such uses as a courthouse and other public buildings, a central marketplace, and in some cases parks or relaxation areas. Elsewhere on the East Coast, colonial governments typically played much less of a role in city planning; charters were often provided directly to cities, and these documents placed the planning power directly in local bodies or individuals. This pattern was especially noticeable in the New England colonies, where almost all planning was done at the "village" level, and it is worth noting that these early arrangements continue to have their effects today. Centralized subnational government, for instance, is far more common in the South than the Northeast, a pattern Alan Grimes attributes to fundamental differences in church organization; in Maryland and the southern colonies, the predominant Anglican system was highly centralized, with most power resting at the higher levels, while in New England, where the Congregational church was dominant, power was in the local parish.[3]

In a sense, the first national planning legislation was provided in the Land Ordinance of 1785. This legislation was approved by the Continental Congress under the old Articles of Confederation, and the measure gave the territories some authority over development and subdivision procedures in their areas. The legislation qualifies as "planning" only in the most general sense, for it did set aside land for different public purposes including schools and defense and established the means by which central and territorial officials were to lay out land and dispose of it. The final stipulations for the part territorial governments were to play in guiding land development, however, were found in the Northwest Ordinance of 1787, a key enactment of the first national legislature.[4] There seems little question that land-use considerations were among the most important subjects not only to early colonial legislatures and local bodies as

noted but central authorities as well. In fact, if the present period is
any indication, it is likely that early planning and land-use legislation
at the national level was itself a result of pressures from powerful
interests that wanted government intervention on their behalf.

American governments then got into the planning business at the
very beginning, even before the creation of the present national and
state governments, and colonial legislatures were included. Government planning was not offensive to early Americans, and they may
have put more stress on it than we do today. It was also not offensive
to the founding fathers, who in meeting in the convention of 1787
seemed to want a government that did precisely this. While their
emphasis was on economic planning, land planning was presumably
included, a line of reasoning suggested in the Federalist Papers
(1787-88) and Alexander Hamilton's Report on Manufacturers (1791).[5]

Nevertheless, the early tradition of public planning and land-use
control in state, local, and national governments did not last long,
and in the 1800s it ran counter to Jacksonian doctrines of free enterprise and antimonopoly and later in the century to social Darwinist
teachings about the survival of the fittest and natural patterns of
evolution. The idea was that it was an artificial interference with the
laws of competition, and all forms of government planning including
state planning were discouraged. However, government help was
apparently all right, at least in the practicing business community.
There was a good deal of state funding and backing of internal improvements like canal, wagon road, rivers, and harbors and later
railroad projects during the 1800s as we have suggested in Chapter 1,
but there was little regulation and even less planning. We had to
wait until the 1930s for more state planning and the advent of the
New Deal.

STATE PLANNING IN THE 1930s

Several states ventured back into land planning as early as the
1920s, most notably New York and Wisconsin, but the 1920s was the
cities' era insofar as planning is concerned as we shall see. New
York was probably the first to set up a direct planning program, and
it had a plan in 1925 although it was never adopted. Wisconsin formed
a state planning agency in 1929; its role was to assist localities
undertake planning and to do some direct planning itself, largely in
the areas of conservation and pollution abatement. Some other states
began to act in the early 1930s, and this included Michigan, New
Jersey, and Vermont, but the real push for state planning did not
occur until after the 1932 elections. It is instructive that it was not
the Democrats as such who initiated state planning in the 1930s, for
Hoover and leading Republicans had urged it long before the New

Deal; nevertheless, it was Roosevelt and the Democrats who actually did it.

The major impetus for state planning in this period can be traced to the National Industrial Recovery Act (NRA), which authorized the Public Works Administration. Acting in accordance with this legislation, Secretary of the Interior Harold L. Ickes established the first federal planning agency in history, the National Planning Board, and named top advisers to it including both a political scientist and a planner.[*] The panel in turn encouraged the states to form comparable planning units of their own, ostensibly for the purpose of aiding the Public Works Administration program and carry out its projects in the states.

The state response was quick and almost overwhelming, and by 1934, a total of 36 states had formed planning boards, either by legislative or executive action, and a year later 45 had. By 1936, only Delaware had not acted to create a planning agency. The early state planning boards dealt mostly with public works and conservation matters. Only to a limited extent did they involve themselves with direct land-use questions. In a few instances, such as West Virginia, emphasis was put on the development of transportation networks and rural highways, but generally the focus was on traditional works projects such as dams and water supply/irrigation improvements. To the extent that the states got into land use, it was mostly in such areas as soil erosion and various forms of geological mapping and studies. At the time, land-use planning was not seen in the comprehensive sense that it is today, and it was also more of a rural matter, having to do with soil and water conservation outside of metropolitan areas.[6] An example of the depression concentration of state planning can be seen in the Iowa State Plan of 1935 as shown in Figure 4.

State planning in the 1930s was triggered by the federal government and specifically by the prospects of federal money, and it could be expected that with the withdrawal of this support, state planning would suffer and perhaps collapse. In fact, while some steps were taken toward comprehensive planning in the states and for a while for the nation as a whole, the newly named National Resources Planning Board was abolished during World War II, with a vengeance, and it was not long after that that most states dissolved their planning boards or transformed them into economic development units (The National Planning Board was then called the National Resources

---

[*]The political scientist was Charles E. Merriam, a member of the so-called Chicago school, which held "power" to be the central focus of political science, and also named to the President's Committee on Administrative Management (1937), and the planner was Charles W. Eliot, II, director of the National Capital Park and Planning Commission, now called simply the National Capital Planning Commission.

Planning Board, having apparently changed its name for political purposes, but even the more conservative and cautious name could not save it. It was formally abolished on August 31, 1943, and Congress was so fearful of its revival that it stipulated that its functions not be transferred to any other agency or be performed in any manner.) Some accounts trace current efforts in state planning to the economic development function, a traditional preoccupation of the states, but this fails to recognize that many states' economic development programs were themselves an outgrowth of an even earlier concentration on state planning.

Economic development was stressed by the states after the war, as opposed to planning, for it was seen as the means of adjusting to a peacetime economy and as the vehicle to stimulate the industry and jobs needed to meet the employment demands of returning veterans. Where state planning boards were retained, as in Rhode Island and Tennessee, they were downgraded and given the virtually

FIGURE 4: Iowa State Plan--Soil Erosion

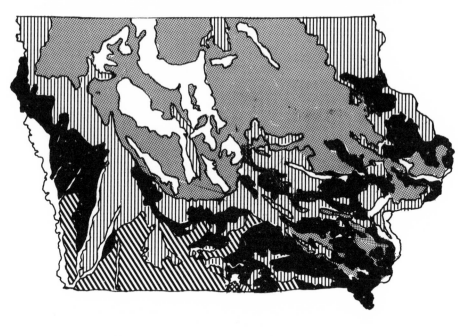

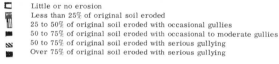

        Little or no erosion
        Less than 25% of original soil eroded
        25 to 50% of original soil eroded with occasional gullies
        50 to 75% of original soil eroded with occasional to moderate gullies
        50 to 75% of original soil eroded with serious gullying
        Over 75% of original soil eroded with serious gullying

Source: Mel Scott, American City Planning Since 1890 (Berkeley: University of California Press, 1969), p. 307.

sole task of assisting localities plan and zone. Today, most states
perform this function. States are now particularly active in helping
smaller cities and towns in this respect and typically serve as con-
duits for the distribution of federal planning money to such units.
Let us now turn to the more recent activities of the states in direct
planning and land-use control.

STATE PLANNING IN THE 1960s AND 1970s

From the postwar period up through the Eisenhower years, state
planning did not amount to much, and in reality there was not much
of an emphasis on the states in any field. One reason was that the
states lost out politically in Washington, in terms of the channeling
of federal grants in aid. The first postwar grant program to be considered by Congress was airports, and legislation was approved in
late 1946 to provide direct federal assistance to the cities for this
purpose, thus bypassing the states. The states and their supporters
in the GOP lobbied vigorously against this pattern but to no avail.
The cities and their Democratic allies in Congress had prevailed;
this seemed to set the mold for future grant programs and intergovernmental relations more generally. At least it did for some
time.[7]
In the late 1940s, important interests began pressing Congress
for funds to rebuild city cores. These forces were found in such
groups as the Greater Philadelphia Movement (GPM), Allegheny
Conference in Pittsburgh, Central Area Committee of Chicago,
Civic Conference in Boston, and Civic Progress in St. Louis.[8] Although not organized specifically on a national basis,[9] these interests
were well represented by the likes of Senator Robert A. Taft (R-Ohio),
who sponsored the legislation to give them what they wanted. The
legislation was also supported by liberal Democrats and Southerners,
an impressive alignment indeed. But the rebuilding of American
cities was an assignment of the federal and local governments, and
the states were left out of any meaningful role here. The states were
not even named in the Housing Acts of 1949 and 1954, which advanced
federal funds to the cities for urban renewal and planning purposes.
Planning was then generally seen as an adjunct of city redevelopment
or renewal, much as it was linked to public works in the depression,
and money was to be used to develop plans designed to pinpoint the
worst areas of the city and to eradicate them. Actually, the 1954
enactment provided federal planning moneys for more broadly based
planning, but again this was seen as a city or county and not a state
function.
The direct federal-city tie was repeated time and time again
through the 1950s and 1960s, in virtually all the planning-related

community development grant areas such as model cities, open space, water and sewer programs, public facilities, mass transit, and the war on poverty. The conflict between the cities and states over grant channeling is usually overlooked in the literature, even though it represents one of the most salient facts of political life in the nation's domestic programs.[10] Both the states and cities are organized into powerful lobbies in Washington, namely, the National League of Cities/U.S. Conference of Mayors and the Council of State Governments/National Governors' Conference, and they are commonly locked in bitter struggle.[11] The states do not lose all the time although they have not fared well in the planning and urban development area. Even where they do win, however, it is less due to their superior arguments than their strength; that is, the strength of the cities and states in Washington varies by the issue area, and where the states have built strong bureaucracies and have powerful interest groups speaking for them, they prevail and the money comes to them and not the cities. The best example of the latter is highways, where all the federal money goes to the states and only after that is distributed to cities and counties.

At the same time, a little-noticed amendment to the federal housing legislation in 1961 made the states eligible for direct planning grants, and this clearly sparked new moves in the states for the development of comprehensive planning programs. In time, most states took advantage of this assistance although at least initially they did very little with the money. In many instances, it was used to do limited mapping of state and private land and to collect studies, plans, and data of local and regional planning agencies. By 1968, the federal government was pumping $7 million a year into state planning, and 44 states in all had been aided, to the tune of $20 million. Today Washington is contributing over triple that figure each year, and it will not be long before the federal government has put out $100 million to bolster state planning. Incidentally, both bills considered on the floor of Congress this time (93rd Congress) authorized $800 million for this purpose, to be used over several years.

The 1961 program should not be confused with the earlier urban planning assistance mentioned briefly above that was made available to smaller communities via the state. In other words, at the time of the enactment of the first broadly based urban planning program by Congress—the "701 program" of the Housing Act of 1954—cities under 50,000 and counties were made eligible, but the money was distributed through the states and not directly; direct assistance was available to larger jurisdictions including metropolitan planning units, and this money was not channeled through the states. States started performing this function for smaller cities and counties in 1955.

One might assume that even though limited, the role given the states under the 1954 legislation would cause them to readdress the

TABLE 1

Organizational Responsibility in States
for Comprehensive Statewide Planning
in 1960 and 1968
(Includes Puerto Rico)

| | Number of States January 1, | |
	1960	1968
Planning and economic development in the same agency	11	13
Independent planning department	6	6
Planning in department of finance or administration	2	4
Planning as staff unit in governor's office	1	22
Statewide planning as interdepartmental committee	—	2
No formal statewide planning program	31	4
	$\overline{51}$	$\overline{51}$

Source: David K. Hartley, "State Planning," in Frank Smothers (ed.), The Book of the States, 1968-69, Vol. XVII (Lexington, Ky.: Council of State Governments, 1968), p. 431.

planning question, perhaps for the first time since the depression. Evidently, however, the response of the states was as limited as the role they were given, and The Book of the States reports that not a single state created a new department "solely for this purpose" and further indicates that by 1955 "very few" state planning boards were still in existence.[12]

The 1961 state planning assistance program apparently did have its organizational effects, thus distinguishing it from the 1954 act. As can be seen in Table 1, well over half of the states had no statewide planning agency in 1960, but by 1968, general planning assistance the direct planning grants were approved, only four states had no planning unit. By and large, state planning in the late 1960s was either a function of the governor's staff directly (and not a line department or Cabinet agency) or the economic development department. The pattern of building planning into the economic development department was especially noticeable in 1960 as might be expected, but by 1968 it began to be broken out and given independent status.

These organizational arrangements continued in the late 1960s and early 1970s, and the number of states with planning as an adjunct

to economic development declined after 1968. In fact, by 1971 only
eight states had planning located in the economic development agency.
In the same year, over half the states had assigned the function
directly to the governor, the pattern backed by most experts.[13] Also
by 1971 and as important, all states had established planning as a
direct state activity and had given it to some state unit, including, in
addition to the two already mentioned, a department of planning, departments of administration or finance, a department of local affairs,
or an independent planning board.[14]

State planning agencies are involved in a variety of programs as
we shall see below, but it is clear that the earlier stress on public
works and rural conservation is no longer evident. This does not
necessarily mean that there is much of an emphasis on comprehensive
planning, for there is not, but it does mean that the depression perspective is being broadened. Probably the major difference is that
state planning now focuses on wider "land-use" considerations than
before, such as the control of critical areas, rural subdivision regulation, environmental impact assessment, coastal zone, wetlands and
flood plain management, power plant siting, surface mining, and the
location of state facilities. While this concentration is considered
"narrow" by some who want all planning including state planning to
deal with the key social and welfare questions of the day, it is broad
by all realistic standards and in comparison with the past.

The current character of state planning as well as an evaluation
of the progress being made can be seen in Tables 2 and 3. Table 2
shows what the states are doing in eight planning areas including
both comprehensive and specialized forms of planning and land-use
control. Outside the tax area, the states have apparently done the
most in such fields as power plant siting and surface mining regulation, while comprehensive planning has definitely lagged. A minority of states has done at least some work on coastal zone management, wetlands control, flood plain regulation, and the designation of
critical areas, and a key motive in the first and last programs has
been federal aid. The national government provides assistance to
the states under the Coastal Zone Management Act of 1972, and about
one-third of the states that are eligible has already been given funds
under this measure.[15] This is the first time incidentally that Washington has advanced money either to the states or local governments
for zoning, typically a local function. Similarly, the recent interest
of the states in "critical area" planning stems from the prospects
of federal grants under the currently pending National Land-Use
Planning Act.

Table 3 provides one measure of the success of the states in
planning and is probably the only evaluation of all 50 states that has
been published to date. It is instructive that in no category has as
many as half the states made "significant" progress, and the best
performance is registered in "technical assistance." Technical

TABLE 2

State Land-Use Programs
(January 30, 1974)

	Statewide Land-Use Planning and Control[a]	Coastal Zone Management[b]	Wetlands Management[c]	Power Plant Siting[d]	Surface Mining[e]	Designation of Critical Areas[f]	Land-Use Tax Incentives[g]	Flood Plain Management[h]
Alabama	—	—	—	—	yes	—	—	—
Alaska	—	—	—	—	—	—	yes	—
Arizona	—	NA	—	yes	—	—	—	yes
Arkansas	—	NA	—	yes	yes	—	yes	yes
California	—	yes	—	yes	—	—	yes	yes
Colorado	—	NA	—	—	yes	yes	yes	yes
Connecticut	E	—	yes	yes	—	—	yes	yes
Delaware	E	yes	yes	—	—	—	yes	—
Florida	E and R	yes	yes	yes	—	yes	yes	—
Georgia	E	—	yes	—	yes	—	—	—
Hawaii	P and R	yes	—	yes	—	yes	yes	yes
Idaho	—	NA	—	—	—	—	—	—
Illinois	—	—	—	yes	yes	—	yes	—
Indiana	—	—	—	—	yes	—	yes	—
Iowa	—	NA	—	—	yes	—	yes	—
Kansas	—	NA	—	—	yes	—	—	—
Kentucky	—	NA	—	—	yes	—	yes	—
Louisiana	—	—	yes	—	—	—	—	—
Maine	P and R	yes	—	yes	yes	—	yes	yes
Maryland	R (limited)	—	yes	yes	yes	—	yes	—

Massachusetts	—	—	yes	—	—	—	—	—
Michigan	P	yes	—	—	yes	—	—	yes
Minnesota	P and R	yes	—	yes	yes	yes	yes	—
Mississippi	—	yes	—	—	—	—	—	—
Missouri	—	NA	—	—	yes	—	—	—
Montana	—	NA	—	yes	yes	—	yes	yes
Nebraska	—	NA	—	yes	yes	—	—	yes
Nevada	—	NA	—	yes	—	—	—	—
New Hampshire	—	—	yes	yes	—	—	yes	—
New Jersey	—	—	yes	yes (cz)	—	—	yes	yes
New Mexico	—	NA	—	yes	yes	—	yes	—
New York	P	—	yes	yes	—	yes	yes	—
North Carolina	—	yes	yes	—	yes	—	yes	—
North Dakota	—	NA	—	—	yes	—	—	—
Ohio	—	—	—	—	yes	—	—	—
Oklahoma	—	NA	—	—	yes	—	—	yes
Oregon	P and R	yes (Partial)	—	yes	yes	yes	yes	—
Pennsylvania	P	—	—	yes	yes	—	yes	—
Rhode Island	—	yes	yes	yes	—	—	yes	—
South Carolina	—	—	—	yes	—	—	—	—
South Dakota	—	NA	—	—	yes	—	yes	yes
Tennessee	—	NA	—	—	yes	—	yes	yes
Texas	—	yes	—	—	—	—	yes	—
Utah	—	NA	—	—	—	—	yes	—
Vermont	P and R	NA	yes	yes	—	—	yes	yes
Virginia	—	yes	yes	—	yes	—	yes	—
Washington	—	yes	yes	yes	yes	—	yes	yes
West Virginia	—	NA	—	yes	yes	—	yes	—
Wisconsin	P	yes	yes	—	—	yes	—	yes
Wyoming	—	NA	—	—	—	—	yes	—
Guam	P and R	yes	—	yes	yes	—	yes	yes
Puerto Rico	P and R	—	—	yes	yes	—	yes	yes

(continued)

31

(Table 2 continued)

a P indicates the state has a land-use planning program under way. R indicates the state has authority to review local plans or has direct control. NA, not applicable.

b State has authority to plan or review local plans or the ability to control land use in the coastal zone.

c State has authority to plan or review local plans or the ability to control land use in the wetlands.

d State has authority to determine the siting of power plants and related facilities.

e State has authority to regulate surface mining.

f State has established rules or is in the process of establishing rules, regulations, and guidelines for the identification and designation of areas of critical state concern (for example, environmentally fragile areas, areas of historical significance).

g State has adopted tax inducements to withhold or delay development of open space (for example, tax on present use, rollback penalty, contract between the state and landholders to provide preferential tax for commitment to open-space usage).

h State has authority to regulate the use of flood plains.

Note: Indications that a state has a program in one of the above categories does not constitute an evaluation of the effectiveness of the program.

Source: H. Milton Patton and others, The Land-Use Puzzle (Lexington, Ky.: Council of State Governments, 1974), pp. 34-35. The first edition of this work was prepared by Professor Richard G. RuBino and William R. Wagner of Florida State University.

32

TABLE 3

Report Card[a] on Emerging Model in Official State Planning Agencies,[b] 1967-72

	Development Plan	Functional Planning Coordination	Regional Coordination and Allocation	Technical Assistance	Information System	Budget Coordination	Development Controls	Applied Research	Stimulation and Support
Alabama	LIM	LIM	LIM	LIM	LIM	LIM	LIM	LIM	MOD
Alaska	MOD	MOD	LIM	LIM	LIM	LIM	LIM	MOD	MOD
Arizona	LIM	MOD	MOD	SIG	MOD	MOD	LIM	LIM	MOD
Arkansas	LIM	LIM	LIM	MOD	LIM	LIM	LIM	MOD	MOD
California	MOD	MOD	MOD	MOD	SIG	MOD	MOD	MOD	MOD
Colorado	MOD	LIM	MOD	MOD	LIM	LIM	SIG	LIM	LIM
Connecticut	MOD	MOD	MOD	MOD	LIM	LIM	MOD	LIM	SIG
Delaware	SIG	MOD	SIG	SIG	MOD	MOD	MOD	MOD	MOD
Florida	MOD	MOD	MOD	LIM	LIM	MOD	SIG	LIM	MOD
Georgia	MOD	SIG	SIG	SIG	LIM	SIG	MOD	MOD	SIG
Hawaii	SIG	SIG	SIG	SIG	SIG	SIG	SIG	SIG	SIG
Idaho	LIM	LIM	MOD	MOD	LIM	LIM	LIM	MOD	MOD
Illinois	LIM	MOD	LIM	SIG	LIM	MOD	LIM	SIG	LIM
Indiana	LIM	MOD	LIM	LIM	MOD	LIM	LIM	LIM	LIM
Iowa	LIM	MOD	LIM	SIG	MOD	LIM	MOD	MOD	LIM
Kansas	MOD	MOD	MOD	SIG	MOD	LIM	LIM	LIM	SIG
Kentucky	LIM	LIM	LIM	MOD	LIM	LIM	LIM	LIM	MOD
Louisiana	LIM	MOD	MOD	MOD	LIM	LIM	MOD	MOD	MOD
Maine	SIG	MOD	MOD	LIM	LIM	MOD	SIG	MOD	MOD
Maryland	LIM	SIG	MOD	SIG	LIM	SIG	SIG	LIM	MOD
Massachusetts	MOD	MOD	MOD	MOD	MOD	MOD	MOD	MOD	MOD
Michigan	LIM	MOD	LIM	SIG	LIM	MOD	LIM	MOD	LIM
Minnesota	LIM	MOD	MOD	SIG	LIM	LIM	LIM	MOD	MOD
Mississippi	LIM	LIM	LIM	LIM	LIM	LIM	LIM	LIM	LIM
Missouri	LIM	MOD	LIM	MOD	LIM	LIM	LIM	LIM	MOD

(continued)

33

(Table 3 continued)

	Development Plan	Functional Planning Coordination	Regional Coordination and Allocation	Technical Assistance	Information System	Budget Coordination	Development Controls	Applied Research	Stimulation and Support
Montana	LIM	MOD	LIM	LIM	LIM	LIM	LIM	MOD	MOD
Nebraska	LIM	MOD	LIM	MOD	SIG	LIM	LIM	LIM	LIM
Nevada	MOD	LIM	LIM	MOD	LIM	LIM	LIM	LIM	LIM
New Hampshire	SIG	LIM	MOD	MOD	MOD	LIM	SIG	MOD	MOD
New Jersey	SIG	SIG	MOD	SIG	LIM	SIG	MOD	LIM	SIG
New Mexico	MOD	MOD	LIM	MOD	MOD	LIM	LIM	SIG	SIG
New York	MOD	MOD	MOD	MOD	SIG	MOD	MOD	SIG	MOD
North Carolina	MOD	MOD	MOD	MOD	MOD	LIM	LIM	LIM	MOD
North Dakota	LIM	MOD	MOD	MOD	LIM	LIM	LIM	MOD	LIM
Ohio	LIM	LIM	MOD	MOD	LIM	LIM	LIM	MOD	SIG
Oklahoma	LIM	MOD	MOD	SIG	MOD	MOD	LIM	LIM	SIG
Oregon	MOD	MOD	MOD	SIG	MOD	MOD	SIG	LIM	MOD
Pennsylvania	MOD	MOD	MOD	MOD	MOD	MOD	MOD	SIG	SIG
Rhode Island	SIG	SIG	SIG	LIM	MOD	LIM	LIM	LIM	LIM
South Carolina	MOD	MOD	MOD	MOD	LIM	MOD	MOD	MOD	MOD
South Dakota	LIM	MOD	MOD	LIM	LIM	MOD	LIM	LIM	LIM
Tennessee	MOD	MOD	MOD	MOD	LIM	LIM	LIM	LIM	MOD
Texas	SIG	MOD	SIG	MOD	MOD	MOD	LIM	LIM	MOD
Utah	LIM	LIM	MOD	LIM	LIM	LIM	LIM	MOD	MOD
Vermont	SIG	SIG	MOD	MOD	LIM	LIM	SIG	LIM	MOD
Virginia	MOD	MOD	SIG	SIG	LIM	LIM	LIM	MOD	SIG
Washington	MOD	MOD	MOD	SIG	MOD	MOD	MOD	LIM	SIG
West Virginia	MOD	MOD	MOD	MOD	LIM	LIM	LIM	LIM	LIM
Wisconsin	SIG	SIG	MOD	SIG	SIG	SIG	SIG	MOD	LIM
Wyoming	LIM	LIM	LIM	MOD	LIM	LIM	LIM	MOD	MOD

34

^aGrades were awarded by using the criteria below.

^bAs designated by governor for various OMB and other federal program requirements.

GRADE	CONTENT ANALYSIS	OPINION SURVEY	INTEREST OF OFFICIALS	EFFECTIVENESS EVALUATION
SIG = Significant	Sophisticated development stage	Generally accepted and desirable	High	Strong
MOD = Moderate	Being developed or modest stage	Some acceptance but varying desirability	Modest	Medium
LIM = Limited	Initial development stage or none	Little acceptance or desirability	Little	Little

Source: Anthony James Catanese, "Reflections on State Planning Evaluation," The Council of State Planning Agencies and the Council of State Governments (eds.), State Planning Issues 1973 (Lexington, Ky.: Council of State Governments, 1973), p. 27.

assistance refers to the aid programs the states have for local governments in planning and land use, and 16 states in all have done well here; nevertheless, this represents a traditional activity of the states and is not a departure from the past. At the same time, over half the states are making "moderate" progress in coordinating functional plans of their own agencies (highway plans, for example), in regional coordination involving substate districts and metropolitan planning agencies, and in "stimulation and support" of planning in general, a vague category at best. Only limited progress is reported in "development planning" and "development controls," and although neither is defined, they presumably refer to "land-use" planning and control. If so, this should shed some light on the first column of Table 2, and it further suggests that the states are accomplishing very little in the way of comprehensive or land-use planning.

Generally, the tables confirm the observations of John Kolesar who just a short time ago said that only a "few states" have made any real efforts at regaining the land-use powers they "handed away." Kolesar, deputy commissioner of the New Jersey Department of Community Affairs, went on to point out that statewide planning is still "largely advisory" and indicated that the states have "little coordinated control" over even their own capital projects.[16]

They are also consistent with the general findings of Vincent Moore on planning in New York State, at least insofar as state power is being used to override restrictive local practices,[17] although they are at odds with the assessment of others including Fred Bosselman, David Callies, Richard Babcock, and Elizabeth Haskell. Bosselman and Callies argue that the "ancien regime" of local land-use controls is giving way to state powers and that local planning and zoning are being "overthrown" through a "quiet revolution" that is taking place all across the country.[18] Babcock and Bosselman are similarly optimistic although slightly more cautious about the states moving in planning and land-use regulation, writing this time in their recent work on exclusionary zoning.[19] And Elizabeth Haskell in a 1971 article saw great promise in state planning and was particularly impressed with the spadework done by Hawaii and Vermont in developing statewide land-use programs.[20]

ASSESSMENT OF DIRECT STATE PLANNING

It is significant that the record of direct state planning is mixed at best, because only a few short years ago the states were being touted as the answer to our land-use problems. The Haskell article suggests this, as does the "quiet revolution" report of Bosselman and Callies done in 1971. And in one of the boldest statements made on the subject, the Washington Post editorialized that same year that the states were the key to "planning the second America."[21]

But the fact of the matter is that by all measures, direct state planning has not succeeded, and this is based on the 1974 data. State planning did not work in the 1930s, and it is not working now. We are not saying that Bosselman, Callies, Haskell, and the Post are wrong, only that the most recent information does not bear out their predictions. It is very possible that early observers had taken the experiences of a few states to represent those of all or most of the states. Hawaii, for example, is the only state to have adopted a master plan and to have approved direct state zoning for its entire territory, and no other state has followed suit; in fact, political conditions may be such in Hawaii that no other state can follow suit, especially in view of highly concentrated land ownership there. And Vermont's achievements in developing state land regulations are by no means symptomatic of what other states are doing, as a general rule, that is. It would be a mistake, we think, to take the progress of a few states as that of all the states, or a majority of them.

This does not mean that we oppose direct state planning or land-use control, for we do not, but it does question a general strategy of land-use planning based on the states. State land-use planning is fine for some states, in essence those states that are doing it, but it is not necessarily right for all states, and it should not form the foundation for national land-use policy as it has up to this point. Perhaps it is not all that serious that Congress has failed to approve legislation making state planning a matter of national policy, basing our hopes for an improved environment on state planning and substantially stepping up the level of federal funding for state planning; in fact, perhaps the House did the nation a favor by voting down the Udall bill in mid-1974. It was voted down for political reasons, but perhaps it was bad substantively. Every major land-use bill to be considered by Congress since 1970 has been premised on state planning, and it appears that it is high time for a new approach. At least the facts point in this direction.

ALTERNATIVES TO DIRECT STATE PLANNING

Other than direct planning and land-use control, the states can perform two functions:

1. Establish planning agencies for particular regions, metropolitan areas, or other districts in the state, with powers over an area extending beyond a single jurisdiction but not to the state as a whole.

2. Concentrate on enabling legislation in planning and land-use control, or authorizing local governments to undertake planning, zoning, subdivision control, official mapping, and other related programs.

The latter role has been a traditional one for the states, and it has meant that virtually all planning and land-use powers are in the hands of localities and not the states, but the former function allows the states to get more directly involved in planning and zoning although not as much as if they did it directly for their territories as a whole. Since direct state planning has made little headway, perhaps the establishment of planning and zoning agencies for particular regions in the state is as much as most states are capable of doing along these lines. Certainly they can continue to provide enabling legislation to localities and they will, and we treat that in the next section after this. Let us now turn to regional planning and the experience of the states here.

DIRECT STATE ROLE IN REGIONAL PLANNING

Most states authorize regional planning, through their general planning enabling legislation, and this is not what we are talking about here. This is treated in the next section. What we are talking about here is the direct creation of regional planning agencies by the state, and this means we are discussing a minority of metropolitan and regional planning agencies and councils of governments; most of the regional or metropolitan planning units have been formed through state enabling legislation and not directly by the state.[*] The enabling legislation route has a major disadvantage—it rarely permits the assignment of enforcement powers to the regional agency. The reason for this is that under this approach the agency is formally established by action of local governments, the object of state enabling legislation, and while local governments may wish to have some form of regional and metropolitan planning, they will rarely give up local enforcement and implementation powers to any regional agency. It is local governments that are in the driver's seat when it comes to state enabling legislation, as we shall see shortly.

When a regional planning agency is created directly by the state, it can be given both planning and enforcement powers, and this is typically the case. Examples of such units are the San Francisco Bay Conservation and Development Commission, created by the State of California in 1965 and given the authority to plan and regulate land use around the bay; the Hackensack Meadowlands Development

---

[*] In the last survey of metropolitan planning that directed itself to this question, 99 of the 126 agencies responding were established under state enabling legislation. See U.S. Housing and Home Finance Agency, National Survey of Metropolitan Planning (Washington, D.C.: Government Printing Office, 1963), p. 4.

Commission, formed by New Jersey state law in 1969 and assigned planning and land-use powers over a 28-square-mile area in the northern part of the state; the Adirondack Park Agency, established by the New York state legislature in 1971 and given planning and zoning powers over both public and private land in the park; the Maryland-National Capital Park and Planning Commission, a regional agency created by the Maryland legislature, with planning, subdivision control, park and advisory zoning authority over the two counties that make up the Maryland suburbs of Washington, D.C.; and the Regional Planning Council, established directly by the state legislature to plan the multicounty Baltimore metropolitan area.[23] All but the last agency have implementation powers, that is, in addition to general planning, and all have local representation on their governing boards, up to and including 100 percent of the seats. Thus, direct state action in this field does not mean the absence of local government influence or control, and in fact may mean the reverse.

Interstate compacts may be included in this category as well, and they are simply regional agencies that extend across state lines. In this light, they require the approval of more than a single state although they are technically created by the states too. In addition, they require the "consent" of Congress, and this may be given in advance. An example of such an agency with some planning duties is the Interstate Commission on the Potomac River Basin, created by acts of the states of West Virginia, Pennsylvania, Virginia, Maryland, and the District of Columbia and assigned limited land-use and pollution control powers over the Potomac River and its tributaries.

An increasing number of states, most notably Georgia and Tennessee, have done quite a bit with "substate districting," a process by which the state legislature establishes subdistricts for its entire territory and forms planning commissions for each district.[24] This generally fits the pattern discussed in this section. At the same time, the procedure rarely involves the assignment of enforcement powers to the district planning commissions, and this has to be seen as a weakness. It seems to have caught on most in the Appalachian states and is backed by the Appalachian Regional Commission, serving a multistate area near the Eastern Seaboard. Let us now turn to the historic and possible future role of the states in planning and zoning enabling legislation.

STATE ENABLING LEGISLATION

For the most part in recent years, the contribution of the states to planning and zoning has been limited to approving enabling legislation permitting local governments to plan and zone. At least this has proved to be about their only permanent contribution. It is important to note that enabling legislation does not refer to all state legislation and is not the special name that is given to state legislation in the planning area as some planners think. It is a special form of state enactment, authorizing and permitting local governments to undertake certain functions or projects. In other words, it "enables" these governments to do something that they otherwise could not do. It does not mandate or require this, as is the case with most state legislation, but "permits" it, under certain conditions. These conditions may have to do with which local governments are authorized to do planning or zoning. Some, say cities over 5,000, may be so authorized; and others, say cities under that figure, or counties, may not. The conditions may also deal with substantive matters, including the nature and composition of the commission to be set up to do the planning or zoning. We get into this later. Enabling legislation incidentally is not limited to planning and zoning and is used by the states in many other fields as well such as public housing, urban renewal, recreation, and sanitation.

In our system of government, the "police power" rests with the states and not with the federal government or directly with local government. "Police power" refers to the general authority of a government or sovereign entity to take action and legislate in the public interest or the general health, safety, welfare, and morals of the people. Federalism, as it is practiced in this country, has placed the police power at the subnational level, and the national government is limited to those functions and duties authorized and listed in the Constitution of the United States (Article I, Section 8). In fact, the unspecified powers or those not given the national government are reserved to the states under the Tenth Amendment; these are generally the police powers. "Police power" has another definition, and it is typically used in this, the more popular sense in planning circles—and that is that it has to do with the regulatory power of the state. In planning and zoning, this means the power of the state to control private land and development in the public interest, and planners commonly see this as the equivalent of "police power." In this definition, however, it can apply to other matters as well, including public utilities (rates, location), restaurants (sanitation), labor unions (elections, use of funds), and corporations (campaign contributions).25

Another legal point is important here. Within the states the political system is "unitary," meaning that all powers reside in the state governments, and the local governments are subservient or merely "creatures" of the former. Local governments in this sense include cities, counties, townships, towns, villages, boroughs, special districts, school districts, and others for that matter. The term "creature" comes from a famous state court decision, in Iowa, a decision that produced the familiar "Dillon rule."26 This rule, so named after John F. Dillon, chief justice of the Iowa Supreme Court

at the time, holds that municipal corporations are creatures of the
state and that the state has total power over them. A contrary view
argues that local government is a matter of absolute right, but it is
the Dillon rule that has been sustained by the Supreme Court of the
United States.[27] The principle is usually applied to other local governments even though the ruling dealt only with municipalities.

Since localities are creatures of the state, they can do only what
the state permits or directs them to do, and this is where enabling
legislation comes in. The history of planning and zoning enabling
legislation is pertinent to this discussion, and by no means were the
states the sole or even the prime movers in this regard, although it
was their action that technically authorized planning and zoning in
this country.

It is instructive that in the modern era or from 1900 to the
present, it is zoning and not planning that has taken the lead. The
states enacted zoning enabling legislation years before they did anything about planning. It has worked the same way at the community
level as well, where the history of zoning is actually longer than that
of planning. This is not the way it was done in early American colonial
history, but it appears to be the way it has been done since then. It
should be noted that planning is only advisory, and although it theoretically should precede actual land regulation (zoning), states and
communities have typically opted for zoning first. Zoning is law, and
it must be "obeyed." It details the use of this or that piece of property—whether a hotel or a house with two acres of land can be built
on it—while planning merely suggests possible uses for the land.
Planning is a guide to future use, while zoning stipulates that use
here and now.

Although ordinances specifying building height limitations and
designating residential and other "use districts" were enacted in
some cities in the late 1800s and the first decade of this century, it
was not until 1916 that the first comprehensive zoning measure was
adopted. This was in New York City, and its foundation was not at
all ideological—having to do with the philosophical desirability of
government intervention in land use—but political. The ordinance
can be traced to concrete pressures, specifically to the Fifth Avenue
Association, an interest group. The association was composed of
leading merchants, and it wanted government help to protect its shops
from factories that were encroaching on its commercial district. It
is also significant that the roots of the first zoning regulations are
traced to a business group and not socialists or others with an elaborate political program. This is not an isolated phenomenon, and it
is important to the understanding of planning and zoning generally,
especially to how it can be altered.

Following the "zoning first" pattern, the U.S. Department of
Commerce published A Standard State Zoning Enabling Act in 1922.[28]
The document was designed to guide states in authorizing local zoning,

although in reality it was to stimulate them in this respect, and it was short by most standards and in comparison to the later model planning legislation. It covered only 13 pages, with 10 of these devoted to the text of the legislation. But needless to say, it was a powerful 10 pages, to the point and precise. The model had nine sections in all, and it was first put out in mimeographed form, revised in 1923 and printed for the first time in 1924; the latest revision was published in 1926.

The membership of the Advisory Committee that drafted the model legislation provides a clue to the original base of support for zoning in the United States. They included

- Charles B. Ball, secretary-treasurer of the American Society of Civil Engineers, City Planning Division
- Edward M. Bassett, counsel of the Zoning Committee of New York and a big name in city planning at the time
- Alfred Bettman, director of the National Conference on City Planning and well known in planning circles, with a base in Cincinnati
- Irving B. Hiett, past president of the National Association of Real Estate Boards, the main builder-developer lobby at the time
- John Ihlder, of the Chamber of Commerce of the United States
- Morris Knowles, also of the Chamber of Commerce and the American Society of Civil Engineers
- Nelson P. Lewis, of the National Conference on City Planning and the American City Planning Institute
- J. Horace McFarland, affiliated with the American Civic Association
- Frederick Law Olmsted, ex-president of the American City Planning Institute, also associated with the American Society of Landscape Architects and a leading name in city planning over the years
- Lawrence Veiller, secretary and director of the National Housing Association

Bassett was the chairman, and he is considered the father of zoning in this country.

Almost without exception, the members were taken from the major interest groups that could be expected to be concerned with planning and zoning and to have a concrete stake in it, and they included not only representatives of professional organizations such as engineers, architects, and planners but business groups as well. To top it off, they were appointed not by a liberal Democrat or an advocate of foreign collectivism, but a conservative Republican, Herbert Hoover, secretary of commerce during most of the 1920s. Hoover, it seems, became so impressed with the prospects of zoning that he decided to lend the weight of the federal government to the movement, and he was clearly the one who sparked the trend politically and on a national scale. The facts so far suggest that it is hard to substantiate the charge that planning and zoning are "antibusiness" and "contrary to the principles of the free enterprise system."

It appears that the states were not the mainstay behind zoning and had little to do with initiating the action at all. In fact, they seemed to be the necessary "vehicle" to getting the word out to localities, and because they were the custodians of the police power, it was mandatory that they act before local governments did. Actually, some states did move on the matter before the model legislation was available; they included Kansas, Nebraska, Missouri, and Indiana, all of which provided their localities with the zoning power before 1922. But the massive authorization of local zoning did not come until after the federal government published the model law.

Within a year of the original draft, 11 states had approved zoning enabling legislation, all patterned after the U.S. act. By 1925, a total of 19 states had adopted legislation virtually identical to the model bill, and by the early 1930s, most of the remaining states had followed suit and authorized their municipalities and other local governments to develop zoning programs. Now all states have approved some form of zoning enabling legislation, and in the vast majority of them, the acts are substantially the same as the federal model, in some cases following it word for word.

The effect in the cities was nearly as marked. In 1921, the year before the Advisory Committee put out its first draft, only 48 local governments in the entire United States had zoning, but by the early 1930s, some 800 cities had approved zoning ordinances. Today about 10,000 cities, counties, and other localities exercise the zoning power, including most local governments in metropolitan areas and an increasing number in rural areas.[29]

It is pertinent that more metropolitan municipalities have zoning than planning, which follows the general pattern as has already been suggested. Planning is apparently seen by cities as being less important than zoning, for reasons previously noted. Planning, it is true, is usually adopted eventually, but in reality not likely for the purpose of "guiding" zoning as the theory would have it, but more for legitimating it. A community zones first, and this gives it the patterns of development it wants—commercial, large-lot residential, apartment—and then it brings in planning to "dress it up" and provide it the Good Housekeeping stamp of approval. It is not even too farfetched to suggest that many local officials consider zoning to be planning and the zoning map to be the master plan, but this is another book.

Apparently even the experts consider zoning more important than planning because they did not come up with model planning legislation until 1928, or some six years after zoning. The idea presumably is that planning would be good to have and theoretically desirable, but it is best to get zoning on the books first and worry about planning later. In any event, planning experts such as Bassett, Bettman, and Olmsted served on both committees, and the planning unit did not issue its report until 1928. In fact, there was considerable overlap in the membership of the two panels, and virtually the

same persons served on both. The planning committee had one local
member, but this was the only difference, with all other members
being carry overs. Thus the organizations represented were the
same, with leading professional and business groups dominating both.
Significantly, labor was represented on neither committee, nor was
the bar or the general public.

The name of the second committee was altered slightly to include
"city planning," or the U.S. Advisory Committee on City Planning
and Zoning. Its official report was entitled A Standard City Planning
Enabling Act, and it contained five sections and 53 pages altogether,
making it four times as long as the zoning model.[30] As with the first
unit, this one was appointed by Secretary of Commerce Hoover, but
unlike its predecessor, it was concerned with more than a single
topic. In addition to city planning, it provided the legislation necessary for the development of local subdivision controls, the official
map, and regional planning. That is, it provided the general rules to
be adopted by state legislatures for the purpose of authorizing local
actions in these areas.

While zoning covers such matters as the type of land use permitted (commercial, residential), density, lot size, and setback
requirements, subdivision regulations seek to assure compatibility
of development from one subdivision to the next and apply to such
things as the dedication of public streets, parks and school sites,
and the provision of public facilities. The "official map" was originally limited to reserving road and street rights of way—in other
words, keeping them from being developed—but may now apply to a
variety of other future public uses such as water mains, drainage
rights of way, parks and playgrounds, and perhaps other public facilities. Incidentally, both subdivision regulations and the official map
are typically administered by the local planning commission, and
this is the way the model legislation reads. Of course, "city planning"
and "regional planning" also covered by the model refer to the process by which future development aims and objectives are determined
and the associated maps, plans, research reports, and other documents, with city planning taking place within the confines of a single
municipality and regional planning occurring across local political
subdivision lines.

Almost certainly one of the most striking features of the 1928
act was the emphasis put on regional planning, which is generally
thought to be of more recent origin. In fact, regional planning never
really came into its own until at least the 1950s and maybe the early
1960s, but the model legislation made it almost simple for a state to
create a regional planning commission.*

---

*A simple petitioning procedure was set up, requiring only the
signatures of 100 citizens or action of a local planning commission.
More generally, see Joint Center for Urban Studies, M.I.T. and

As in zoning, most states quickly adopted the national model, and by the mid-1930s, over half the states had approved measures permitting local planning. Today, all states authorize their localities to plan, either through enabling legislation or in other ways such as city charters or direct legislation. It is instructive that state enabling legislation was so closely patterned after the national model and that very few of the states have altered that legislation substantially since the 1930s. The same is generally true of the zoning legislation, and presently most state enabling laws are still based on the model of the 1920s.

The model planning act and therefore the state statutes go into planning organization and powers in some detail, and specificity is the rule. For example, the standard legislation calls for the establishment of independent planning commissions. The reasoning behind this was that planning was too important a function for politicians and politics and that it should be protected from these influences. This assumes that politics cannot influence the "independent" planning commission, but more recent research shows this is not true. The result of this stipulation was the creation of planning commissions that were not responsible to the city council or chief executive, at least directly, and that were independent of the general political and policy processes in the community. The provision was backed by Bassett, Bettman, and Olmsted, but it has been taken to task by contemporary students of city planning including Richard Babcock, the National Commission on Urban Problems, Robert Walker, T.J. Kent, Jr., and others.[31]

The more recent arguments hold that there is no way to divorce planning from politics, that planning should be put under officials who are politically responsible and accountable, that planning has to be implemented to be effective, and that it cannot be implemented if not integrated into the mainstream of local government, along with sewers, water supply, zoning, highways, mass transit, parks, and other functions. Also it is claimed that the independent planning commission has not worked the way the proponents had hoped and that the quality of local politicians is higher than it was in the 1920s. These arguments seem to be the generally accepted ones today, at least in the planning community.*

Harvard, The Effectiveness of Metropolitan Planning (Washington, D.C.: Government Printing Office, 1964).

*Planning directors do not feel a transfer of planning to the mayor or council will impair the quality of planning. See Francine F. Rabinovitz and J. Stanley Pottinger, "Organization for Local Planning: The Attitudes of Directors," Journal of the American Institute of Planners (January 1967): 27-32.

Other stipulations of the model legislation provided for a multi-membered planning board to administer the planning agency, established the terms of planning board members, set forth the duties of planning commissions, determined what municipal unit would be responsible for adopting the plan (the planning commission or city council), and named the planning commission as the administrator of key planning-related ordinances. They also set the ground rules and criteria for making planning decisions.

The incidence of planning and subdivision powers in American localities today is as follows:

Communities with	Total Number	Portion of Universe
Planning board	10,717	59.6 percent
Subdivision regulation	8,086	44.9 percent

Over 10,000 communities have planning boards, and this represents about 60 percent of those that might reasonably be expected to exercise planning powers. In 1972, there were over 78,000 local governments in the United States, and thus the universe considered here is by no means as broad as that; actually, most local governments are school districts, special districts, or other units that are not the general-purpose variety that are set up to do planning.[32] In addition, about 8,000 local governments have adopted subdivision regulations, and both the planning and subdivision authority can normally be traced directly to the early state enabling legislation.

Planning boards exist in nearly all cities with a population of 50,000 or more and in over 90 percent of the cities with a population ranging from 5,000 to 50,000. Furthermore, about three-quarters of American cities have a published master plan, although this says nothing about their having adopted or implemented this plan. In addition to local planning commissions, there are now about 400 metropolitan planning boards, including multijurisdictional agencies, city-county units, county commissions, and increasingly councils of governments.

This pretty much completes the picture of state involvement in planning and zoning at the local level, although the states do provide "technical assistance" to localities as has been noted above. David Ranney terms the state input in this respect "not very helpful" and outdated, and he is particularly concerned that the states have not seen fit to make many changes in either their zoning or planning enabling acts; he says that this indicates a "lack of state concern" with the planning of urban areas.[33]

At the same time, it would be wrong to place the entire burden on the states, for as we have seen with the model acts, the states do pretty much what they are pressured to do. And if in fact urban areas

have inadequate state authorizations or are operating under outmoded
state laws, the cities and counties are not helpless to do anything
about it. To the contrary, the municipal lobby in state legislatures
is one of the most important around, and in all but one or two states
the cities are organized into interest groups called municipal leagues
or associations. Examples are the Florida League of Cities, the
Georgia Municipal Association, the League of California Cities, the
New York State Conference of Mayors, and the Utah League of Cities
and Towns. Counties are similarly organized (Maryland Association
of Counties), and they have a great deal of power in many states. A
recent study shows the influence of localities in state legislatures,
and this influence appears to be particularly marked in some of the
urban and industrial states like New York, where the city government
lobby ranks right up there with major business and labor groups.[34]
Politics means pressure, and the states are subject to it just like
other governments are; they are not exempt.

As we have pointed out, direct state planning has not produced
much. A far preferable approach, we think, is a reform of state
enabling legislation, by bringing it more up to date and more in line
with contemporary conditions and thinking. The goal should be to
widen the inputs into the local planning and zoning decision-making
process, along the lines proposed by the Douglas Commission,
Richard Babcock, and others; this would include the development of
new criteria on which local planning decisions are based and increasing the number and variety of interests that are involved in these
decisions. Perhaps the independent planning commission issue
should be reconsidered as well, although this is not as important as
the substantive changes. This would not require any transfer of
direct powers to the state, but it would probably involve the state
more in local decisions.

In short, the criteria should be broader than they are at present,
and they should include "regional," "metropolitan," and even "statewide" factors, that is, in addition to the purely "local" ones that are
considered now. They should also include the impact of land-use
decisions on matters not considered under existing enabling legislation or local ordinances, and this would include the effect on the
supply of housing, especially for low- and moderate-income people,
and on the need for facilities to serve entire regions or areas
broader than one community. State enabling legislation is generally
silent on these points and leaves much discretion to local governments. The local governments, in turn, have tended to neglect the
wider variables.[35] Luther Gulick said over a decade ago that there
is no way that one community can isolate itself from others, but the
suburbs of our great metropolitan areas are clearly trying, and
zoning is typically the means.[36]

In one community that we have in mind, a zoning decision on a
gas station at the intersection of a local road and an interstate

highway can be based only on "local" need, or the needs of the immediate neighborhood for gas services. (This is the way the ordinance
reads, and it is based on state enabling legislation.) The fact that the
interstate highway has a traffic count of 40,000 cars a day and that
there is no gas station in any direction for 10 miles cannot, as a
legal matter, be considered in this decision. Clearly, state enabling
legislation should be revised to require, and not merely permit, consideration of need as it in reality exists in the wider context, and not
in the artificially narrow frame in which it presently exists.

It is clear that more groups and interests are affected by local
land-use decisions than are represented in the hearings and other
deliberations associated with these decisions. Citizens in one jurisdiction may well be affected by a decision of a neighboring community
on a shopping center, for example. The decision may affect them not
only as consumers needing commercial facilities, but the ultimate
need for shopping facilities in their own neighborhood. Yet these
citizens are not, as a matter of course or legal right, included in
zoning and planning decisions in jurisdictions other than their own.
They receive no notices of public hearings, no reports of the planning
commission, and no official communication on the matter at all. Most
enabling legislation says nothing on this point and provides only that
the needs of communities be taken into account and that public hearings be held. The legislation could be phrased to encourage the consideration of the needs and views of these people even though they
are not voters in the jurisdiction and perhaps in the state in question.
Since this would normally take place within a single metropolitan
area, it would add a metropolitan dimension to decisions that are now
purely local. The idea here would be to add political reinforcement
to the criteria changes suggested above; that is, metropolitan interests should be brought into the locality to back up metropolitan
needs.

The political step would perhaps force decisions into broader
channels and make a reality out of the legal stipulation that wider
factors be taken into account. That interests outside a particular
jurisdiction do not vote in that jurisdiction and therefore would have
no political weight there is an argument that cannot be substantiated.
The fact of the matter is that voting is not the only way to influence
public officials and government decisions, and it may not even be the
most important.[77]

FORMAT FOR THE REST OF THE BOOK

These are a few of our recommendations, and we develop the
points throughout the book. We also examine other forms of state
involvement in planning and land-use control in more detail, including

direct planning and zoning, and make suggestions on these matters. We do not present a dogmatic view, one that must be followed under any and all circumstances, but hopefully we do provide some realistic options and a central theme that will be workable. With B. F. Skinner, we see planning as a tool that can be shaped and molded to the ends we want. But to be successful, that tool must operate within certain practical and political constraints, and it is in identifying these constraints that this book may make its greatest contribution.[38] It is in this sense that our work can most valuably be used as a guide to future national land-use policy.

NOTES

1. Tom McCall, "Oregon: Come Visit but Don't Stay," State Government XLVI, no. 3 (Summer 1973): 167-171. See also Innovations in State Government: Messages from the Governors (Washington, D.C.: National Governors' Conference, 1974), especially Parts II and III on state planning and land-use control.

2. See John W. Reps, The Making of Urban America: A History of City Planning in the United States (Princeton, N.J.: Princeton University Press, 1965), pp. 95-103.

3. Alan P. Grimes, American Political Thought, rev. ed. (New York: Holt, Rinehart and Winston, 1960), p. 24.

4. Richard Hofstadter and others, The American Republic, 2nd ed. (Englewood Cliffs, N.J.: Prentice-Hall, 1970), Vol. 1, p. 236.

5. See Hamilton, Madison, and Jay, The Federalist Papers (New York: Mentor Books, 1961); and Alexander Hamilton, "Report on Manufacturers," in A. T. Mason (ed.), Free Government in the Making, 3rd ed. (New York: Oxford University Press, 1965), pp. 341-348.

6. Mel Scott, American City Planning Since 1890 (Berkeley: University of California Press, 1969), p. 304.

7. See Daniel J. Elazar, American Federalism: A View from the States, 2nd ed. (New York: Thomas Y. Crowell, 1972). Professor Elazar describes the direct federal-local tie as a "squeak point" in the federal system (Chap. 8). In other words, he does not like it and wants all money to go through the states.

8. Edward C. Banfield and James Q. Wilson, City Politics (Cambridge, Mass.: Harvard University Press, 1963), p. 267.

9. Mills argues persuasively that businessmen do not have to be formally organized to have influence. C. Wright Mills, The Power Elite (New York: Oxford University Press, 1956), p. 294.

10. See, for example, two of the most recent books on intergovernmental relations: Arthur W. Macmahon, Administering Federalism in a Democracy (New York: Oxford University Press, 1972);

and Michael D. Reagan, The New Federalism (New York: Oxford University Press, 1972).

11. See Suzanne Farkas, Urban Lobbying (New York: New York University Press, 1971).

12. David K. Hartley, "State Planning," in Frank Smothers (ed.), The Book of the States, 1968-69, Vol. XVII (Lexington, Ky.: Council of State Governments, 1968), p. 433.

13. See, for example, James Dolliver, "State Planning and the Governor's Office," in The Council of State Planning Agencies and The Council of State Governments (eds.), State Planning Issues 1973 (Lexington, Ky.: Council of State Governments, 1973), pp. 39-40; and Deil S. Wright, "Governmental Forms and Planning Functions: The Relation of Organizational Structures to Planning Practice," in Thad L. Beyle and George T. Lathrop (eds.), Planning and Politics (New York: Odyssey, 1970), pp. 68-115.

14. Vincent T. Smith, Jr., "State Planning," in Robert H. Weber (ed.), The Book of the States, 1972-73, Vol. XIX (Lexington, Ky.: Council of State Governments, 1972), p. 445.

15. See Proceedings of the Conference on Organizing and Managing the Coastal Zone, June 13-14, 1973 (Washington, D.C.: Council of State Governments, 1974).

16. John N. Kolesar, "The States and Urban Planning and Development," in Alan K. Campbell (ed.), The States and the Urban Crisis (Englewood Cliffs, N.J.: Prentice-Hall, 1970), p. 131.

17. Vincent J. Moore, "Politics, Planning, and Power in New York State: The Path from Theory to Reality," Journal of the American Institute of Planners XXXVII, no. 2 (March 1971): 66-77.

18. Fred Bosselman and David Callies, The Quiet Revolution in Land-Use Control (Washington, D.C.: Government Printing Office, 1971), p. 1.

19. Richard F. Babcock and Fred P. Bosselman, Exclusionary Zoning: Land-Use Regulation and Housing in the 1970s (New York: Praeger Publishers, 1973), Chaps. 11 and 12.

20. Elizabeth Haskell, "New Directions in State Environmental Planning," Journal of the American Institute of Planners XXXVII, no. 4 (July 1971): 253-258.

21. "Planning the Second America," editorial from The Washington Post, November 20, 1971, in U.S. Senate, Committee on Interior and Insular Affairs, Background Papers on National Land-Use Policy (Washington, D.C.: Government Printing Office, 1972), pp. 21-22.

22. E. Jack Schoop and John E. Hirten, "The San Francisco Bay Plan: Combining Policy with Police Power," Journal of the American Institute of Planners XXXVII, no. 1 (January 1971): 2-10.

23. Another example may be the Lake George Park Commission in New York, an agency with wide powers including zoning over a broad area, although it is not clear whether it is created directly by the state or through enabling legislation. See William H. Whyte, The Last Landscape (Garden City, N.Y.: Doubleday, 1968), p. 52.

24. See James L. Sundquist, Making Federalism Work (Washington, D.C.: Brookings, 1969), pp. 158-163; and Advisory Commission on Intergovernmental Relations, Regional Governance: Promise and Performance (Washington, D.C.: Government Printing Office, 1973). The latter is Vol. II of a six-volume series on Substate Regionalism and the Federal System.

25. The two definitions are discussed in the dated but valuable book: Donald H. Webster, Urban Planning and Municipal Public Policy (New York: Harper & Row, 1958), pp. 270-272. Unfortunately this book is out of print.

26. See City of Clinton v. the Cedar Rapids and Missouri River Railroad Co., 24 Iowa 455 (1868).

27. This view is found in People v. Hurlbut, 24 Mich. 44 (1871). For a discussion of the conflicting interpretations of local governments vis-a-vis the states, see Anwar Syed, The Political Theory of Local Government (New York: Random House, 1966).

28. U.S. Advisory Committee on Zoning, Department of Commerce, A Standard State Zoning Enabling Act Under Which Municipalities May Adopt Zoning Regulations, rev. ed. (Washington, D.C.: Government Printing Office, 1926).

29. Allen D. Manvel, Local Land and Building Regulation (Washington, D.C.: Government Printing Office, 1968). This report was done for the National Commission on Urban Problems, chaired by former senator Paul H. Douglas of Illinois, and represents the only comprehensive survey of local planning and zoning ever done. The panel's main report was Building the American City (Washington, D.C.: Government Printing Office, 1968).

30. U.S. Advisory Committee on City Planning and Zoning, Department of Commerce, A Standard City Planning Enabling Act (Washington, D.C.: Government Printing Office, 1928).

31. Richard F. Babcock, The Zoning Game (Madison: University of Wisconsin Press, 1966), Chap. 2 (Babcock calls the planning commission a "dodo," "neither expert nor responsible"); Building the American City, pp. 238-239, cited above (Note 29); Robert A. Walker, The Planning Function in Urban Government (Chicago: University of Chicago Press, 1950); and T. J. Kent, Jr., The Urban General Plan (San Francisco: Chandler, 1964), especially Chap. 1.

32. U.S. Bureau of the Census, Census of Governments, 1972, Vol. 1, Governmental Organization (Washington, D.C.: Government Printing Office, 1973), p. 1.

33. David C. Ranney, Planning and Politics in the Metropolis (Columbus: Charles E. Merrill Publishing Co., 1969), pp. 66-67.

34. Wayne L. Francis, Legislative Issues in the Fifty States: A Comparative Analysis (Chicago: Rand McNally, 1967), Chap. 3. This study employed sophisticated statistical techniques to reach its conclusions and was based on the perceptions of state legislators. See also Harmon Zeigler and Michael Baer, Lobbying: Interaction

and Influence in American State Legislatures (Belmont, Calif.: Wadsworth, 1969).

35. See, for example, Raymond and May Associations, Zoning Controversies in the Suburbs: Three Case Studies (Washington, D.C.: Government Printing Office, 1968), especially pp. 72-78 on "Land Development Decisions: Analysis."

36. Luther Halsey Gulick, The Metropolitan Problem and American Ideas (New York: Knopf, 1962).

37. See David B. Truman, The Governmental Process, 2nd ed. (New York: Knopf, 1971).

38. In this respect we build on a tradition started by Edward Banfield. See John Fridemann and Barclay Hudson, "Knowledge and Action: A Guide to Planning Theory," Journal of the American Institute of Planners 40, no. 1 (January 1974): 13.

3

DIRECT STATE PLANNING: AN OVERVIEW

Perhaps the most important point we can make in this and the next chapter is that direct state planning is so limited. It is not the accomplishments and achievements of Hawaii and one or two others like Vermont, as significant and real as they are. The fact is that most of the states have done little or nothing in this category, and this has been shown in Chapter 2. Table 2 suggests that few states have received the highest rating in direct state planning. The column "Statewide Land-Use Planning and Control" contains only the states of Hawaii, Vermont, Florida, Maine, Minnesota, and Oregon as those with the greatest powers in this area.

In addition, Table 3 shows nine states making "significant" progress in "development planning," or the category treated here, and they are Delaware, Hawaii, Maine, New Hampshire, New Jersey, Rhode Island, Texas, Vermont, and Wisconsin. However, it should be noted that making "significant" progress is not the same as having the program or doing much about it; it may only measure the progress of a state in moving toward a program. At the same time, Maine, Florida, and Oregon are generally recognized as being in a sort of "second level" of states directly involved in planning and land-use control, that is, right behind Hawaii and Vermont, and they are treated in Chapter 4.[1] Even Vermont may belong is this "second level" of states since its controls are generally limited to areas outside towns and cities with zoning powers. Hawaii's zoning, on the other hand, applies to every square foot of land in the state's inhabited islands, putting it in a special class. John Kolesar puts Alaska as well in this "second" level, but we feel the situation in that state is such that there is little to distinguish it from the others; thus, we do not accord it any special status.[2]

Even the recent State of the States 1974 report of the governors
admits that the states have been slow to adopt "strong, comprehensive
planning measures," and perhaps part of the reason is the governors
themselves—that is, their lack of power to do anything about it.[3] But
maybe the problem is deeper than this and can be traced to broader
political factors; at least the facts in this chapter point this way.

For comparative purposes and to build on the literature to date,
our first class, the one reserved for Hawaii, is the same as the
Council of State Governments' "Approach A," Statewide Comprehensive Land-Use Management, and to William James' Category (1),
Statewide Comprehensive Land-Use Management; our "second level,"
containing perhaps Vermont and a few others, is generally the equivalent of the Council of State Governments' "Approach B," Land
Management According to Functional Criteria, and to Senator James'
Category (2) with the same title.[4]

MEANING OF STATE PLANNING AND ZONING

Before getting into the details of the states with direct land-use
authority, let us define our terms. Direct state planning means that
the state government does planning for the state as a whole or a substantial part of it, and this refers to comprehensive or land-use
planning. Generally, this involves the preparation and adoption of a
master plan for the state's entire territory or most of it. This plan
will include proposed land uses such as urban, rural, conservation,
or more detailed categories like residential, particular kinds of residential, commercial, industrial, and so on. In other words, the plan
indicates where each type of use should take place, and it contains a
map that specifies these uses for particular areas or land in the state.
This does not necessarily mean that localities do no planning, and in
practice it clearly does not mean this; it only means that the states
are in the direct planning business. Local planning may be more
detailed as in Hawaii, or cover areas not treated by the state plan
as in Vermont. Similarly, the plan may extend to all areas in the
state as it does in Hawaii or only to selected ones as is the case in
other states.

The state master plan may also get into other aspects of planning,
that is, in addition to land use per se, and in Hawaii this includes
public facilities and transportation planning.[5] This can be confusing.
As T. J. Kent points out, public facilities and highways are also "land
uses" and can be considered part of land-use planning.[6] In Vermont,
state planning is generally limited to the narrower version of "land-
use planning" and has a more traditional land-use focus. In the other
states mentioned—Maine, Florida, and Oregon—planning is also more
or less restricted to conventional land-use considerations. Again it
is Hawaii that stands out and that seems virtually isolated from the rest.

"State zoning" is shorthand for state land-use controls, and this refers to direct state powers to control development on a wide scale or a fairly widespread basis. It may include zoning per se as it does in Hawaii, or it may fall under a broader or different classification such as "land regulation." In fact, the states on the mainland seem to be avoiding the term "zoning," and this has to be for political reasons; "zoning" is local, and the states do not want to be infringing on a local power. Presumably if another name is used, local authorities will not object as much, perhaps because they do not know what is happening. Vermont, for example, calls their zoning by another name, and the administration in Maryland denied seeking zoning when they asked for powers to regulate "critical areas" in the state. As with planning, state zoning may apply to all land in the state (Hawaii) or most of it (Vermont).

Zoning regulates land uses and indicates where commercial, various forms of residential, industrial, recreational, and other uses may be permitted. Unlike planning, zoning carries the force of law; planning, of course, is merely advisory. Zoning includes both a text, which sets forth the rules for each zoning class (set back requirements, building height, and minimum lot sizes), and a map, which designates uses for each tract of land to which it is applied. Some of this was covered in Chapter 2, but that was in an exclusively local context. State zoning is more general than the local variety, and in the only state that has it pure and simple, Hawaii, it deals with broad categories of land uses within which localities determine more specific uses. Some states such as Oregon have direct state subdivision regulations, governing layout patterns and the provisions for various public facilities like streets, sewer, and water. Again, as with zoning, subdivision control in the states is typically more general than in localities.

"Land regulation," or the more general definition of zoning, may refer to a variety of land-use controls including subdivision powers, a "permit system" under which developers are required to secure a use permit, and zoning per se in the narrower sense. State land regulations may apply to both public and private land, but they have the greatest meaning in the private sphere. The federal government is not required to follow state land controls or local ones for that matter, and the record of state and local compliance with their own land regulations is mixed and spotty at best. The nature of politics seems to make land regulation a matter between public authorities and private developers, as government agencies do not seem to control each other very well. In addition, the states doing direct state planning and regulation may also be engaged in other land-use programs such as coastal zone management, power plant siting, or the designation of critical areas, but this is of importance in this and the next chapter only insofar as it relates to more broadly based planning and land regulation.

DIRECT STATE PLANNING
AND NATIONAL LAND-USE POLICY

   Direct state planning has been a part of every major land-use
bill introduced in Congress in recent years. Here we are talking only
about "planning" the advisory function and not, for the moment, zoning
or land regulation. It was part of the original Jackson bill in 1970,
and it is part of the two measures to have gone the furthest in the
House and Senate this Congress (93rd).[7] The administration has
supported it as have most of the Democrats in both houses, and so
have some conservative Republicans like Senators Goldwater and
Buckley. Interest groups have backed it, including the home-builders,
developers, the labor unions, conservation organizations such as the
Sierra Club, the governors, state legislators, and the Rockefeller
brothers.[8]
   Planning, as we are treating it in this section, is not the same
as direct state creation of regional agencies (Chapter 1). It involves
only the state government itself, dealing with its entire territory or
a major part of it; agencies established by the state for particular
portions of the state or other forms of regional, subdistrict, or local
planning in the states are excluded. Neither does it refer to coastal
zone planning or planning for critical areas alone (with one exception
cited below); these are only limited kinds of state planning even though
they are direct. It also excludes functional planning done by state
agencies such as highway planning of the state roads department or
commission. The meaning is highly specialized. To qualify, it must
be done for the state as a whole or a substantial part of it; it must be
done by the states directly or by a central agency of the state such
as a planning department; and it is limited to the "master plan"
process.
   The proposed Land-Use Planning Act of 1974 provides for direct
state planning.[9] It authorizes the federal government to make annual
grants to the states to assist in the development and administration
of a "comprehensive land-use planning process." The bill defines
this process as one that provides for the "development of an adequate
data base for comprehensive land-use planning," the coordination of
the planning activities of all state agencies (as the activities impinge
on land use), the consideration of "aesthetic, ecological, environmental" and other values and conditions, the identification of land to be
used for agriculture and forestry, industry, transportation, urban
development, and other purposes, and the establishment of a method
of assuring that local government programs are consistent with state
planning objectives. The measure also calls for the "substantial and
meaningful" public and agency involvement in "all significant aspects"
of the state planning process and requires the states to take into
account the planning activities of interstate agencies.

These are very broad and general factors, not subject to precise definition or specific limitations. They leave scarcely anything for the imagination and include virtually "everything" as far as we can tell. The one limitation seems to be "land use," but most things can be related to land use in some way or another. The measure provides little protection for local planning and local planning agencies and seems to hand the entire planning job over to the states; within the states, the task is given to a central planning agency.

It is important and in fact crucial to see that the "planning" provisions of this legislation do not contain the same thrust as "land regulation." Land regulation is limited in quite specific terms to "critical areas" or "areas of critical environmental concern" and to certain land uses of "regional," "statewide," or "more than local" impact. No such limitations are put on planning, and federal money can be used for any and all purposes or territory in the states. It must only fall in the "land-use" category.

The latest Senate bill calls on the states to develop a "statewide land-use planning process" within three years, and planning funds under the legislation can be withheld if the states fail to act. Yet the Senate's definition of "statewide planning" is not as broad as the House's and in fact represents a watered down version of the bill the Senate approved in 1972 (the latest Senate action was 1973). In other words, the role of the states in comprehensive land-use planning has been cut back in these two respects.

The committee report accompanying the Senate bill makes a point of this and specifically says that the bill does "not require state planning over all land within the state."[10] The Senate version restricts state planning to five categories of planning, and these are areas of critical environmental concern such as flood plains and coastal districts, key facilities like airports and major highway interchanges, large-scale development such as industrial parks, public facilities, and utilities of regional benefit, and land sales and development in recreation areas. The land-use bill passed by the Senate in 1972 provided for a wider role for state planning and authorized federal grants for state planning of their entire territories; to be eligible for grants, "adequate statewide" land-use planning was necessary.[11]

The reasons for the change are not clear, but it may have had something to do with pressures from cities and counties. Local officials have generally been concerned that state planning would interfere with their prerogatives, but their lobbying has been low-keyed in this regard. In essence, the Senate bill restricts state planning to areas outside cities and counties with planning, and even then to areas meeting certain criteria. If the House language is accepted, there seems little question that tension would arise between the states and localities over planning. This apparently the Senate has tried to avoid.

However, there is another factor here. The House, while more liberal in the planning area, is more restrictive on "land regulation."

Here it is the House that cuts back on state powers and the Senate
that expands them. Perhaps the House chose to bow to local influence
on regulation and to take the broader view on planning, the "safer"
of the two. The Senate's reasoning may have been that quibbling over
planning should not impede action on regulation. Regulation is generally
considered more important, and the idea would be to get the states
into actual land control first and to worry about planning later. This
view was reflected in the model state planning and zoning legislation
provided in the 1920's, and it is found in the more recent Model Land
Development Code of the American Law Institute.[12] In this light, it
is probably the House bill that most significantly restrains the states,
a position quite consistent with the traditional role of this chamber.[13]
Incidentally, both the House and Senate measures advance $800 million
to the states for planning and regulation. We are thus talking about a
large sum of money, much more than is presently available to the states
for planning alone.

The argument for statewide planning is that for the states to regulate critical areas they have to know something about all land in the
state. That is, critical areas or uses of more than local concern cannot be adequately planned unless it is known how they relate to the
broader picture. The point is that there are interrelationships, and
only the wider form of planning can show them. This is truly "comprehensive" planning, and there is much merit in it.[14] It is hard to
contest in purely abstract and ideal terms.

In fact, the opposition has not suggested that in theory the wider
planning role is not desirable, but they have argued that localities are
already planning and that general state planning would lead to confusion and duplication. Planning for critical areas is one thing, but
statewide planning is something else. This says nothing of the political
rivalries that would be triggered if the states tried to plan in the
broader sense; this would be particularly true if state plans conflicted
with local ones and were not simply reflections of them. The political
realities seem even more important than the considerations of merit
(confusion and duplication). Few people deny the value of state planning
as a general matter, and in practice few dispute state planning that is
limited to critical areas or uses of more than local concern. This
says nothing of their position on regulation of such areas or uses.

There is a strong possibility that the House approach will prevail,
and this is the approach favored by most experts in the field. This
does not make it "right," but it is a fact worth noting, and it is certainly consistent with planning theory. In this sense, the experiences
of the states in broadly based direct planning are especially pertinent.
If the federal government is going to support this kind of planning,
we should at least know what the record is in the states. Have they
shown capabilities? Is there any reason to assume they can do this
sort of planning? For national policy to be based on this state planning,
there should be some evidence showing that the states can do the job
and hence justifying sharply expanded federal outlays for this purpose.

DIRECT STATE ZONING
AND NATIONAL LAND-USE POLICY

Direct state zoning as used in this section refers to any form of
state land regulation applying generally or to most land in the state.
In fact, proposed national land-use policy is more limited than this
and, unlike planning (House version), is restricted to state control
of critical areas. The one state discussed in this chapter, Hawaii,
and one in the next, Vermont, have gone beyond the federal mandate.
Both the House and Senate land-use bills authorize federal assistance
for state regulation of "critical" or other areas of more than local
concern.

It is widely assumed that this will involve only a portion of any
state, and the committee reports accompanying both bills cite the Model
Land Development Code as the source of the point that no more than
10 percent of the state, and this would include areas impacted by key
facilities (House), uses subject to development of "regional" benefit
(House), the location of new towns (Senate), and areas of significant
historic and cultural value (Senate).

The House report says:[15]

the Model Code estimated that decisions affecting such areas
and land uses might constitute 10 percent of all land-use decisions within a given state. Development and land-use decisions
of only local concern, approximately 90 percent, would remain
under the control of local governments.

Similarly, the Senate report says: "According to an estimate . . . of
the American Law Institute, at least 90 percent of the land-use decisions currently being made are of local significance only."[16] The
idea is that they would not be affected by the legislation, and the
purpose for stressing this is to dispel fears of local officials. However, there is no way to know just how much land the federal legislation will affect, and it could be as much as 100 percent in some cases.
The 10-percent figure represents a judgment on the part of the repor-
ters of the American Law Institute and is not part of the Code per se.
Thus there is no way of knowing the accuracy of the figure. A state
wanting to limit regulation would be well advised to put the specifics
in the legislation. Florida did this in its Land and Water Management
Act of 1972, and Maryland followed suit in 1973 (both use 5 percent;
in Maryland it applies not only to the state as a whole, but to each
county separately).

Now let us turn to the experiences of Hawaii and, in the next
chapter, to the other states most known for the development of direct
state land controls. We consider both the unique and unusual as well
as the typical aspects of these states, in an attempt to see the extent

to which they can serve as a model for national policy makers. Direct state planning and zoning are treated together.

HAWAII

Background and Politics

The history of Hawaii is pertinent to this discussion, and traditional patterns of land control and ownership make this state special if not unique. At the same time, the state faces some of the same problems of urbanization, conservation, preservation of farmland and open space, and housing that are found in other states; in fact, it has been having these problems for some time.

The fact that Hawaii has a different background than the other states has some bearing on its use as a "model" for the others. The most important point that can be made in this respect is a tradition of centralization. This goes for both the control and ownership of land. In the early days, land was controlled by a small set of Hawaiian "chiefs" or tribal heads who exercised authority over most aspects of the islands' life. Although there was the "Great Land Division of 1848"–or the "mahele"–this involved no substantial redistribution of property, and it was not land reform as we understand it today. Land reform now generally refers to such actions as breaking up large estates, creation of farm cooperatives, redistribution of major land holdings to peasants and small farmers, and perhaps even nationalization of land.[17]

Following the Land Division, the number of owners was slightly enlarged, but land ownership remained in the hands of a few. During most of the 1800's, the Hawaiian islands were governed by a tight monarchy, and in 1898 they were "annexed" to the United States by treaty and given territorial status. The monarchy carried on the tradition of the chiefs, and while local officials existed the major decisions were made by authorities in the capital. Central control extended to land use, and all land was given a designation indicating the permitted use–all of this long before the advent of "zoning" on the mainland. Under Hawaiian law, all contrary uses were ruled "kapu," and significant penalties were imposed on the owners. Land ownership continued to be concentrated throughout the late 1800s, and much of it was titled to the king or queen. Monarchical rule was characterized by Professor RuBino as a sort of "centralized feudalism," apparently suggesting the combination of aspects of both centralization and decentralization.[18] However, it appears that decentralization was limited to minor administrative questions and that policy control was in the hands of a central hierarchy. The islands remained in territorial status until 1959, and the basic authority over development was retained in the territorial government.

Today over 85 percent of the land in the state is owned by less than 100 individuals, corporations, trusts, or the government; about half of this is privately held.[19] Only a handful of families and groups own about 90 percent of the private land in the state, with one organization controlling about a tenth of it alone. The private holdings include nearly all the tillable agricultural land, with government land generally being less productive. Several corporations and conglomerates each own from 1 to 4 percent of the land. Castle & Cook, for example, a conglomerate, holds about 4 percent; the Alexander & Baldwin Corporation owns 2 percent; AMFAC, another conglomerate, owns 2 percent; and the Campbell Estate, a family concern, owns 1 percent. Much of the property in large holdings is used for pineapple and sugarcane, although some of it near urban areas is being converted to development. The pattern is clearly a carry-over from an earlier age, and it shows no signs of disappearing.

Hawaii thus draws on a long and strong tradition of central control of land and concentrated land ownership, factors that provided a foundation for action of the part of the new state. What was needed was the landowners' support for land-use controls in the new government. This support was given, and the state acted. Hawaii became a state in 1959, and it moved swiftly to approve a land-use law. By 1961, Hawaii became the first state to adopt a statewide land-use plan and, more important, statewide zoning. And it remains the only state to this day that has done either.

Another political factor has to be considered, and that is the other side of the concentrated ownership pattern, or the absence of any sizable bloc of small farmers. Much research suggests that this group has been traditionally hostile to public land controls throughout the United States. They voted out zoning in Charlevoix County, Michigan, early in 1974, and Babcock shows how they worked against a zoning ordinance in Ogle County, Illinois.* Furthermore, it was representatives of this group that came to Washington in massive numbers to

---

*The Charlevoix vote was a referendum on a legislatively adopted zoning ordinance, and it was taken in April 1974. Leading the opposition were small cherry farmers who feared the controls would restrict their options in this mixed agricultural and luxurious resort area in northern Michigan. Babcock says the following ad was taken out by the farmers of Ogle County: "The peasants of Europe came to America and became free men. If we allow this zoning law to pass, we will be on the road back to peasantry in Ogle County." Richard F. Babcock, The Zoning Game (Madison: University of Wisconsin Press, 1966), p. 25. Similarly in cities like Houston (1948, 1962), Witchita Falls (1963), Baytown (1969), Pasadena, and Laredo that have voted down zoning, the strongest opposition came from the smallest property owners. All these cities are in Texas.

defeat the national land-use bill in 1974; this included such organizations as the Mississippi Forestry Association (speaking for over 4,000
tree farmers in the state), Louisiana Forestry Association (2,200
farmer members), Texas Forestry Association (representing 150,000
timber owners), North Carolina Forestry Association (speaking for
220,000 landowners in North Carolina), Nebraska Farm Bureau Federation, Illinois Agricultural Association, Missouri Farm Bureau
Federation, Iowa Farm Bureau Federation, Forest Farmers Association, New Mexico Cattle Growers' Association, South Dakota Stock
Growers' Association, Texas Sheep & Goat Association, National
Cattlemen's Association, Oklahoma Cattlemen's Association, Colorado
Soil Conservation Board, Wyoming Association of Conservation Districts, Kansas Association of Conservation Districts, Texas Association of Soil and Water Conservation Districts (the soil and water
districts, although public agencies, speak for farmers and landowners),
and many others. Small farmers simply do not have this kind of influence in Hawaii, and they have virtually no organizational voice at all.

English philosopher Harrington said it over 300 years ago that
land ownership and public policy are directly linked: the wider the
distribution of land the less the control of a single power, and the more
concentrated the ownership the greater the likelihood of central control.
He also said that government could not act outside an economic base,
lest instability result.[20] Perhaps this helps explain the Hawaii situation and also the decentralized patterns of land-use planning elsewhere
in the country.

The action in Hawaii did not come because of some special leadership qualities on the part of the officials or because of logical arguments as to the desirability of government land regulation—at least
it did not come from this alone. It came because of a strong political
base on the side of the controls, centrally exercised. Without this
base it is doubtful the action would have been taken, and it is not even
clear that they would have tried. These are fundamental rules of politics, and they can be ignored only at great risk.

The motives of the landowners were these: They saw their property under increasing development pressure, and they wanted to keep
their land in agricultural use. They had thriving businesses, and they
wanted them protected. This they could not do without the help of
government. Local governments would not do because they were too
divided and weak—only the control government could do the job.
Besides with strong central zoning, taxes on agricultural land could
be kept constant and not rise with property values and urbanization
pressures. This has been a key factor in getting approval of preferential assessment for farmland in other states, although it is sometimes overlooked (attention is focused on the "public" benefits, or
the preservation of open space).[21] Zoning, in short, would prevent
urban pressures from forcing a conversion of prime agricultural land
to subdivisions, and it would keep taxes low; this, of course, is an

ideal combination from the landowners' standpoint. It is also important that the land supply in Hawaii is strictly limited, and landowners
cannot simply sell off their land and move to equally productive land
elsewhere, a point we come back to later.

There were other payoffs as well. The planners got comprehensive, statewide land regulation and planning. It may be too farfetched
to suggest as one source does that planners used the dwindling supply
of land as an "excuse" to get planning, but the general idea is correct.
Planners want planning however they can get it, and this way is no
doubt as acceptable as any other, politics and all. The conservationists got zoning for remote areas unprotected by local interest groups,
areas they wanted reserved because of their scenic and environmental
qualities.

The state got something too—a program and a bureaucracy, several
of them in fact. Even the counties were not left out, and they got the
detailed control of their land, within state guidelines. The city and
county of Honolulu got something too, in a sort of negative sense; it
was spared direct state controls and given the right to make specific
land-use and planning determinations as it pleased. It got nothing it
did not have all along, but at least it did not get direct state control.
In reality, the state program affected Honolulu very little as we shall
see shortly. And the public got something—a preservation of open space
and the remaining agricultural lands. At least it got the promise of
this, and in practice it appears that land has been urbanized at a
slower rate than it would have been without the state controls. This
can be considered a public benefit, but the public may also be paying
for it in terms of higher housing prices, a point we treat later. We
now turn to the state legislation, to see how it works in practice.

1961 Land-Use Law

Although Hawaii contains eight major islands, more than four-
fifths of the population lives on one island—Oahu, which contains
Honolulu. The other islands, with the exception of one used as a military target, are known as the "Neighbor Islands," and altoge ther the
Hawaiian islands have a land area of 6,000 acres. Only three states
are smaller. The state has less than a million residents (ranks 40th
in population), and this again puts it in a minority status.[22]

Hawaii's Land-Use Law was adopted in 1961, two years after
statehood, and it has been amended on several occasions. The law
also constitutes the state's General Plan which is not a separate
document but merely amounts to the zoning act. This follows the
zoning-planning link described in Chapter 2—the "zoning first" philosophy—and suggests a similarity in practice to mainland localities.
This is important since there is, in reality, no independent plan;

zoning is adopted, and it becomes planning. Again, it is almost an
afterthought. Zoning is put on the books with no plan to guide it, and
when authorities are questioned about it, they simply respond by
saying that the zoning is the plan. It is instructive that the state
spends two pages in a recent report explaining in rather obtuse language that zoning is planning and vice versa.[23] At the same time,
Bosselman and Callies note that a separate state plan was approved
in 1960, prior to the land-use legislation, but this was apparently
superseded by the 1961 law and in any event is now considered out of
date and "obsolete."[24] This is confusing, but what facts we can
uncover suggest that the 1960 plan did not form the base of the 1961
legislation and did not guide it as planning theory would require.[25]

    The Land-Use Law applied zoning to all the inhabited islands.
This did not take effect immediately and was subject to an administrative determination of the state Land-Use Commission; the panel
was to set the boundaries for the different zoning districts, which it
did some three years later.

    The legislation established four zoning classes: 1. urban, 2. rural,
3. agricalatural, and 4. conservation. The urban, rural, and agricultural designations were in the original law in 1961, and the conservation zone was added by legislation approved in 1963. Although the
text of each zone was enacted immediately into state law, the "map"
did not go into effect until 1964 with action of the land-use body. In
other words, the zones were not applied to specific parcels until 1964.

    The urban zone was for land that is developed or substantially
developed, or land that can be expected to be developed over the
coming 10 years. There was to be an element of planning in this, and
it was not simply to be an extrapolation of present patterns. The idea
was that a supply of land is to be reserved for urban use by being put
in the urban class, and this is to be based on what planners think
should be made available for planned urban purposes. It was not to
be based merely on the laws of economics and the demands of the
marketplace.

    The rural zone was to be applied to land that is in relatively
low-density urban uses or that contains smaller farms and land holdings.
This is significant because it is the character of the improvements
or ownership patterns and not the land itself that serves as the basis
for the zone. The practice is not all that typical and is not followed
in most of the other states. Quasi-public uses were also permitted
in the rural zone, and this includes utility buildings and private educational institutions.

    Agricultural zoning was to be given land that is under intensive
cultivation or is capable of such farming and that is developed or
planned in residential uses of one acre or more (that is, estates).
This includes crop and grazing land and the processing operations
associated with large-scale agriculture on the islands (sugarcane
mills are an example).

The conservation zone was originally designed for state-owned forest and water reserve districts, but with time it was applied to other areas. Under previous law the state holdings were restricted to conservation uses anyway; so the new regulations had little effect. The new land was largely privately owned and included mountainous areas and other property with significant scenic and environmental value. The application of the zone to private holdings had to be politically sensitive, although we can find no research on the matter.

The bulk of the land area on the islands is zoned agriculture and conservation; this includes the islands of Kauai, Niihau, Maui, Molokai, Lanai, Hawaii, and Oahu. An eighth island is used for military purposes and is not zoned. The Island of Oahu, which contains Honolulu, was given no rural zoning, and in fact the category has been used only to a limited degree on the other islands. Only Oahu has any significant urban zoning.

State zoning in Hawaii governs both public and private land, a practice that varies widely elsewhere. In other words, zoning in many areas of the country applies only to private land, and public agencies are free to do as they please. But in Hawaii public land is subject to the same restrictions as private land is, and this includes land leased to developers but retained in public ownership. In fact, probably most of the land in the conservation zone is publicly owned, and its use is regulated strictly by the state.

To administer the legislation, the state formed the Land-Use Commission, a unit composed of seven lay members and the heads of two state bureaucracies, the director of the Department of Planning and Economic Development and the director of the Department of Land and Natural Resources. This detail is provided not simply for informational purposes but because it allows some insight into the political pressures on zoning. The panel is appointed by the governor with legislative confirmation and is served by the staff of the Planning Department. The latter point is important since although the commission is given key planning duties, it has no planning staff of its own and relies on professionals responsible to another set of leaders. Anyone who is familiar with the operations of planning agencies knows what kind of problems this can create, and the pattern overlooks the realities of the relationship between the quality and character of work performed and lines of authority.[26] We return to this point later.

The land-use panel has the authority to set the boundaries for the zoning districts and to review them every five years. These responsibilities are all assigned by law, and the initial boundaries were established in 1964. A comprehensive review was undertaken in 1969, by the firm of Eckbo, Dean, Austin & Williams, but no general adjustment in the districts has been approved since 1964. The changes that have taken place have been in the form of individual rezonings, which has meant, in most instances, the expansion of the urban zone.

The political system of the Hawaiian islands is very simple: a
state and four local governments. Both the state and local governments,
all counties, are given a role in all categories but one. This is the
conservation zone, which is solely a state responsibility. The general
classification and specific uses for all land in the rural and agricultural zones are governed by state controls, and determinations are
made by the state Land-Use Commission; still, the counties have
some important powers in these zones as we shall see shortly.

Uses in the conservation zone are set exclusively by state controls
as noted, specifically by the Board of Land and Natural Resources;
the Land-Use Commission has no administrative authority in this zone,
and its implementation powers are restricted to the other three zones.
Uses in the urban district are determined jointly by the state and the
counties. What this means is that land in all zones, but the conservation district, is subject to a dual system of regulation, and local
powers are not minor. In the ''intergovernmental'' zones, state controls are typically broad and general, and county ones more specific. In some cases, state controls may be specific as well.

Let us take a closer look at how it works. The counties have the
authority under state law to issue ''use permits'' in the agricultural
and rural zones, and while this is subject to state veto, the local
position generally stands.[27] This amounts to a delegation of the ultimate ''specific'' powers to the county in these zones, as a practical
matter, that is. To illustrate, officials of Kauai County turned down
a proposal for the development of the old Kilauea sugar plantation
into large-lot residences. The property is in the agriculture district,
and it was put there by state action, but its subdivision had to be
approved by the local government. Had the county given its nod, it
would still have been technically subject to a state review. It works
much the same way in the rural zone.

The urban zone is slightly different. But even there the final
authority rests with the county, and state powers are limited to the
designation of the zone per se. Even this designation can, in effect,
be reversed by the counties, and this has to be crucial. The state
sets the urban district for various areas in the state, and the counties
then determine more specific uses such as apartments, commercial,
single-family residences, industrial, and institutional. They may,
in reality, overrule the state by specifying, for example, agricultural
or rural use of land put in the ''urban'' zone by the state. Of course,
it is urban land that is under the greatest development pressure and
therefore where land-use controls have the greatest impact. And
this only goes to show the importance of local government in the whole
zoning picture in Hawaii.

In the urban districts, the counties have the real power and in
fact almost the exclusive say. Local control is so great there that
Shelley Mark, head of the Hawaii Planning Department, says urban
zoning is ''adminstered solely by the counties.''[28] In reality then,

zoning powers are shared by state and local authorities and are not exclusively under the state. And in three of the four districts including the urban district, it is local government that for all practical purposes has the final control. This suggests an underlying pattern not too dissimilar from that on the mainland.

Effects of the Law

The state Land-Use Law never really went into effect until 1964 since that was the date the land-use body put its final blessing on the district boundaries. The pressure on the state since 1964 has been for the reclassification of land from the other three categories to urban, and this has pretty much set the politics of the matter. The goal of the developers has been to try to get the state to rezone land to urban uses. The land-use panel has derived its political bargaining power by withholding approvals or at least "charging a price" for them. Nothing improper is suggested here, and the words are used in a purely neutral sense.

In fact, the commission has apparently rationed its power wisely, and of the 100,000 acres proposed for reclassification, only 30,000 have been rezoned.[29] About a tenth of the acres reclassified were considered "prime agricultural" land according to Mark, and if the preservation of this land is the principal objective, the legislation has been successful. This requires us to make the assumption that more land than that would have been converted to urban use had there been no Land-Use Law in the first place. In any event, the record shows that a request for rezoning is not the same as its approval.

One of the criteria applied by the commission in the switches to urban zoning has been "need," and need has been determined through planning and land-use studies cataloging existing undeveloped "urban" land and future population and development pressures. This suggests that the decisions are not arbitrary and that professional data have been brought to bear on the process, but it does not tell us how much "politics" has had to do with it. Conclusions along these lines are hard to come by, although some critics have charged "conflict of interest" and political bias in the Land-Use Commission.

A recent inventory has shown that Oahu's urban needs can be met under existing zoning for the next 18 years. This has likely had an effect on reclassification decisions, as the Land-Use Commission has turned down rezoning requests on that island with a greater degree of regularity. This is a "need" consideration, and it is significant since retaining land in one of the other three categories, especially the conservation zone, means more state authority and presumably more central direction. The panel, however, has not turned down all urban rezonings on Oahu, and this raises the prospects of other factors playing some role.

Assessment of the Law

On the positive side, it has to be said that the state has undertaken to plan and zone its entire territory. And the original enactment
has stood up for over a dozen years. That no other state has sought
such wide powers, let alone implemented them, has to be to Hawaii's
credit; it is easy to do something "everyone is doing," but it is harder
to go it alone. In fact, states do tend to copy one another, especially
in the same region, and this has to be comforting if nothing else.[30]

In addition, a number of groups with divergent and often conflicting
interests are in the same harness, on a statewide basis. This would
include planners, developers, administrators, politicians, landowners,
conservationists, citizens, and others, and it has to be a plus. Hawaii
has apparently achieved this goal with enviable precision.

The law has also preserved agricultural land from development,
contained urban pressures, and "forced" the more efficient use of
land in urban areas—and this all falls on the positive side of the ledger.
The state has further moved cautiously in relations with local authorities and has not sought to preempt local powers in the administrative
sphere. All of this points to a very admirable state role, one that is
highly unusual if not unique.

Yet the picture is not entirely bright. In the first place, the state
has no plan independent of zoning. Simply the time dimension (zoning =
present; planning = future) would suggest there should be a separate
plan. Second, has the state involvement in land use brought "wider"
interests and "broader" perspectives to bear on the decision-making
process? The theory of state planning suggests these benefits, but
whether this has happened in Hawaii is not at all clear. It is true that
the urban district has been contained, but most specific zoning decisions are made by the localities and not the state. There is little
evidence that the state has overruled local government but some
suggesting the reverse.

Third, how different is Hawaii's experience from that of the other
states? The real power over land use in three of the four zones seems
to be in the hands of local authorities, and this includes land in the
urban zone, which has to be the key one in terms of the effects of
controls. We have already suggested that the counties can override
the state will in the urban district, and it is the counties and not the
state that appears to have the basic powers in the agricultural and
rural zones. Besides, if Honolulu has enough urban zoning for the next
two decades, how much influence can the state have there in any event?
Honolulu contains 80 percent of Hawaii's population, and the county
has full authority within that zone. What this amounts to is state control over the conservation zone, which is mostly state land anyway,
and state administration of this zone has been sharply criticized (see
below). If the state is to provide guidance and a perspective different

from that of localities and if this pits more general conceptions of
the public interest against narrower ones, there is scant evidence of
it in Hawaii. The tendency seems for power to "fly off the common
center," and land-use regulation in Hawaii is apparently no exception.
This goes no matter who has the formal authority, and much research
shows that the pattern is by no means limited to this situation.[31]

There have been other problems. Housing prices are high in
Hawaii, and they have gone up in recent years. They have risen sharply
since the enactment of the Land-Use Law, and some observers attribute the extent of the rise to the legislation.[32] It is held that while
containing the urban district, the measure has forced land and housing
prices up, in view of the pressure this causes in the existing urban
areas. Babcock and Bosselman have suggested that the land-use
legislation is "not an ideal instrument to achieve balanced housing
policies" and claim that the absence of specific tools in the legislation
to deal with housing makes it "cumbersome" for this task.[33] Others
have proposed government subsidies as the only way of solving the
housing problem. This seems to be saying that no matter how the
zoning law is rewritten, it cannot do the job. It also suggests that
zoning is exclusionary and drives up housing prices regardless of the
specifics, which has been Siegan's argument all along. Siegan, an
attorney-turned-professor, argues persuasively that zoning has significantly cut into the housing supply and that zoning is exclusionary
by definition. Zoning must therefore raise housing prices, and this
is so regardless of how it is structured.[34] In fact, zoning in Hawaii
has probably cut most deeply into the supply of low- and moderate-
income housing, or at least this is where the problem seems the
greatest. Of course, to know the effects of the legislation on housing
per se, it would be necessary to hold constant the influence of other
factors such as inflation and rising wages. This, of course, is no
simply undertaking.

Developers hold that too much land has been put in the agriculture
district and that urban land is under too much pressure. They also
complain that state standards of "need" are indefinite and vague,
making it difficult for them to prove the desirability of converting
agricultural and rural land to the urban classification; the burden of
proof incidentally is on the applicant, or the developer. Developers
have further argued that state and county administrative requirements
are too stiff and involve excessive and needless paperwork. Still no
prominent developer has proposed the law's repeal, and they seem
generally to support it.

Conservationists have their complaints too. They contend that
the Land-Use Commission is "pro-development," and some have
suggested "conflict of interest" on the part of individual commission
members. In fact, interest groups are represented on the land-use
panel, following a pattern used widely in mainland states, and the
unions and the landowners both have their spokesmen. The unions

in Hawaii are not "antidevelopment" or "antibusiness," and the construction trades in particular have given strong backing to promotional growth and tourist policies. The longshoremen have generally sided with these policies as well. To the extent that it exists, a union-developer-landowner alliance seems entirely natural and may suggest broader political ties likely to emerge elsewhere with time. In the meantime, the conservationists are unhappy. The pattern may have something to do with the desire of some environmentalists to form a "third force" as an alternative to the two parties, a move backed by such leading state planning advocates as Governor Tom McCall and others.

There are also complaints with the administration of the legislation. Duplication, overlap, confusion, inefficiency, as well as lack of communications, enforcement, and expertise have been familiar charges. Critics say that the assignments under the law are confusing and that there is overlap and duplication. They argue that all powers should be lodged in a single agency and not the several that presently share responsibilities for decision making. The Land-Use Commission sets the boundaries and makes rezoning decisions; the Planning Department supplies the professional staff for the commission; and the Board of Land and Natural Resources rules on the conservation zone. The governor also has a role, as do the heads of two state bureaucracies. This is too much and should be changed according to this view.

It is also said that the "commission" form is obsolete in administration and not the way to make key decisions in important policy areas like planning and land use. This position is generally supported by the experts and is consistent with traditional public administration thinking.[35] The argument is that determinations of this nature should be made by a single administrator, someone appointed by the governor or perhaps even the governor himself. This would promote political responsibility and administrative accountability. It is also suggested that the commission has no professional staff employed by it directly and that this is contrary to good administrative practice.

Some hold that there is little coordination between state and local government on zoning decisions. Specifically, it has been suggested that the state has little or no information about the local situation when it makes rezoning decisions. As an example, it is argued that when the state reclassifies land to the urban district, it has no idea as to whether the county had the public services and facilities available to serve the new uses. This is attributed to a lack of communication between state and local officials and an apparent lack of concern and sensitivity on the part of either to the problem.

It is further alleged that the state does not enforce zoning. More particularly, it is charged that many land uses exist that are not in conformity with state law and that the state does not even follow up on its own zoning approvals. Examples of developers not complying with state regulations have been cited, and presumably they are not

too uncommon.. Along these same lines, it has been noted that the
Board of Land and Natural Resources, which has the zoning responsibilities in the conservation district, has no expertise in land-use
planning and in fact has prepared no plan for this land to date. Thus
it has no basis on which to make specific decisions and is without
policy guidelines. This is an especially noteworthy charge since it is
only in the conservation zone that the state has exclusive power, and
if the state is not doing the job there, this suggests a real problem.

Finally, it is said that the state planning staff is too small and
underfinanced and that the quality of personnel has suffered under a
strict three-year residency requirement for all state employees. Of
course, without professional expertise state planning is not apt to
amount to much, and it is also not likely to gain much respect. We
do not imply that all the criticisms are valid or that they are fully
backed up with the facts. We only note that they have been made and
that there may be some merit in them.

The record of state planning and zoning in Hawaii has been mixed.
We do not say that it has been a bad one and the facts will not support
this, but it is nowhere near perfect. One evaluation sums it up, and
it has it that although much has been accomplished under the legislation, "much more" has not.

It seems that the state's action in land use stems from its special
tradition and unique political circumstances. This has facilitated state
zoning, almost unheard of in this country, but it does not necessarily
mean that it can make it "work." In operation, state zoning in Hawaii
has many weaknesses, and the same goes for state planning. This
policy is subject to most of the same political pressures found in the
other states, and in the final analysis the bulk of its planning program
has been forced into many of the same channels. The facts of this
chapter suggest that where the state has retained exclusive control
(as in the conservation zone), state planning and zoning are by no
means unqualified successes and that where it has shared power
with local governments, it is local control and local views that have
tended to prevail.

The Future

Bills were slated for introduction in the 1974 session of the
Hawaii legislature to correct some of the deficiencies in the land-use
program; this followed inaction in the 1973 session.[36] Probably the
most important of these had to do with low- and moderate-income
housing.The proposal is to establish direct state controls in special
areas designated for such housing, and this goes for urban districts
as well. This could be a significant breakthrough, because such a
target is rarely seen as part of the "critical areas" package in other

parts of the country. If it works, it may well provide a model for other
states. A bill was also offered providing for a stronger state planning
program, one separate from zoning. This has been a definite lack,
and in fact the state provides very little planning leadership in any of
the zones. Only time will tell whether improvements can be made
through state planning and zoning legislation, but in the meantime,
building national land-use policy on the experiences of one state would
seem unwise and premature. Besides, a close examination of this
state reveals some very real problems. State planning is by no means
a panacea, and Hawaii's performance suggests it is a mixed blessing
at best.

We now turn to direct planning and land regulation in other states.

NOTES

1. Systematic reports on the activities of the states in direct
planning and zoning can be found in the following sources: Council on
Environmental Quality, Environmental Quality 1973 (Washington, D.C.:
Government Printing Office, 1973), pp. 215-222; Environmental Quality
1972 (Washington, D.C.: Government Printing Office, 1972), pp. 183-
186; Environmental Quality 1971 (Washington, D.C.: Government
Printing Office, 1971), pp. 60-68; H. Milton Patton and others, The
Land-Use Puzzle (Lexington, Ky.: Council of State Governments, 1974);
and Richard G. RuBino and William R. Wagner, The States' Role in
Land Resource Management, Supplement (Lexington, Ky.: Council of
State Governments, 1972). "Land-Use Planning Reports," cited in
Chapter 1, is attempting to provide current information for all 50
states on the subject. The U.S. Senate Committee on Interior and
Insular Affairs and the House Subcommittee on the Environment have
also compiled data for all the states.

2. In Alaska the state has control over land in "unorganized"
areas, but this does not amount to much (in power), and the state's
urban areas are exclusively under local authority. See John N. Kolesar,
"The States and Urban Planning and Development," in Alan K. Campbell (ed.), The States and the Urban Crisis (Englewood Cliffs, N.J.:
Prentice-Hall, 1970), p. 130.

3. The State of the States In 1974. Responsive Government for
the Seventies (Washington, D.C.: National Governors' Conference,
1974), p. 39.

4. See RuBino and Wagner, op.cit., pp. 9-13 (main text, not the
Supplement as in Note 1); and William S. James, "Why a State Role
for Land Use?" State Government XLVI no. 2 (Summer 1973): 166.

5. See Department of Planning and Economic Development, State
of Hawaii General Plan Revision Program. Part 5, Land Use, Transportation, and Public Facilities (Honolulu: State of Hawaii, 1967).

6. See T. J. Kent, Jr., The Urban General Plan (San Francisco: Chandler Publishing Co., 1964), p. 19.

7. For a discussion of federal land-use policy, see Lance Marston, "Land Use and Environmental Quality–Crisis or Opportunity?" in Richard H. Slavin and H. Milton Patton (eds.), State Planning Issues 1973 (Lexington, Ky.: Council of State Governments, 1973), pp. 1-4.

8. See The Wall Street Journal, February 2, 1973, p. 8. See also Policy Positions, 1973-74, National Governors' Conference and National Legislative Conference.

9. As reported by the committee to the floor of the House. See U. S. House of Representatives, Committee on Interior and Insular Affairs, Report on Land-Use Planning Act of 1974, H. R. 10294 (Washington, D. C.: Government Printing Office, 1974), pp. 3-6.

10. U. S. Senate, Committee on Interior and Insular Affairs, Report on Land-Use Policy and Planning Assistance Act, S. 268 (Washington, D. C.: Government Printing Office, 1973), p. 62. This was 1973 legislation, and it was approved by the Senate.

11. Emphasis added. See U. S. Senate, Committee on Interior and Insular Affairs, Report on Land-Use Policy and Planning Assistance Act of 1972, S. 632 (Washington, D. C.: Government Printing Office, 1972), p. 6.

12. See American Law Institute, A Model Land Development Code, Tentative Draft No. 3 (Philadelphia: American Law Institute, 1971), Article 8, pp. 53-95. A more recent draft is cited in Chapter 1.

13. Lewis A. Froman, Jr., The Congressional Process (Boston: Little, Brown, 1967).

14. See James G. Coke, "Antecedents of Local Planning," in William I. Goodman and Eric C. Freund (eds.), Principles and Practice of Urban Planning (Washington, D. C.: International City Management Association, 1968), pp. 7-28.

15. Report on Land-Use Planning Act of 1974, p. 29.

16. Report on Land-Use Policy and Planning Assistance Act, 1973, p. 45.

17. Land reform is currently an issue in some Latin American and Asian nations. See Gabriel A. Almond and James S. Coleman (eds.), The Politics of the Developing Areas (Princeton, N.J.: Princeton University Press, 1960).

18. See RuBino and Wagner, op. cit., p. 9. The history of Hawaii is treated in Richard Hofstadter and others, The American Republic, 2nd ed., Vol. 1 (Englewood Cliffs, N.J.: Prentice-Hall, 1970), pp. 278-280.

19. Fred Bosselman and David Callies, The Quiet Revolution in Land-Use Control (Washington, D. C.: Government Printing Office, 1971), pp. 13-15.

20. See James Harrington, The Commonwealth of Oceana, 1656, pertinent excerpts of which are found in A. T. Mason, ed., Free Government in the Making, 3rd ed. (New York: Oxford University Press, 1965) pp. 38-44.

21. See William H. Whyte, The Last Landscape (Garden City, N.Y.: Doubleday & Co., 1968), Chap. 6. Whyte does not overlook the point.

22. See Robert H. Weber and Ralph J. Marcelli (eds.), The Book of the States 1972-73, Vol. XIX (Lexington, Ky.: Council of State Governments, 1972), p. 572.

23. The report says: "State policies and concerns with respect to proper land use are thus evinced through implementation of the Land-Use Law. The State Plan for land use on each island is in reality indicated by the district boundaries established in the process." State of Hawaii General Plan Revision Program, pp. 21-22, cited above (Note 5).

24. Bosselman and Callies, op. cit., p. 11.

25. Planning theory is discussed in our co-authored The Politics of Land Use: Planning, Zoning, and the Private Developer (New York: Praeger Publishers, 1973), pp. 7-8.

26. One of the best sources on the realities of administrative operations is Anthony Downs, Inside Bureaucracy (Boston: Little, Brown, 1967).

27. "Trends in Land-Use Control: Statewide Land-Use Enactments," in J. Ross McKeever (ed.), Shopping Center Zoning, Urban Land Institute-Technical Bulletin 69, 1973, p. 66.

28. Shelley M. Mark, "It All Began in Hawaii," State Government XLVI, no. 3 (Summer 1973): 190. He also says counties are "responsible" for the "administration" of land uses in the agriculture and rural districts (p. 191).

29. We use "power" as Banfield developed it in Political Influence (New York: Free Press, 1961), Chap. 11.

30. See Ira Sharkansky, Regionalism in American Politics (Indianapolis: Bobbs-Merrill, 1969); and Jack L. Walker, "Diffusion of Innovations among the American States," in Richard I. Hofferbert and Ira Sharkansky (eds.), State and Urban Politics (Boston: Little, Brown, 1971), pp. 377-412. Interstate emulation is encouraged by the mere existence of such groups as the Council of State Governments, the National Governors' Conference, and the Council of State Planning Agencies; in fact, it is their policy as well.

31. Bertram M. Gross, The Managing of Organizations, Vol. I (New York: Free Press, 1964), Chap. 3. See also Philip Selznick, TVA and the Grass Roots (Berkeley: University of California Press, 1949).

32. Marshall Kaplan, Gans, Kahn, and Yamamoto (consultants), Housing in Hawaii (Honolulu: State of Hawaii, Department of Planning and Economic Development, 1971).

33. Richard F. Babcock and Fred P. Bosselman, Exclusionary Zoning: Land-Use Regulation and Housing in the 1970s (New York: Praeger Publishers, 1973), pp. 162-165.

34. Bernard H. Siegan, Land Use Without Zoning (Boston: D. C. Heath, 1971). Siegan has become a controversial figure because he

has proposed scrapping of zoning as the only way of solving housing and other problems.

35. This thinking came from the "high noon of orthodoxy" period of public administration, but it is quite popular today in most practical circles. See Don Allensworth, Public Administration (Philadelphia: J. B. Lippincott Co., 1973), Chap. 8. See also Wallace S. Sayre, "Premises of Public Administration: Past and Emerging," Public Administration Review XVIII no. 2 (1958): 102-105.

36. U. S. Senate, Committee on Interior and Insular Affairs, State Land-Use Programs (Washington, D. C.: Government Printing Office, 1974), p. 81. This is part of a 50-state survey of state land-use controls prepared by "Land-Use Planning Reports." The information was collected in September of 1973.

4

DIRECT STATE PLANNING
AND ZONING: THE EXCEPTION
ON THE MAINLAND—VERMONT

THE NEW STATES?

Much has been heard lately about the "new states" and their programs. We have been told to watch them, for there is a "revolution" taking place. Daniel Elazar feels that they have advanced so that they are now the "keystones" of the American government arch.[1] Beer and Barringer have told us what they are doing for the poor; Elizabeth Haskell, what they are doing for the environment; Professor Macmahon, what they are doing for federalism; and Theodore Lowi, what they are going to do for us in the future.[2] The age-old problems of outdated constitutions, cumbersome executive branches, the long ballot, obsolete state legislatures, rural control, and special interest influence are apparently to be neglected, and we are to concentrate on a virtually reborn institution. All of this follows on the heels of charges that the states have "outlived" their usefulness, that they have "largely ceased" to be innovators, and that they were "irrelevant" and should be replaced with new political and administrative forms.[3]

As evidence, partisans have pointed to what Oregon has done in regulating bottles, what Delaware has done in controlling the shoreline, what Minnesota has done in promoting metropolitan planning, what Maryland has done in state financing of school construction, what California has done in welfare reform, and perhaps more than any of the others, what Vermont has done in land use.* The reason Vermont is stressed is that it is the only mainland state to have done anything really notable in the area of state planning and land regulation. Hawaii, of course, has done more, but one can always point to the

---

*See citations in the Notes from the National Governors' Conference and other sources.

special conditions there to disqualify it as a "model." Vermont is
put forth, and its land-use programs are cited as what the states are
doing and can do. Thus, Vermont has the number-one spot in land use,
and this suggests the importance of this chapter and an evaluation of
the progress the state is making in this area. Do the facts justify its
being touted this way? A positive answer suggests that state partisans
may be right. A negative one may cast some doubt on the matter.

SIGNIFICANT QUESTIONS ABOUT VERMONT

Let us raise a few questions about this state. We do this not to
take up space, but to condition the readers as to the kinds of things
we looked for in studying the state. Some of the questions are not
obvious and suggest some penetrating considerations that are often
overlooked or taken for granted. The facts in this chapter suggest they
have to be raised. Some readers will find some of them offensive or
insignificant, but we feel that after examining the chapter, they will
agree the facts are pertinent.
What is Vermont doing? Is it important? Is the state protecting
local rights and still not overlooking the wider public interest? Does
it represent "broader" points of view than local government? Can it
overrule local interests? Or is it merely a vehicle of local groups?
Can local governments override the state? (The entrance of states
into land use does not automatically mean the rule of "wider" and
"broader" interests, for state policy may simply be a manifestation
of local wills, stamped with state approval.)
Is Vermont enough like the other states to permit the adoption
of its programs by other states? Does the heavy recreation orientation
of its economy make it undesirable for emulation? Are there political patterns that make it an undesirable model for other states?
Is Vermont's land-use program working in actual practice? Is
the state actually regulating land directly? Is Vermont really doing
planning? Or is it merely "working on" a plan as most other states
are? Does it have a state plan? Is this a comprehensive land-use
plan? Is there a map with this plan showing desired future land uses
for specific parcels? Has the plan been adopted? By whom?
Are actual regulation decisions based on a plan, especially an
adopted one? Or are they based on political influence patterns of the
moment? Or on other factors? If there is a plan and it forms the
base of decisions, does the plan merely reflect political influence
"backed up" one step (that is, put in the plan)? Is there professional
input into state land-use decisions? Do the citizens have a role?
Are public hearings held to get popular and interest group views?
What has been the effect of state controls on housing? On housing
prices? On housing supply? Do state regulations concentrate on

"outsiders" or "locals"? What is the effect on development and on
the environment?

Is there a special political base for the legislation? Especially
one that is not likely to be found in other states? Are citizens generally satisfied with the program? Is there any evidence that they support
it? Are developers satisfied? If they are not, is it because they are
opposed to all controls? Or is it because of specific conditions associated with this legislation? Are developers represented in the process? Do they dominate it? How about conservationists and environmentalists? Are they happy with it? Are there any particular problems
with the legislation, now that it has been in effect for several years?
Are there any special problems with its administration?

These are just a few of the questions that should be addressed,
and it is particularly important that we keep them in mind, as well
as their answers, before coming to conclusions about this state. This
is especially true when it comes to judging the efficacy of the Vermont
experience or the possibilities of its adaptation in other states. Just
to "have" a land-use program, we submit, is not enough. It must be
"working" or at least perceived to be such by enough groups to justify
a favorable assessment. Just to "have" state planning is not enough.
More is needed, such as a plan, especially an adopted one, and one that
has some meaning (it specifies land uses). These are by no means
foregone conclusions in states with land-use programs and planning,
and the issues have to be raised no matter how unpleasant their implications.

In this chapter we take a look at some of these questions, hopefully all of them, and much more. Toward the end, we examine three
other states, namely, Oregon, Florida, and Maine, which wind up the
list of states with significant direct planning and zoning programs.

BACKGROUND OF THE VERMONT LEGISLATION

Vermont had no tradition of central control to draw upon as did
Hawaii. In fact, it is part of New England, and this section is known
for "local" control and grass-roots democracy. Special priority
is put on public policy that is made in person by all the residents,
through the "town meeting." For town government does not necessarily mean "progressive" government, and it certainly has not meant,
at least in Vermont, a government exercising strong land-use controls.
Much evidence, to the contrary, suggests considerable hostility to
zoning and other forms of government regulation among the "select-
men" or town governors in Vermont, a hostility that has not been
erased with the enactment of state controls. In reality, romantic
notions notwithstanding, the towns in Vermont or elsewhere in New
England are not run by the citizens directly, but by their represen-

tatives, and they resemble city, surburban, and rural government in other parts of the country in this respect. Vermont, then, unlike Hawaii, had no history of central control or land-use regulation. This makes its achievements all the more remarkable in a sense, or at least all the more worth studying.

Over the last two decades, Vermont had become popular with vacationers and with others seeking a new home or a "second home" away from the cities. Its proximity to such metropolitan complexes as Boston, New York, and even Philadelphia made it especially inviting. It also has a good "image" in many circles and has attracted the likes of the Kennedys and others in the "jet set." It was where the "beautiful people" wanted to go. Many fly in or even drive there just for the weekend, especially in the winter.

Developers came with the influx of the newcomers, to provide the recreational, residential, commercial ski and resort facilities and services demanded. But by the mid-1960s, residents and officials in the state began to wonder out loud whether they could accommodate the new pressures. They were especially concerned about government controls on land and whether they were adequate or even existed. There was definitely a "carpetbagger" element here, and this has been used to elicit support for decisive state controls. The state government represented the "native" Vermonter in other words, and the target was the "outsider" whether he be tourist, newcomer, or developer. Even the "beautiful people" were tagged, perhaps especially. But this gets into the politics of the situation, and this is covered in the next section.

In 1967, the legislature acted to widen the authority of local governments to regulate land use, and in 1968, with the backing of Governor Hoff, the body approved the Municipal Planning and Development Act, which gave localities and regional planning commissions greater authority over land. Legislators also adopted a sign and outdoor advertising law, and all this suggested that the first wave of an environmental movement had already swept the state. Governor Deane Davis spearheaded other drives along these same lines in the late 1960s, and in 1970, under his leadership, the legislature enacted the landmark Land Use and Development Control Law, popularly known as "Act 250." Other legislation was passed that year, and some of it dealt with land use, including measures on shoreland zoning, pollution, and mobile home parks, but Act 250 was the big one and the one that is most widely discussed outside the state.

The current governor (1975), Thomas P. Salmon, attributes the legislation to the realization on the part of Vermonters that land is a finite resource which, if not properly managed, will be exploited. Other factors that contributed to the enactment of the legislation, according to the governor, are a decade of misuse of land in the state, the rapid conversion of agricultural land to nonfarm uses and the resulting disruption, the expansion of the interstate highway system, the popularity of outdoor sports and concomitant problems, the back-to-the-land "affliction" which has apparently "seized" urbanites, rising taxes on farmland near new development, and an environment in Vermont which the citizens wanted protected. In short, the governor said:

> By the late 1960s, it had become all too evident that the state was in the grip of new economic and social forces with which it was powerless to cope. New techniques and strategies were called for, and they have been forthcoming.[4]

POLITICS

The preceding section provides some insight into the politics of the matter, and it appears that the legislation was strongly backed by the "insiders" or "old-timers" who were suspicious of the new arrivals. Of course, it was opposed by some of these people, and it seemed that they were generally the ones (the "natives") who were contesting its administration. Native Vermonters who supported it included farmers whose land was being pressed by new uses and whose taxes were sharply escalating where the land was not taken for some new use. But it would be wrong to underestimate the "negative" motive, and that was a resentment of outsiders and the feeling that the legislation would somehow "punish" them, and perhaps keep them out altogether.

The two parties gave their support too. In a state whose legislature has been traditionally dominated by Republicans, recent Democratic governors were in the forefront of the general movement that led to the approval and administration of the 1970 legislation. This included Philip Hoff (mid-1960s) and Thomas Salmon. Salmon was the Minority Leader in the Vermont General Assemby at the time the law was approved. Democratic legislators, what there were of them, also backed the measure by good margins. However, it was the Republicans that put it through. Vermont has a "modified one-party" system at present, and this represents a change over the "dominant one-party" arrangement it had only a decade or so ago.[5] During the earlier period, Duane Lockard detected a "shifting bifactional" one-party system, with both liberal and conservative factions in the dominant Republican party.[6] It is the conservative wing of the party that has led the opposition to the legislation, although not all conservatives oppose it.

Proof of the GOP foundation is as follows. At the time of the bill's enactment, the lower house of the Vermont legislature had a Republican majority of 98 to 50 (plus 2 independents). Many of the Democrats come from Winooski and other "French-Canadian" areas of the state, and the Republicans come from everyplace, especially

the rural areas and small towns. In the Senate, the GOP margin was
a similarly lopsided 22 to 8. In addition, the governor in 1970, Davis,
was a Republican. In terms of its administration, the power has been
shared by Republicans and Democrats, but both have backed it. Davis
was in power for the first two years after its enactment, and Salmon,
a Democrat, has been governor since 1972 (he was elected for another
two-year term in 1974). During the early "implementation" period,
the Republicans continued to control the legislature by sizable margins. They had a majority in 1971-72 in the lower house of 95 to 52,
with 3 independents, and in the upper chamber the same 22 to 8 edge.[7]
In short, the Republicans put it in, and the Republicans and Democrats
have carried it out.

Interest group activity in Vermont is hard to uncover. This is
not a bustling urban state that has received the kind of research
directed to New York, California, New Jersey, and Pennsylvania.
Elizabeth Haskell has examined the politics of land-use programs in
nine states including Vermont, and although she mentions the role of
interest groups like sportsmen, fishermen, farmers, businessmen,
industrialists, public health and environmental protection advocates
in states like Wisconsin, New York, Washington, and Illinois, she
says nothing of the positions of these groups in Vermont; in fact, she
does not even mention them in this context.[8]

Vermont has a particularly active lobby that is opposing state
planning and land-use control, and that is the Institute for Liberty and
Community in Concord, but this group was obviously not strong
enough to defeat the legislation and has concentrated on its administration.

Perhaps one factor is that interest groups are not all that strong
in this state. Some research suggests this. Vermont has been classified by political scientists as having a "moderate" pressure group
system.[9] What this means is that it is moderately weak or moderately
strong depending on how you view it; the three categories are "strong,"
"moderate," and "weak," and Vermont falls right in the middle.
Vermont has labor unions, including the AFL-CIO, although membership is low, a state Farm Bureau, and an influential manufacturers'
organization, the Associated Industries of Vermont. Its legislature
is noted for its "amateur" status (high turnover), and this might be
expected to facilitate interest group influence although it could work in
the opposite direction as well. In fact, one study suggested that it
meant the former and that the Associated Industries group was able
to "manipulate" committee chairmanships and assignments without
the knowledge of the legislators.[10] Paper companies are important
in the manufacturers' lobby, and it would be surprising if they had
no interest in the 1970 measure, or at least its adminstration. Another
study found teachers' associations and utilities among others to be
influential in state legislatures, and presumably Vermont is no exception.[11]

From everything that can be gathered, traditional interest groups
played little role in the Vermont environmental legislation either in
support or opposition. This does not mean none of them took positions,
only that the groups themselves were not responsible for the legislation. If they were, we cannot find the evidence. It would appear that
interest groups have directed their attention to the measure's implementation instead. The experience of the Liberty Institute suggests
this, and so does the activity of the recently formed Landowners'
Steering Committee (against the legislation), the Vermont Citizens'
League (opposes the legislation) established in 1973, the Vermont
Natural Resources Council (formed in 1971 and a backer of the legislation), and the paper companies as suggested. In addition, a group
of farmers recently filed suit on the proposed Land-Use Plan, charging
failure by the state to produce a map showing how property would be
affected. Bosselman and Callies cite some interest groups that are
interested in the measure, but this is exclusively in the context of
"administration" and not enactment; these include builder and realtor
organizations as well as "conservation societies."[12] The local government lobby in the state is the Vermont League of Cities and Towns,
but it apparently has not opposed state moves in this field as it has in
other states like Maryland and Michigan.*

Vermont's interest group situation seems to give public officials
a stronger hand, and the same goes for the state's one-party system.
Strong competition in either sphere appears to weaken public authority
and shift power to interest groups or parties, both private institutions.
In more specific terms, it would appear that the legislation was engin-
eered by an especially popular and ambitious governor and continued
by a similar figure. In 1969, the then executive Davis appointed a
Governor's Commission on Environmental Control and named to it key
citizens and legislators. Capitalizing on adverse public sentiment
and concern over a proposed development of the International Paper
Company and on a general fear of new developments in the southern
part of Vermont, the panel recommended a statewide system of planning
and land-use controls that was later to be accepted almost verbatim
by the state legislature.

The role of the chief executive is all the more remarkable in
view of his generally limited formal powers. This is shown in a statistical study by Joseph Schlesinger, and out of a possible 20 points
Vermont scores only 13, a low figure; only 13 states are lower.[13]
The Vermont executive has important budgetary and appointive powers
but little authority in the area of veto authority; he also has limited

---

*In Maryland, the Maryland Association of Counties successfully
opposed a strong state land-use measure, and in Michigan, the Michigan Township Association successfully bottled up similar legislation
in committee (Maryland in 1973, Michigan in 1973 and 1974).

tenure potential. This seems to demonstrate the importance of informal powers, personality, and skill in tapping political resources, a point Richard Neustadt make in relation to the presidency.[14]

ACT 250 IN PRACTICE

Governor Salmon says that Act 250 is "not zoning." Even it it was, he argues, the people of Vermont would favor it (he cites a sample showing 51 percent of the residents back "fairly rigid restrictions" on development), but it "decidedly" is not. The facts do not entirely support this position. It is true that the legislation is not labled "zoning," but it is, by any reasonable standards. It meets the definition we advanced in Chapter 3 and falls within the general "state zoning" category, and it does what zoning does all over the United States—regulate land including commercial, industrial, residential, and other uses. In fact, it is zoning plus since it really includes subdivision controls as well. Most communities divide their land regulations into "zoning" and "subdivision controls," and they represent separate processes and specifics; they are generally two independent ordinances. This was the way it was set up in the model enabling legislation, and it is the method stipulated by most state laws. This applies to Vermont localities, although their zoning and subdivision ordinances are known as "bylaws." In reality, as we shall see shortly, the Vermont legislation even goes beyond this, that is, zoning and subdivision, and gets into other areas not treated by most communities in the country.

About the only points supporting the governor's argument are that the state controls are more flexible than most zoning ordinances elsewhere and that they combine aspects of different regulations. Also, to this point, they do not specify in advance what land uses are permitted and which are ruled out; to a certain extent, this difference will no longer be applicable once the new Land-Use Plan is adopted.

The legislation, as amended, set up a series of nine district commissions and a state Environmental Board to consider and approve development plans. The regulations apply to subdivisions of more the 10 units and commercial or industrial developments of more than 10 acres in towns with zoning and subdivision regulations. In other areas, that is, in areas unregulated by local government, they apply to residential developments of more than one unit, and to commercial-industrial projects of more than an acre. Thus, a bonus is given towns and cities with local controls. Basically, this means that the state controls are used outside major urban concentrations and that local controls apply inside them. The legislation was clearly aimed at large-scale development, especially that which was not reviewed by any local authority. Small-scale projects, on the other hand, were

seen as falling within the scope of local powers and plans. The measure
incidentally applies to all development regardless of its nature or size
above the elevation of 2,500 feet. In other words, state controls are
used directly in these areas, and the purpose is to protect the state's
mountains from unplanned development.

Act 250 established a procedure, whereby state <u>planning</u> would
be put into effect. It thus dealt with planning as well as <u>regulation</u>,
although the emphasis was on the latter (also regulation went into
effect immediately, and planning was to wait). Ultimately, it was
assumed that specific decisions would be based on a statewide master
plan, specifically a Land-Use Plan, and in the interim on certain
criteria set forth in the legislation. The criteria actually will be
applied even after the adoption of the plan, for even though the plan
supposedly is based on them, conditions change making the criteria
a permanent ingredient in the regulation process.

Once the Land-Use Plan is adopted—and it is now under active
consideration—it will contain a map, and this will show each parcel of
land in the state and how it is to be used. This will amount to the final
argument that Act 250 is zoning, for although no such map exists now,
it soon will. In fact, there is much controversy over this map, and
the state, if it has it, will not release it. No doubt the "zoning" argument has something to do with it, but there is something else as well,
and we return to this later. Farmers have recently filed suit, as
noted, to require the state to produce the map and bring it before
public hearings.

The legislation provides that the state must issue a permit on
proposals subject to its authority before development can proceed.
There are several criteria on which the review is to be based, and
these include a determination of the effect of the proposal on air and
water pollution, the water supply, soil erosion, highway congestion
and safety, the public schools and other services of local governments,
scenic and natural qualities and historic sites, growth, agricultural
land, forests and earth resources, public and private utility services,
and public investments of various kinds, as well as its consistency
with appropriate state, local, and regional plans and capital programs.
In other words, the state has the authority to reject proposals that do
not meet these standards for example, the proposals that "unduly"
pollute the air or water, put an "unreasonable burden" on the existing
water supply, cause a "dangerous" or "unhealthy" reduction in the
capacity of land to hold water, have an "adverse" effect on the scenic
or natural beauty of the area, and are "not in conformity" with duly
adopted plans and capital improvement programs. That development
proposals can be turned down on the basis of aesthetic factors like
scenic and natural beauty raises some potential legal questions, ones
that have by no means been resolved in the courts. In addition to zoning
and subdivision powers, these criteria suggest the existence of "adequate public facilities" and "staged land-use" authority, which are
exercised by few communities in the United States.

Loudoun County, Virginia, recently adopted an ordinance requiring developers to prove that they will not put an excessive burden on schools and other facilities and, if they do, to pay for these facilities, but this is atypical. Montgomery County, Maryland, has adopted a watered-down version of the Loudoun (adequate public facilities) ordinance and made it part of its subdivision regulations; Ramapo, New York, not long ago approved a "staged growth" program, assigning proposed developments points (development scoring too low is not permitted), but again this is virtually unique. Vermont in essence has all these things.

Three plans are required under the 1970 measure: an Interim Capability Plan which was to catalog existing land uses (and "quickly"), a Land Capability and Development Plan or the final form of the first plan, and a Land-Use Plan. The state has gone through the first stage, and the final Land Capability and Development Plan was enacted by the legislature and signed into law by the governor in 1973. The latter plan addresses itself to the impact of development on land considered most useful in the classes of agriculture, forestry and mineral extraction, historic, scenic, or recreation; to the effect of development on public facilities and services; and to the impact of proposed and future development on certain private utilities, facilities, buildings, and land. In addition, it deals with very generalized forms of desired future land uses.

The Land-Use Plan has been proposed by the administration and has received the formal approval of the governor, but it faces an uncertain future. It has generated considerable controversy and is politically sensitive because it gets into the specifics of particular parcels and the uses to be permitted on them. This "tips the hand" of the state and adds an element not currently part of the picture. It is bound to have a significant effect on land prices, to increase them where high densities are allowed and to decrease them elsewhere. To head off certain problems, the governor has stated publicly that there should be some way to compensate landowners whose property values are lowered by the plan.[15]

The Land-Use Plan may be the most important step the state has taken to date, because it takes Vermont out of the "permit" system (and simply reacting to proposals) and into more conventional zoning. The permit system will be retained of course, but decisions with the plan will have the benefit of specified uses established prior to development proposals. This is about the only thing that distinguishes Vermont's present "zoning" from zoning as we know it elsewhere; that is, it does not pinpoint actual uses prior to the submission of development plans. With the Land-Use Plan all this will change. Currently, the only time that the state controls take on this character is where there are "local" or "regional" plans available (most likely zoning maps) and, in a few instances, state functional plans that specify actual land uses.

Here is what the Land-Use Plan does. First, it in effect mandates local planning and zoning. The draft of the plan specifically says that "all . . . lands" in Vermont "shall be classified" in one of seven zones, and the "boundaries" and "limitations" of each zone "shall be established by plans and bylaws . . . prepared by the towns or the regional planning commissions. . . ." Local and regional plans, in addition, must "further" the state land-use plan and be consistent with it. If the towns fail to do this—and this is important—the state is directed to step in and draw up and adopt the plans and the zoning maps itself. Of course, if the statewide plan is detailed enough, this problem should take care of itself. Second, a statewide system of land uses is set up, and local and regional plans and zoning are to be governed by it. Specifically, the Land-Use Plan says that towns and regional planning commissions "shall establish uses of lands generally in accordance" with the system.

The proposed plan provides for the following uses:

1. urban, or residential, commercial, industrial, and other development in cities including lands needed to accommodate growth for at least 30 years and at densities of about 2,000 per square mile or higher (statewide density at present is 48 per square mile);

2. village, or uses that are settled at a density significantly greater than the surrounding area and that have an intensity of development of one or more principal buildings per acre, with supporting public and private facilities;

3. rural, or land near urban and village concentrations, shopping, employment, and containing residential development including "second" or "vacation" homes, and suitable for low-to-moderate densities;

4. natural resource, or lands that generally have potential for agricultural, forestry, or mineral extraction and not conveniently located to employment, shopping facilities, and improved roads;

5. conservation, or lands generally of a size of five square miles or more and which are undeveloped or predominantly forested and which have potential for commercial forestry, are in excess of 1,500 feet in elevation or have significant natural, recreational, scenic, and other similar features;

6. roadside, or lands that are located within 100 feet of an interstate, state, or local highway in a rural, natural resource, or conservation area;

7. shoreline, or land immediately around or beside lakes and waterways.

For each of the seven areas, the plan sets forth "permitted" and "conditional" uses. So, for example, in the rural area, single- and multiple-family detached dwellings are "permitted" uses, and mobile home parks and vacation homes are "conditional" uses. The difference is that more stringent requirements and stipulations are established for the second category, and it is more difficult to qualify. It is clear, by the nature of the uses set in each category, that the conditional variety is more likely to be controversial and politically explosive; thus, additional standards are provided, giving neighbors and others a better chance at defeating them and making approval by no means a certainty. A "mobile home park" is a good example, and it is certain that residents would object much more to this use than, say, another like "single-family detached." Obviously politics has been built into the plan.

The fact is that these "areas" or "uses" are not exactly the same as a typical set of "zones" in a zoning ordinance. They are somewhat broader, and they are not presented in the legal detail found in most ordinances. They seem to follow the practice that has been backed by such organizations as the Urban Land Institute—that is, "flexible" land-use controls. It is true, they represent zoning, but the zoning is not as rigid and not cast in concrete as most zoning is. Most zoning ordinances, for instance, establish strict set-back requirements, covering front, side, and rear yard setbacks from neighboring property lines (this applies, incidentally, to both residential and nonresidential property). Similarly, the residential zones of most zoning ordinances set lot-size minimums, for example, one-acre, two-acre, half-acre zones, and so on. The Vermont system contains none of this.

This gives greater discretion to planners and public officials, and it could well cut housing costs and promote better layout patterns. This is an argument that we develop in some depth in our Politics of Land Use: Planning, Zoning, and the Private Developer (Praeger, 1973). A good illustration of the principle is the section on conditional uses in the "shoreline" area; they may include "any reasonable use of lands within a shoreline area that is consistent with the natural, scenic, or historic character of the body of water and the surrounding area. . . ." Many planners hold that this kind of "zoning" makes more sense than the more detailed variety. We agree.

EFFECTS OF ACT 250

One source calls the state effort so far a "massive holding action," and this seems to sum it up pretty well. Some proposals have been approved and others disapproved, and we have no information on the percentages. But it is clear that a proposal for development is by no means the same as approval, a pattern similar to rezonings in Hawaii. Most of the rejections have come from the district commissions, and generally the statewide Environmental Board gets into specific proposals only on appeal. Developers have been turned down on the basis of undue traffic congestion that would be caused (an apartment complex) and inconsistency with a state plan (a recreation plan—and it was a proposed service station) among

other reasons, and many proposals have been held in abeyance until
informal agreements, covenants and compromises can be worked
out. In some instances, a small minority it appears, denials have
been appealed to the courts (the procedure is from the district commission, to the state Environmental Board, and then the courts); in
one such case, the owner of a mobile home park has sued to gain the
right to expand his facilities, having been turned down at both the
district and board levels. Some have suggested that the "holding
action" notion is based on the reasoning that little development should
be permitted until the state prepares its Land-Use Plan. Thus, proposals are being held up for a variety of reasons.

It appears that the law has slowed the growth rate of Vermont
and cut back on development, as this suggests, although hard-and-fast
data are difficult to come by. This represents the judgment of observers who have watched the law closely in the first years of its operation. Probably the greatest effect in this regard has been the influence
in terms of discouraging applications. That is, if developers know
what they are up against, they will simply not apply and perhaps go
to another state or do something not covered by the law in Vermont.
The assessment therefore is not based on formal "rejections" alone.
This has seemingly had the most significant repercussions in remote
rural regions of the state, where local authorities are reportedly most
dissatisfied with the measure. There the sentiment against zoning of
any kind, state or local, runs high, although there has to be some
ambivalence here as well since these are the same people most likely
to be convinced by the "Vermont for Vermonters" slogans (this is
familiar campaign rhetoric, used by liberals and conservatives alike).
That the "Vermont for Vermonters" sloganeers are also "zoners"
has apparently not crossed their minds.

Of the three plans provided for in the law, the only one that
"counts" (to date, that is) is the Land Capability and Development
Plan. As noted, this was approved by the state legislature, and it is
law. Yet if offers only the most generalized of guidelines to the district commissions and Environmental Board. It is not a zoning map,
and its land-use maps are quite broad and provide little specificity.
These maps cannot be used in any practical way as the base for decision making, and it seems that for "planning" to make any headway
and to form the foundation of implementation decisions, we shall have
to wait for the Land-Use Plan. This may be a long wait, and major
battles over it can be expected. It all gets back to a general principle—
that is, the experts say for decisions to be "legitimate" they must be
founded on specific criteria; they must be made "rationally," in other
words.[16] Yet the politics of the matter is that decision makers are
rarely anxious to provide these criteria or rationales. To do so
restricts their options and makes them much more subject to criticism;
it makes them much more vulnerable. This is all in the political
sense. By keeping their justifications (the base of their decisions)

general, vague, and abstract, officials protect themselves politically, and this is the reason the state will not release the land-use map that specifies proposed development, parcel by parcel in the state. This would restrict their options in specific decisions, "tip their hand" in advance, and make it much harder to "pull any political capital" out of the decision. It makes no sense politically (to release the maps). This is also "rationality" incidentally, political rationality, perhaps the highest kind.

State officials will release the maps when they are "forced" to and no sooner, and this will be at the last possible moment (the law requires the maps; so they have little choice in the matter). The longer they can hold the maps off the market, the longer their options will remain open. They increase their importance immensely by declining to act. Their perspectives are short run, and the experts' standards long run. It is, of course, the politicians' perspectives that will prevail.

There have been some technical difficulties with the law, and there have been a number of exemptions because of the way the law was written. Some observers believe that the law's coverage should be expanded. Strip development such as motels and service stations and small-scale industrial operations around limited residential concentrations are excluded for example, and yet it is argued that since they have their effects on the environment, they should be subject to state review. Also subdivisions that offer individual lots in excess of 10 acres are similarly excluded. These, too, have their impact on the environment.

ASSESSMENT OF THE LAW

All in all, Bosselman and Callies report that the law is "progressing well."[17] Here are some pluses. In the first place, "planning" is being done, and it is separate from zoning as it should be. This has to be a plus, for as we have seen in Hawaii, it is entirely possible to combine the two and therefore to downgrade planning; in a direct confrontation, there is no question that the zoning will "win." It seems imperative if we are to have planning in this country that it "mean" something, that it represent the "future" dimension, and that it not simply reflect existing realities as zoning does. Vermont does not have this problem. At the same time, its "planning" is running into trouble, perhaps because of its independence, and this may hold up the entire program.

In addition, in Vermont planning is law. This is important, and it is not at all typical. In fact, we know of no other place where this is true, state or local. (Hawaii may be an exception, but there the two are fused.) The Land-Use Plan that we were quoting above is not merely "advisory"; it carries the "force of law." In other words, it must be obeyed. Planners should ask for more. Zoning is subject to it, as are particular implementation decisions. Of course, other criteria are involved, but presumably the plan has already taken these into account and reflects them. This is nearly ideal, we suggest.

There also seems to be a good working relationship between state and local authorities. The state includes both the state Environmental Board naturally and the district commissions, and "local" authorities include town, city, and regional officials. Generally, the state has dealt with large-scale developments as we have noted, leaving smaller ones to local zoning and decision making, and where the local government has zoning, the state has typically deferred to local controls. Few complaints have been registered so far as we can tell, and it is among local officials where the opposition to state planning is the greatest. This amounts to "creative federalism without Washington," and it is working. Professor Reagan may have to add a new chapter to his recent book on "permissive" federalism because the federal government is permitting nothing here.[18] It is not involved at all. Reagan argues that subnational authority should be exercised within a frame set by the national government.

The state has moved into areas not treated by local regulations. Thus, it has filled a vacuum and served to control development that would otherwise not be subject to any public scrutiny. This cannot be criticized, and it can serve the public interest. If some local governments are upset—and some town officials are, at least on ideological grounds—they have every opportunity to pass local controls and implement them themselves. We are not saying that this must be the best for all concerned, but the fact is that public planning and zoning can improve the environment, and all areas are going to have it anyway, in time. The only choice is whether it is going to be exercised locally or by the state, or perhaps by Washington (a few people are suggesting the latter, at least by implication).[19] If communities do not want the state to do the job, they should do it themselves; what choice is there? It appears that state action has stimulated local zoning, and in part from this reason, and we generally view this as a plus.

Furthermore, zoning in Vermont is flexible. If indeed the state has zoning—and we say it does—it is flexible zoning, exhibiting few of the canons of traditional land-use controls. The argument has already been developed in detail. This gives decision makers, developers, and citizens greater latitude in shaping land-use patterns in accordance with current desires and local needs, and it represents a significant advance over earlier practices, which put communities in a straitjacket (this goes for controls and development patterns).

In fact, Vermont's legislation covers planning, and it is the generalized version of state plans (so far) that forms the base of specific land-use decisions, which is as it should be. Schuyler Jackson, the present chairman of the Environmental Board, has been quoted as saying that these plans are only "advisory," but it is still true that they are "law." Thus, they can be drawn on to turn down proposals inconsistent with them, and this will be especially important when the Land-Use Plan is adopted. The current governor, Salmon, has said that the Vermont system is "reactive" and "negative" in terms of its relationship to particular proposals for development, but with broad plans based in law, this "reactive" and "negative" system can work. We know the governor would agree. It is only when plans and guides are rigid and cast in cement that the terms (reactive, negative) take on their normal connotations and make zoning "unworkable"; such zoning puts officials on the defensive as the governor says, and this is not good. The system, as it is unfolding in Vermont, provides for a "positive" government role and puts public authority in the driver's seat. Most planners would say that this is where it belongs, and we do not disagree.

Vermont is also enforcing its law, and this may give it an edge on Hawaii. In a recent situation, a developer was found to have cleared his land for a recreational development, with ski trails and roads all carved out of the wilderness, even though the proposal was still pending. In a routine check, the state discovered what was being done and promptly got a court order to stop the action.

Finally, as the governor is fond of saying, the law provides for extensive citizen involvement and, in his words, "control." The point is that laymen dominate the formal decision-making process; that is, they constitute the membership of the district commissions and the state board. Elizabeth Haskell reports that they include representatives of conservationists, developers, builders, general businessmen, public officials, and college professors.[20] The governor feels that this pattern differs from that stipulated in the American Law Institute's model state land development code. Regardless of the validity of this point, the law does encourage citizen participation in a variety of ways, both through service on state commissions and public hearings, and this has to be a plus. At the same time, it does not discourage professional input, but provides a blending of the two. This seems an ideal combination.

The Vermont system, however, is far from perfect. There are some problems; some of them are inherent in the successes and perhaps cannot be avoided. For example, there is still much confusion over planning and zoning and what they mean. Is the state in the zoning business or is it not? Different people have different answers. Is the state truly drawing on plans for its decisions, or just the appearance of this? Probably most officials in Vermont do not know the difference between zoning and planning, and this likely includes some on the district and state commissions. Whatever the difference is in theory, many officials confuse them in practice. Both officials and citizens view the Land-Use Plan as a zoning map, and

the district commissions seem to consider "plans" of the towns and
regional planning agencies to be "zoning maps" and vice versa.

Similarly, while there are generally cordial relations between
state and local officials, there is some overlap between the two, and
few people are sure where local authority stops and state authority
begins. As an illustration, the state (district commission) approved
a development under state law, but it was turned down by the town
government. The law covers the reverse of this—and clearly the state
can overturn a local decision that conflicts with state laws or plans—
but what of the state being overruled by localities? Some would argue
that, as a practical matter, local governments should be able to set
"higher" standards if they wish, but what does this mean in practice
and is it consistent with state law? Presumably, if the state law is
well written—and this one seems to be—it takes into account all the
factors that should be considered; if the local government reverses
the state, is this proper?

Along these same lines, getting two levels involved in the same
decisions can be good for intergovernmental cooperation but costly
for developers. In point of fact, developers often have to go to two
levels of government for approvals, in part because of the confusion
over who has the final authority. This involves a "dual system" of
regulation to them. It can be expensive to developers, and they are
bound to pass on the costs to the public. Also the developers complain
about the time-consuming process for review and approval, and some
feel that this is not due to their actions (their not doing their plans
right in the first place) but state inefficiency and footdragging (see
above). Some believe that state officials feel "time is on their side,"
the idea being that regulations are getting stronger all the time and
the hands of public authorities strengthened. The longer the state can
hold off a developer, this line of reasoning holds, the better its
bargaining position. There are some unpleasant realities, and they will
not go away if we overlook them.

Until the adoption of the state Land-Use Plan, there will still be
some problems with plan priorities. That is, which plan or plans
have priority? Plans are done by these agencies, all separately and
all referred to already: town government (town plans), regional
planning agencies (regional plans), regular state departments (functional plans, like the state recreation plan and the state highway plan),
and state land-use plans (the Interim Capability, the Land Capability
and Development, and the Land-Use Plans) Which has priority in
any given situation, or any given decision? It is not clear. Once the
state Land-Use Plan is formally adopted, there will be little doubt
(we think), but until then, how are decisions to be made? Obviously,
it depends on the particular decision, the particular district commission,
the particular decision maker, or particular circumstances. This
can be confusing and can cause real problems for developers, landowners, and citizens, not to mention the different state and local

agencies. In reality, planning decision premises are rarely clear or
"exclusive" (and thus meaningful), and thus it is hard to pin them down
in any event. But at least clear ground rules to start would help.
There is enough confusion even then.

Further, and similar to Hawaii, state controls in Vermont have
cut into the housing supply and have apparently forced higher housing
prices. At least this is the conclusion of Babcock and Bosselman, who
have researched the matter. They attribute the higher prices to a
"wide variety" of conditions including ecological, aesthetic, and
traditional zoning and subdivision requirements imposed by state and
local governments, and they say that a "concern for the cost of housing"
is "not evident" in the Vermont law or its administration; they also
cite the "dual regulation" system as pushing costs upward.[21] As
already suggested, the law may also be cutting into development potential, not so much because of its specific features but its general psy-
chological effects; to the extent that the state depends on new development and the tourist trade this attracts, this can pose a problem, and
it is not a minor one.

Finally, there has been a good deal of criticism that the state law
has infringed on private property rights. This is the argument of such
organizations as the Institute for Liberty and Community and the Landowners' Steering Committee, and their positions are put forth regularly
in the Vermont Watchman (a cartoon from a recent issue demonstrates
their concerns—see Figure 5). Their arguments include the following:
The state law represents an "invasion of private property rights";
it takes property "without compensation"; it "undercuts" local government; and it assures "bureaucratic rule." These groups are especially disturbed about the prospects of the proposed Land-Use Plan
mandating statewide zoning, and their harshest criticism is reserved
for it and for the chairman of the Environmental Board which is pre-
paring it. Although many planners tend to discount such groups, we
do not, and we feel that their charges should be examined carefully
since there may very well be merit in them. If necessary, the state
law should be revised, which is no more than the liberal Democratic
governor has suggested (a form of compensation for landowners whose
property values are lowered by state planning). We support public
compensation where state controls decrease land values.

In sum, we think that the Vermont law stands up pretty well. It
has problems, but these are to be expected. In many respects, it
would seem that the Vermont experience would serve as a better
model than Hawaii's because of the similarity in traditions between
Vermont and the other states. This is a tradition of local control and
a certain degree of hostility to land controls of any kind. Vermont
has developed state planning and "zoning" in spite of this tradition,
and its actions bear watching.

Still, this is a small state and one based heavily on a tourist-
recreational trade. It is also a predominantly rural state. Its 1970

FIGURE 5

Vermont Watchman Cartoon

Source: Vermont Watchman, January 1974, p. 9. The Vermont Watchman is published by the Landowners Steering Committee, Box 729, Lyndonville, Vermont. Reproduced by permission.

population of 445,000 makes it smaller than all but two states, and its
land area of 9,000 square miles puts it in the 43rd position (seven
states are smaller). Its population density is 48 persons per square
mile, and this is to be compared to over 381 persons per square mile
in New York, 276 in Delaware, 623 in Connecticut, 199 in Illinois, and
396 in Maryland. To what extent these population and economic characteristics make Vermont unique or unusual cannot be known, but they
should be taken into account.

While the claims made at the beginning of the chapter may be too
broad, Vermont's record does not disprove them, and it supports them
in many respects. Vermont may be in the "backwash" geographically
and economically, but it is among the front runners in land use. About
this there can be little doubt.

OREGON

Unlike Vermont and Hawaii, Oregon has no single piece of legislation we can point to to distinguish it. It has a series of measures.
Governor Tom McCall referred to the situation as being like "spokes
on a wheel," and he cited a number of interrelated laws in land use
and planning that have been enacted over the last four or five years.[22]
Its actions in this field may, in fact, have something to do with its
being ranked as high as it is among "innovative" states, a finding in
a recent study by Jack Walker.[23]

In 1973, the Oregon Legislature created the Land Conservation
and Development Commission and gave it sweeping powers over certain kinds of land uses and review authority over local planning and
zoning. Under the measure, the state is given direct land-use controls
over certain activities of "statewide significance," including public
transportation facilities, sewerage and water supply and solid waste
systems, public school construction, and certain "priority" areas such
as freeway interchange development and flood plains. In addition, the
state is provided review power over local plans, zoning, and subdivision ordinances, to assure conformity with state goals and guidelines.
If localities do not have such controls, the state is authorized to step
in and regulate directly. In reality, although similar in some ways to
Vermont's 1970 law, this legislation is not as broad as Vermont's, or
clearly as Hawaii's, as local governments in the state generally have
land controls.

As of October 1973, one source reports that 23 of the state's 36
counties had the controls and that the others were in the process of
adopting them. Of the 238 cities in the state, 148 reportedly had
planning and land regulation ordinances; 76 were in the process of
getting them; and only 13 had made no moves in this direction.[24]
The state's role in direct state planning seems unclear (are state

"goals" and "guidelines" plans?), and its role in direct state zoning
conditioned on local inaction (which appears limited) and thus does
not amount to much.

Other legislation in the state has been approved in the areas of
coastal planning, scenic waterways, "greenbelts" (preferential assessment), and open-space preservation. In a celebrated case, however,
the state enacted a law in 1973 providing strong and direct state subdivision control. The law was aimed at recreational developers, but
its provisions were so stringent that the developers stormed the
capital and the state backed down; it promised to bring such construction to a standstill, and the old subdivision law, much weaker, was
reinstated. The action embarrassed the governor, and it is a subject
he prefers to avoid and that his opponents like to remind him of.

FLORIDA

The key legislation in this state is the Florida Environmental Land
and Water Management Act of 1972. The measure provides for the
establishment of "areas of critical state concern" and the pinpointing
of "developments of regional impact." Both of these are loosely
defined, but in general they may include the usual, or areas of special
environmental, historical, natural, regional or statewide importance,
areas significantly affected by or having a significant effect on existing
or proposed major public facilities, areas of major development including new communities, and uses because of their character, magni-
tude, or location would have a substantial effect on the health, safety,
or welfare of more than one county. This language is not ours, but
is taken directly from the legislation, and it makes the point. The final
assessment of this law will clearly have to await implementation
since the provisions are so vague and no one can tell for sure what
they mean. It is worth noting that no designations have been made to
date; perhaps Florida officials are confused too.

The legislation sets up a complicated administrative procedure
designed to carry out the program and in short involves several
agencies including a new unit established by the measure—the Florida
Land and Water Adjudicatory Commission, the state land planning
department, local governments, and regional planning commissions.
It is actually local governments that designate the "critical areas"
or uses of "regional impact" and not the state; however, the state is
given the right to move in to designate and control these areas and
their uses if local governments do not. Thus, the state authority is
not minor, and in reality its leverage under the legislation is quite
impressive. The state is, in essence, the "supervisor" and "over-
seer" of the measure, but the actual planning and regulation are done
by localities. Regional planning agencies are "advisory" to local

governments in this regard, and the state gets involved only if the mechanism breaks down.

It is instructive that the act restricts critical areas and regional uses to 5 percent of the state, or about 500,000 acres. It also is generally patterned after the American Law Institute's Model Land Development Code and is the only state to date to follow it (this is probably the reason the 1972 measure is given such wide attention).

MAINE

Maine's 1970 Site Selection Law set up a "permit system" regulating commercial, industrial, and residential developments in excess of 20 acres or occupying a single parcel or structure of over 60,000 square feet in floor area, and natural resource drilling and excavating operations. Although no state plan per se was envisioned under the measure, it did require conformance on the part of proposed development with environmental quality standards, sound soil management practices, and the availability of adequate transportation services; developers are also required to show "financial capacity." a novel stipulation so far as we know.

Oil companies and recreational developers were apparently the main "targets" of the legislation, and the administration was assigned to the Environmental Improvement Commission, a preexisting agency. Specifically, developers must obtain a license from the state before going ahead with plans.

In 1971, the Maine legislature approved enactments extending planning, zoning, and subdivision controls to all "unorganized" and "deorganized" (apparently counties) areas, and this applied mostly to the northern half of the state. If local governments adopt these controls, state regulation is dropped, although the localities must meet certain state standards. In a similar move, the state passed legislation requiring local regulation of shoreline areas and providing for direct state controls if localities fail to act. The administration, however, under the shoreline measure is to remain in the hands of local government even if the state provides the controls.

The head of the Maine planning department says that the state is developing a definite land-use policy in view of these and other laws, but he does not say that the state is engaged in land-use planning as such.[25] Obviously, this is a politically sensitive matter, and the states can be expected to tread slowly, at least for the most part. Let us now turn to other forms of state involvement in land use.

NOTES

1. Daniel J. Elazar, American Federalism: A View from the States, 2nd ed. (New York: Thomas Y. Crowell, 1972), p. 1.
2. See Samuel H. Beer and Richard E. Barringer (eds.), The State and the Poor (Cambridge, Mass.: Winthrop Publishers, 1970); Elizabeth Haskell, "New Directions in State Environmental Planning," Journal of the American Institute of Planners, XXXVII, no. 4 (July 1971): 253-258; Arthur W. Macmahon, Administering Federalism in a Democracy (New York: Oxford University Press, 1972), Chap. V; Theodore J. Lowi, The End of Liberalism (New York: W. W. Norton, 1969).
3. See Charles R. Adrian, State and Local Governments, 2nd ed. (New York: McGraw-Hill, 1967); and Rexford Guy Tugwell, Model for a New Constitution (Palo Alto, Calif.: James E. Freel, 1970).
4. Thomas P. Salmon, "Vermont: Public Support for Land-Use Controls," in Robert H. Weber and Ralph J. Marcelli (eds.), State Government XLVI no. 3 (Summer 1973): 197.
5. Austin Ranney, "Parties in State Politics," in Herbert Jacob and Kenneth N. Vines (eds.), Politics in the American States, 2nd ed. (Boston: Little, Brown, 1971), pp. 82-121.
6. Duane Lockard, New England State Politics (Chicago: Henry Regnery, 1959).
7. Robert H. Weber and Ralph J. Marcelli (eds.), The Book of the States 1970-71 (Lexington, Ky.: Council of State Governments, 1970), p. 65; and The Book of the States 1972-73 (1972), p. 66.
8. Elizabeth Haskell and others, Managing the Environment (Washington, D. C.: Smithsonian Institution, 1971), pp. 24-28.
9. L. Harmon Zeigler and Hendrik van Dalen, "Interest Groups in the States," in Jacob and Vines (eds.), op. cit., pp. 122-160.
10. Harmon Zeigler, "Interest Groups in the States," in Jacob and Vines (eds.), op. cit., 1st ed. (1965), p. 116.
11. Wayne L. Francis, Legislative Issues in the Fifty States (Chicago: Rand McNally, 1967).
12. Fred Bosselman and David Callies, The Quiet Revolution in Land-Use Control (Washington, D. C.: Government Printing Office, 1971), p. 66.
13. Joseph A. Schlesinger, "The Politics of the Executive," in Jacob and Vines (eds.), op. cit., 2nd ed., pp. 210-237.
14. Richard E. Neustadt, Presidential Power (New York: John Wiley, 1960). For an application of the same principle and in the context of urban planning, see Martin Meyerson and Edward C. Banfield, Politics, Planning, and the Public Interest (New York: Free Press, 1955).

15. At least he has said this nationally. See Governor Salmon's comments on "Land-Use Regulations and Property Tax Relief," in Innovations in State Government: Messages from the Governors (Washington, D. C.: National Governors' Conference, 1974), p. 97. He writes in a section on "New Approaches to Land Use and Environment."

16. The question is treated at length in Alan Altshuler, The City Planning Process: A Political Analysis (Ithaca, N.Y.: Cornell University Press, 1965). See also Edward C. Banfield, Political Influence: A New Theory of Urban Politics (New York: Free Press, 1961).

17. Bosselman and Callies, op. cit., p. 89.

18. See Michael D. Reagan, The New Federalism (New York: Oxford University Press, 1972).

19. See, for example, The President's Committee on Urban Housing, A Decent Home (Washington, D. C.: Government Printing Office, 1968).

20. Haskell and others, op. cit., p. 298.

21. Richard F. Babcock and Fred P. Bosselman, Exclusionary Zoning: Land-Use Regulation and Housing in the 1970s (New York: Praeger Publishers, 1973), pp. 165-168.

22. See testimony of Governor McCall in U. S. House of Representatives, Committee on Interior and Insular Affairs, Subcommittee on the Environment, Land-Use Planning Act of 1974, H. R. 10294 (Washington, D. C.: Government Printing Office, 1974), pp. 68-84.

23. See Jack L. Walker, "Innovation in State Politics," in Jacob and Vines (eds.), op. cit., 2nd ed., pp. 354-387.

24. U. S. Senate, Committee on Interior and Insular Affairs, State Land-Use Programs (Washington, D. C.: Government Printing Office, 1974), p. 57.

25. Phillip M. Savage, "Toward a State Land-Use Policy: The Maine Experience," in Richard H. Slavin and H. Milton Patton (eds.), State Planning Issues, 1973 (Lexington, Ky.: Council of State Governments, 1973), pp. 5-10.

5

SPECIALIZED STATE ZONING:
WILL IT WORK?

DIFFERENCE BETWEEN SPECIALIZED
AND COMPREHENSIVE CONTROLS

Chapters 3 and 4 have dealt with comprehensive planning and land-use controls. They have treated the states that have been most prominently involved in these controls, although, as we have seen at the end of Chapter 4, not all the states are exercising them in too comprehensive a manner. What it amounts to is that the comprehensive controls are used by two states, Hawaii and Vermont, and that is it. The other three states maybe moving in this direction, but they are not there. This means that we have little to go on in this area; few models are possible and we do not know what the future holds. What, then, are the prospects of the states developing more limited controls?

The specialized controls generally refer to limited forms of zoning, but some states use other terms, preferring to reserve "zoning" for what local governments do. They may use simply "regulation" or "control," but the idea is the same—authority over certain land uses. Others use the term directly and qualify it to say it is done for particular purposes or geographical areas (and not others). This, then, is what specialized controls means, that is, zoning or other forms of land controls that apply to specific uses such as power plants or surface mining, or to specific areas such as flood plains and land around state buildings. This is to be distinguished from the more general form of zoning or land regulation, covering all the land in the state (as in Hawaii) or most of it (Vermont).

This chapter concentrates on these kinds of control, when exercised by the state directly, and not on planning per se; however, when planning is involved and is pertinent to the controls, it is treated. The last part of the chapter is devoted to one state that sought to adopt strong state land-use controls over key areas, and hopefully the experience of this state, Maryland, can give us some lessons as to the likelihood of getting particular kinds of state zoning approved and therefore as to their "workability."

INCIDENCE OF SPECIALIZED STATE ZONING

There are generally two types of specialized state land-use controls: traditional controls such as shoreline and wetlands regulation and "critical areas" controls, a more recent development. There is currently a tendency for the states to get more involved in both kinds of controls, and that the regulations are "traditional" does not necessarily mean that the states have used them to any extent or even have them on the books at all. Indeed, many of them have been tapped sparingly as we shall see. All forms of zoning in this country have been local, and the states have typically given zoning responsibilities to localities including the traditional specialized variety.

States have been encouraged in the past several years to adopt "critical areas" controls, in anticipation of federal money to be provided by the Land-Use Planning Act (if it ever passes; it was defeated in the House in 1974). There is virtually no experience with "critical areas" planning and control, and conclusions here must be somewhat speculative. We come back to this point later and in some depth.

Table 2 in Chapter 2 shows the incidence of specialized state zoning. The data in the table, as of January 30, 1974, will be updated with more recent material wherever this is possible (through mid-1974). We have collected most of the pertinent legislation in each of the categories we are about to examine and shall refer to it directly in the following paragraphs without citation.

STRIP MINING CONTROL

The most common form of specialized state controls is surface or strip mining regulation, and states like Ohio, West Virginia, Pennsylvania, and Illinois have been in the business for some time. Basically, this involves controls over excavating activities and the reclamation of the land once the strip mining operations are completed. The controls vary in strictness and effectiveness, and "weak" state regulations have caused some people to press the federal government for direct, stronger ones.

In all, 30 states now have these controls, out of an estimated 36 that might logically have them, representing a slight increase in the number (27) in Table 2. Recent additions include Wyoming and Idaho. Some states are also revising their surface mining legislation, perhaps in response to possible federal controls (such a bill recently passed the House), and North Dakota, for example, approved amendments to its strip mining law in 1973, with a view toward strengthening it. The state was concerned by the prospects of stepped-up mining activity in the western part of the state. The new legislation requires stricter reclamation procedures among other things.

Similarly, Kansas in 1974 amended its law along the same lines. The amendments cut the time permitted for reclamation and gave the state greater discretion in requiring early grading and seeding (for instance, a provision was stricken prohibiting reclamation and grading under wet conditions). They also compel the submission of more detailed reports from mining operations covering such matters as the dates of grading, planting, seeding, and the area planted.

POWER PLANT SITING CONTROL

The next most popular kind of specialized zoning is power plant siting, and this is a new power in many states and has come in large part as a result of pressure from environmentalists. At the same time, public service and public utility commissions in the states (called "corporation" or "railroad" commissions in some cases) have traditionally had control over power utilities including siting, but presumably environmental and conservation considerations played little role in their determinations. Generally, it appears that the new controls are also administered by these commissions. This has to affect their application and the perspectives used in making decisions. There are probably no better examples of old-line agencies in the states, dominated by traditional power structures in the utilities, and liberals, conservationists, and citizens' groups are seldom represented on them. Little research can be cited on the subject, especially the politics of decision making; this is unfortunate in view of their importance. The situation may even be more revealing than that uncovered by Nader's Raiders at the national level as it would appear that persons with close ties to the utilities are often named to these state bodies.[1]

To date 25 states have power plant siting legislation on the books, and this includes states like Montana, Rhode Island, Arkansas, and Alabama. Altogether, two additional states, Kentucky and Massachusetts, have approved such legislation in 1974. This makes an even half of the states to have acted on the matter (23 are shown in Table 2).

As an example, the state of Washington exercises regulation through the Thermal Power Plant Siting Act. The legislation creates a special commission to administer the program (thus likely deviating from the normal procedure)—a thermal power plant site evaluation council, and this panel has the power to adopt rules, regulations, and policies to carry out the act and to consider applications for siting.

While its authority is advisory—the governor makes the final decisions—
it holds public hearings and takes evidence and is the chief recom-
mending body. Proposals must meet high standards. For instance,
they must demonstrate "minimal adverse" effect on the environment
and ecology of the land, as well as on the state waters and their aquatic
life. The law applies to major power plants or those with a generating
capacity over a certain amount; it gives the council control over the
location of associated transmission lines as well. In some states, the
latter power is given to local government and is covered by "special
exceptions" (requiring a special permit); this is true in Maryland,
for example.

Arkansas approved, for the first time, a siting law in 1973, known
as the Utility Facility Environmental Protection Act. It extends to the
siting of all major public utilities including electric generating plants,
electric transmission lines, and gas facilities and transmission lines.
Utilities under the measure are required to secure a "certificate"
showing both environmental compatibility and public need before
going ahead with plans. Regulatory authority in this state, incidentally,
is given to the Public Service Commission, and as indicated this is
probably the typical pattern.

FLOOD PLAIN CONTROL

Flood plain controls are given to state agencies in 15 states, and
there has been no change in the number in this category since January
1974. States with powers here include Montana, Nebraska, New Jersey,
Oklahoma, and Washington, and most of these have controlled their
flood plains for a decade or longer. This is not an especially new
control, but it is being stressed to a greater extent now as part of the
overall land-use package that states are expected to adopt.[2] The sever-
ity of recent floods may have had some effect as well, with Agnes
being a good example.

Generally, flood plain legislation sets the criteria for the designation of drainage basins, waterways, rivers, and lakes to be affected
and the area near them that is to be regulated. In some cases, no
construction is permitted at all (rare), and in others limited improvements such as off-street parking in connection with a close-by shopping
center or floodproof facilities may be allowed. The tendency has been
to tighten the requirements and to bar any permanent residences as
well as most businesses and industrial construction or improvements.
Still, what is and what is not a flood plain is by no means a settled
question (even among experts), and specific determinations are
usually required; these may be built on detailed studies by geologists,
hydrologists, and others who can predict the prospects of an area
being flooded at periodical intervals such as 25, 50, or 100 years.

The administration of the legislation takes this kind of consideration into account.

Legislation in the state of Connecticut authorizes the commissioner of environmental protection to establish "encroachment lines" delineating flood plain areas. This is done after extensive study and public hearings, and once designated, no "obstructions" may be placed there without a "permit" from the state. Whyte says that the Connecticut controls are working well and that local governments in the state "welcome" the state role in this regard. He says that it has "stimulated" rather than "inhibited" local initiative.[3] In Michigan, by the same token, all development in flood plains is subject to a state "licensing" system, that is, directly (and not through local government); the procedures are outlined in the state's Inland Lake and Streams Act.

Recent legislation in Indiana (1973) sets up minimum standards for state and local regulation of flood plains. "Flood hazard" areas are defined as those along rivers or streams having a drainage area of one or more square miles (in urban districts), or ten or more square miles in rural districts. This updates and supplements "flood control" regulations enacted by the state in 1945. Under the recent act, either the state or local government may issue "permits" for uses in flood plains, depending on who has the authority (varies by area). "Permitted uses" requiring no permit include agriculture, forestry, parks, golf courses, and play areas, while "special exceptions" that must be licensed include pipeline, railroad, floodproof industrial or commercial uses, and sewerage facility uses.

COASTAL ZONE REGULATION

Although a few states have been in this for a long time, the interest in coastal zone regulation has increased greatly in the last two years due to the enactment of federal legislation in this area. This was covered to some extent in Chapter 2, but the measure was the Coastal Zone Management Act of 1972, and it provided federal grants for this purpose. This was the first time, incidentally, that Washington has granted funds to either state or local government for zoning per se. Planning money has been available to the cities since 1954 and to the states since 1961 (through the "701 program" of the federal housing act), but no money was previously provided for zoning.[4]

Funds under the 1972 legislation are given only to the states and not to local governments, and about a dozen states have been assisted so far. Most of the money has been used for "tooling up" and not planning or actual zoning. It is probably worth noting that "zoning" is not used in the federal legislation—only "management."

This had to be strategic to some extent (zoning is local, and no one, not even Washington, wants to alarm localities). There has been no change in the number of states involved in coastal zone regulation since January of 1974.

States that have adopted coastal zone legislation include Maine, Michigan, Minnesota, Mississippi, Texas, and Virginia. Wisconsin has had such legislation on the books for years, and it applies to the state's shoreline on Lake Michigan. From the looks of things above Green Bay, it appears to be working. In fact, Wisconsin has been a leader in protecting its shores, waterways, highways, and other areas from harmful development and unplanned uses. It has also received high scores on soil management practices.

All in all, 14 states have laws and programs in the area, and this represents just under half the total number that border on "qualified" bodies of water such as the Atlantic and Pacific Oceans and the Great Lakes.[5] The universe in this category is projected at 32, meaning that this is the number of states with boundaries on this water.

Likely the best-known state in this field is California, and it takes precedence over Delaware in this respect. Delaware's landmark Coastal Zone Act of 1971, regulating industrial development on the state's shore and going beyond most other states' measures, was widely heralded as a breakthough in coastal zoning. It may have had something to do with triggering the federal program since federal grants often come after one or more states have done the spadework (the "laboratory" theory).

The California Coastal Zone Conservation Act of 1972 is popularly know as Proposition 20. It applies strict controls on all land within 1,000 yards of the ocean, extending from the mountain range near the Oregon border on the north to the Mexican boundary in the south.

The regulatory powers under the act took effect right away and did not wait for the development of a coastal plan, also provided for. This follows the procedure elsewhere. Hawaii never did adopt a separate plan after its comprehensive zoning controls were approved, and Vermont has yet to give its nod to the pending Land-Use Plan. In the meantime, land regulations in those two states are being applied. (In Hawaii, in fact, the zoning legislation was the plan.) The California Coastal Zone Plan is due in December of 1975 and is to consider such matters as the maintenance, restoration, and enhancement of the quality of the coastal environment as well as the availability of such services as transportation, recreation, and others.

The law also set up the California Coastal Zone Conservation Commission and six regional commissions; all are state bodies, and their purpose is to administer the program. Specifically, the regional commissions have control for the shoreline within their geographical areas, and they may grant "permits" for certain limited uses allowed under the act. The regional units also have planning duties, but it is

the statewide board that makes the final decisions in this area.
Although the measure never went through the whole legislature the
two houses were in a stalemate over it—it was approved by the voters
in a special referendum. This is the derivation of "Proposition 20."

An effort was made in the California case to build affected interests
into the administrative mechanism, and perhaps something can be
learned from this. For example, the district commissions contain
representation of the local governments in the area, and the representation is direct (not appointive). One-half the seats are, by law, provided them, with the other half going to the "public" and named by the
legislature. The state body is composed of six members from the
regional commissions and an equal number from the public.

The most important interest group participating in the process
is "local governments," and they are in on the ground floor, enjoying
cumulative representation as a result. This is significant as we have
seen in the chapters on Hawaii and Vermont, because it is the local
government that seems most threatened by state land-use controls and
is most likely to block them. Apparently California headed off this
opposition by giving the localities the key voice in the administration,
and while this may make decisions more "parochial," it is good politics. Another factor in this regard is the fact that the matter was
taken out of the hands of the state legislature, where studies have
shown local governments to be strong.[6] The League of California
Cities is the chief lobbyist of local governments in this state, and it
is influential. One case has been taken to court so far, and that involved
a ruling of the San Diego Coast Regional Commission; the matter is
presently before the California Supreme Court (late 1973).

WETLANDS CONTROL

The final zoning category in the traditional class is wetlands
management, and as can be seen in Table 2, a total of 16 states have
legislation in this area. This represents no change in the first half
of 1974. States with this authority include Delaware, Georgia, Louisiana, Massachusetts, New Hampshire, and New Jersey, and New York
recently enacted legislation here, the Tidal Wetlands Act of 1973.
The New York third measure puts a moratorium on development in tidal
wetlands and requires a state permit for plans in these areas. It
extends to proposals to drain, dredge, fill, or develop any of the state's
wetlands, and permits are required from the state's new Department
of Environmental Conservation.[7] The New York law also authorizes
the preparation of land-use regulations and directs that an inventory
of the wetlands be undertaken.

Mississippi approved wetlands legislation for the first time in
1973, and its Coastal Wetlands Protection Law regulates dredging,

excavating, soil, sand, gravel, flora, and fauna removal in wetlands, dumping, actions that might damage the wetlands, and the erection of structures in them. However, there are significant exemptions, including oil and gas exploration, production, and transportation. This suggests that the legislation may have been tailored to meet the needs of certain interests, although it may also have been felt that these groups were sufficiently regulated by other agencies.

ZONING AROUND STATE PROPERTY
AND STATE SUBDIVISION CONTROL

Not included in Table 2 are two forms of specialized state controls that should be mentioned. States like Oklahoma, Kansas, and Maryland have authorized direct state zoning of land around certain state institutions, buildings, or other holdings, including the Capitol, state farms, and state-owned airports, and some states have also adopted direct subdivision regulations. Subdivision control, of course, is largely a local function, a key one under state planning enabling legislation, but some states have assigned this function to an agency of state government. State subdivision regulations deal mostly with health matters such as sewage, water supply, and water courses, and only to a limited extent if at all with layout. They may be administered by the state health department as in New York and probably most states, and they again are directed mostly at rural areas where local governments have no subdivision ordinance.

Oregon's ill-fated subdivision control legislation of 1973 may have been the strongest anywhere, and it was aimed mostly at the recreation industry. As an alternative to direct state control, some states have sought to strengthen their subdivision enabling legislation and to mandate it statewide. Oregon appears to be taking this route now that direct controls have been blocked. Colorado approved such a measure in 1972. Under the Colorado law, land sales are barred throughout the state unless minimum subdivision standards are met covering such factors as site plans, impact on streams and lakes, topographic maps, effects on vegetation, and geological conditions.

Before leaving the "traditional" zoning section, it might be well to make one more point; that is, it seems this kind of zoning is "working." At least there is little evidence to suggest it is not. There are exceptions of course, as Oregon's infamous subdivision law suggests, but by and large it appears that the states are quite well suited for this kind of regulation even though not all of them have engaged in it. They seem to be much better equipped to deal with this sort of thing than with the newer forms of specialized zoning including control of "critical areas" or "uses of more than local concern." We get into the reasons for this in detail later, but let us now turn to a more general discussion of the matter.

CRITICAL AREAS CONTROL

Controls over "critical areas" are found in a few states, and the number is not all that large In a way this is surprising since so much has been made of it, in Congress and in conferences, but the action in the states has not matched the hopes. According to Table 2, only seven states have approved such legislation. While there was a spurt a couple of years ago, critical areas legislation is running into trouble all over the country, and the figure may now be leveling off. The states with these powers are Colorado, Florida, Hawaii, Minnesota, New York, Oregon, and Wisconsin. The legislation generally covers a dozen or more possible areas or uses, namely, those with certain special characteristics (wetlands is an example) or with a regional or statewide impact.

It is not clear that all seven of these states truly have this power, and we know of no examples of its being exercised. Even Hawaii does not have it in the strictest sense, for it has only "general" zoning authority over most the state's lands, having delegated the specifics to local government; in urban districts, in fact, the state can be reversed, and this would include "critical areas." Besides, according to a recent report of the Senate Interior Committee, critical areas legislation is currently pending in the Hawaii assembly. The section on Oregon in Chapter 3 does not suggest the existence of this specific type of legislation there, and unless there has been a change in the last few months, the same goes for Colorado. As for Florida, although it has it, no areas have been designated to date.

Minnesota does have such a measure, having approved it in 1973; under it, the governor is handed the power to designate critical areas. The legislation defines a critical area as one affected by development of more than local impact, containing historic, natural, scientific, or cultural resources of regional or statewide importance, significantly affected by an existing or proposed major public facility, or possessing certain other characteristics.

New York apparently falls in this category because of its laws that set up regional commissions to plan and (possibly) regulate land uses in the Adirondacks and a few other key ares of the state (such as the Catskills, the Tug Hill Plateau and the Hudson River Valley). We have no information on Wisconsin. We now look at one state's attempt to put critical areas legislation on the books.

MARYLAND LAND-USE LEGISLATION, 1974

Background

Maryland legislators took up a new land-use bill early in 1974, one that had just emerged from a blue-ribbon committee appointed to study the matter. The legislation had to do with state control of critical areas. This followed on the heels of the defeat of another bill on the same subject during the 1973 session of the assembly. The earlier measure was unacceptable to most of the states' big local governments and to a host of others including developers, builders, and citizens' groups; under rather intense pressure from the powerful Maryland Association of Counties, lawmakers in Annapolis voted it down. This was so even though it had the general backing of the administration and seemed to be a personal favorite of the governor's. The feature that interest groups were most concerned about was the one giving the state direct land-use controls in certain instances, where statewide or regional impact could be shown. Yet even when that feature was removed (as it was later in the session), the bill failed to gain the legislators' approval.

Now what had happened to change the situation? Three things had taken place that many assumed would alter the course of events. First, the momentum across the nation to put the states into the land-use business had apparently picked up steam. One conference and seminar after another had been held in the intervening year, sponsored by such organizations as the Council of State Governments and the National Governors' Conference, and in them speakers had been systematically drumming up support for state land-use legislation. Invariably, the advocates pointed out how state land-use controls would improve the environment, save the wetlands, preserve the shorelines, clamp down on unplanned development, curtail pollution, and strike a blow at localism and parochialism. Although scant evidence was provided to back up these claims, this did not stop state land-use control proponents from pressing their case.

Second, Maryland named a state land-use advisory commission following the 1973 legislative session and appointed prominent local officials such as Montgomery County's William Sher, then the president of the Montgomery County Council. It was the county lobby, as noted, that so vigorously opposed the Maryland land-use legislation initially, and Sher and most of his colleagues in the counties naturally agreed with this position. The appointment of Sher and his selection as a top officer of the study panel had special significance, for Montgomery was not only the state's wealthiest county, but it was also one of the most populous and influential, and its voice would almost certainly be important in determining the outcome of the upcoming struggle over land use. Montgomery is on the outskirts of the District of Columbia, and it is the home of many high federal officials. Sher, who later in 1974 announced for Montgomery County executive, became one of the strongest advocates of a state land-use law. He convinced his own County Council and likely others of the law's merits.

Other county officials were named to the advisory unit—formally the the governor's Study Commission on Intergovernmental Relations in Land-Use Regulation—and these included the president of the Charles County Commissioners, the chairman of the Garrett County Board, the planning and zoning officer of Anne Arundel County (near Baltimore), and the general counsel of the Maryland-National Capital Park and Planning Commission, the bicounty agency serving the Maryland suburbs of Washington, D. C. Legislators from Baltimore, Prince Georges (also a Washington suburb), and Montgomery Counties, and the Eastern Shore were also picked, as were representatives of developers and the state chamber of commerce.

Clearly, the goal was to build all major affected interests into the proposal and to provide it an advance political base, especially in the counties. Still, there were some important omissions, and whether this was by design or refusal to serve we do not know; these included the county executives in Baltimore (surrounds Baltimore City but does not contain it), Anne Arundel, and Prince Georges Counties, or the chief officers of three of the four biggest suburban jurisdictions in the state, jurisdictions with about half the state's population and pro-bably more than half the voters. It was also the suburbs and not the farm bloc as the newspapers had it that were most threatened by state controls since they already had the controls (the rural areas had few of them); besides, the suburbs had the votes, and the farmers did not.

In addition, the administration in Annapolis, everyone believed, would almost certainly give as much backing to the land-use law in 1974 as they did the year before, and evey indication was that they were going to support it even more strongly this time in view of its greater political attractiveness. It is also worth noting that the governor used his powers of persuasion to change Lieutenant Governor Blair Lee's position on the matter. Lee, a former member of the Montgomery County Planning Board and for years a private land use consultant, probably had more technical expertise in urban planning than anyone else in the state capital, and had he stuck to his original position against state involvement, it would have clearly made the administration's job much harder. (Lee was a member of an influ-ential Maryland family and had a political base outside Annapolis.) Shortly before the administration's original bill was introduced into the state legislature, Lee wrote in a blistering letter to the Washington Post that the "prospect of having local zoning disputes settled by a

state bureaucrat in Baltimore is abhorrent to me. . . ."[8] He also rhe-
torically asked the Post, a backer of the legislation, "What is a 'critical area'?"

Third, Congress was closer than ever in early 1974 to approving
a national land-use policy measure, or so it appeared, and this meant
that the states were under pressure to move all the faster to "tool
up" for the grants the legislation was to supply. The federal policy,
as we have pointed out in earlier chapters, was designed to induce the
states to undertake comprehensive planning and "critical areas"
control programs and it had been pending for several years at the time.

What the Bill Would Do

The measure introduced in 1974, the one to come out of the
governor's "blue-ribbon" committee, was really quite simple. It
provided for direct state planning for the state as a whole and direct
state controls over areas of "critical state concern." The latter was,
of course, just another way of phrasing "critical areas," and they were
defined as areas in which "any substantial development will have a
state or regional economic or environmental impact." Examples
included shorelines and coastal areas, land around water reservoirs
and impoundments, historical sites, circumference areas around
major highway interchanges, areas of regional interest in which
development decisions will have a substantial impact on the plans,
natural resources or public facilities of another jurisdiction, and
areas where development would result in an irretrievable loss of
natural resources. These were named specifically in the proposed
legislation, but it was not to be limited to them.

While the state was not given direct control over critical areas
under normal conditions, it was to designate them and to have at least
an influence over their development, and it might, under certain circumstances, step in and regulate them directly. The bill also set up
a State Land-Use Board, and it was to draw up the controls.

Existing Controls on Land Use in the State

In Maryland, planning and zoning decisions are in the hands of
local and not state authorities; this, of course, follows the arrangement
elsewhere. More specifically, planning and zoning in the Free State
are the responsibility of counties and, to a lesser extent, cities. The
buld of the land area outside Baltimore and Washington, D. C., for
example, is subject to county development controls, and this is the
area under the most intense growth pressures and where land regulation can have the greatest impact.

In land use, Maryland differs from most other states in only one key respect, that is, its greater reliance on counties as the basic planning and zoning authority. Typically, other states give more land-use power to cities, townships, towns, or other political subdivisions "beneath" the county. In some cases, "regional" agencies have been granted direct or indirect powers over development; these would include the planning and water/sewer commissions in the Washington suburbs. These agencies still contain much "local" character, however, in that they do not cover the entire state or even a significant portion of it, and their boards are named exclusively by local governments and not the state.

It is a misconception—and this is important because it is so widely misunderstood—to say that present development in Maryland is a result of the absence of planning and land regulation. State planning partisans often talk as though the country has no planning and that our governments do no regulating. This is not true. The development we can see all around us has resulted from government controls on land, specifically in Maryland local or county controls. The major county governments in the state have had these powers for decades, and the same goes for the regional units just mentioned. There is little question where the responsibility for existing land use and development belong—if is local government.

If the state were to step into this area, it would not represent the first input of government authority or the "public interest" into the process, only a shift from one level of government to another. Neither would it represent the first example of "regional" planning since the bicounty agencies in the Washington suburbs have been doing this for some time and with mixed results. The same is true of Baltimore, where the "Regional Planning Council" has been planning for the multicounty city-suburban area for at least a decade. All these agencies were set up directly by state legislation.

Arguments for State Planning

The main argument for state planning is that local planning is not working. The idea is that the local nature of the current decision-making process involves parochial decisions, and that when only the interests of small areas are involved, land-use decisions do not reflect the needs of the broader universe. The contention is that since the wider public is not included in the process, its wishes are therefore excluded. Sometimes it is suggested that local governing bodies are no match for developers and that only the state can handle them. For some reason, most of the discussion in the Maryland legislature dealt with the problems in rural areas and with rural local governments, but the fact is that most of the literature deals with urban areas and the problems with urban governments.

For example, the National Commission on Urban Problems noted that a wide array of governments now exercise zoning powers in the typical metropolitan area, governments in most cases covering only a limited area and commonly representing only a small number of residents; the panel, whose report was issued in 1969, went on to point to the "abuses" of this "multiplicity" of units in terms of land-use controls, and its central conclusion was that zoning was "rigged" in the interests of the suburbs.[9] Particularly concerned with the plight of minority racial and income groups and their needs for suburban housing, the commission called for prompt state intervention. In his remarkable book, The Zoning Game, Richard Babcock similarly proposes relief from suburban zoning restrictions by aggressive state action, specifically through the establishment of state standards by which local decisions can be structured to benefit wider areas.[10] And in his work, Administering Federalism in Democracy, Professor Arthur Macmahon urges a "delocalization" of zoning and a shift of powers to the states, citing fragmentation and the use of zoning to block moderate-income housing as key reasons.[11]

No specific mention was made of housing needs or the use of the legislation to fulfill these needs, and to the contrary there was a definite "conservation" and "environmental" ring to the measure. No doubt the adminstration felt that stressing housing would make it too politically explosive, and the same would be true of pointing to the need to override suburban zoning. Yet all of this can be subsumed under the general argument, and apparently at least the suburbs thought so, for they worked against the bill.

Existing State Role in Land-Use Decisions

It might be noted that at present in Maryland, the state is not without some influence over local planning and land-use decisions. The general legislation governing zoning and land-use decision making is provided by the state, and local codes must be consistent with this. In some cases, in fact—such as the Maryland suburbs of Washington or the Baltimore metropolitan area—it is state legislation that has established the regional planning agency and that may more directly set the ground rules for county governing bodies. Still it is the localities that adopt the zoning ordinances and make the final zoning decisions. The ultimate responsibility is theirs.

The state also has a Planning Department, but its role is largely advisory, and at least until recently it has served principally as a conduit for the distribution of federal planning funds to smaller local governments. It also collects data and undertakes studies on the state capital improvements program, natural resources, and certain other matters.

There is, in addition, a state Planning Commission, which "advises and assists" the department, but neither it nor the department has any direct powers over local planning and zoning and rarely, if ever, has even any informal influence over local planning, zoning, and development decisions. One of the chief reasons for the limited assignment of land-use powers to Annapolis has been the lobbying of the "public interest groups" representing counties and cities, as they have effectively guarded such local prerogatives from state "interference." Moreover, zoning is, of course, subject to judicial review in the state courts.

Localism in Maryland Politics and Administration

Perhaps the most important point that can be made in this section has to do with the strong tradition of localism in the state. Next to one or two states in the Union such as Georgia, Maryland may be the most "local" of all. It stands up well against Vermont in this regard and probably has more organized local strength to protect local powers from the state than the Vermont towns. Almost certainly the Maryland Association of Counties is more powerful than the Vermont League of Cities and Towns, and these are the two most influential "local government" lobbies in their respective states.

The Maryland tradition is discussed by John Fenton in Politics of the Border States, and it is manifest in fiercely independent local voting patterns in the state.[12] But more to the point, state policy in Maryland is often little more than what powerful local and county groups want. This applies to both statewide and "local" legislation of the state. The defeat of the state land-use bill in 1973, reflecting the influence of the counties in general, suggests the first pattern, and the continual overrriding of the "state will" for any county by local legislative delegations suggests the second. This "overriding" is not atypical, but it is rarely apparent.

Much state legislation and other policy in Maryland are approved and carried out in a local frame, and this includes the administrative variety. More so than probably most states, Maryland still permits its legislative delegations from each county to determine pretty much what state policy it wants for that county or, if that fails (which is rare), in determining how the policy shall be implemented in the county (almost as important). The county delegations form separate commit-tees in the state legislature—that is, just like the Finance Committee (state Senate) or the Appropriations Committee (state House of Dele-gates). In fact, there are only a few subject-matter committees to speak of in the legislature, six in the House and three in the Senate. This means much of the power is in the hands of numerous "local" or geographical committees composed of the different county dele-gations. Each delegation in the two houses constitutes a formal standing committee, and bills are actually referred to it and reported out just like they are in other committees. So, for example, the five senators from Montgomery County form a committee in the upper chamber, and they consider and act on bills affecting the county. The same is true in the House, where delegates from a given county like Montgomery are organized into a committee for legislative purposes.

It is infrequent that one of these geographical committees is overriden by the chamber or legislative body as a whole, and the politics are such that is is really almost unthinkable. The procedure seems especially well designed to keep the state from acting in any substantive or geographical area, where any important local bloc such as a county governing body, county administration (the county executive in the suburbs), developers, or citizens' associations opposes this action. All that a local interest has to do is to convince a majority of either its county's House or Senate delegation to vote "no." In Montgomery, this means convincing as few as three people, or a majority of the Senate delegation.

The process extends to administrative decisions as well. It applies, for instance, to decisions of the State Highway Administration, a key executive agency that, while formally under the governor and secretary of transportation, has close and direct ties to county legislative delegations in both houses. The delegations have actual veto power over proposed new or improved roads going into the long-range highway plan (20 years) and have the informal negative over current highway programming (5 years). Formal requirement or not, it is scarcely conceivable that the roads agency would build a new highway or widen or otherwise substantially alter an existing one without the approval of the two legislative delegations from the county in question. Of course, many and perhaps most state roads projects originate within the county delegations in the first place, possibly put there by some key local interest. There is really no reason to assume that state land-use policy could operate outside this pattern, and there was much in the proposed legislation in 1974 in fact to put it quite firmly inside it. No doubt the difference between Maryland and most other states in this respect is that Maryland has made local rule a legal and formal matter, while elsewhere it works this way without this institutional blessing.

Another indication of this process is the extent to which geographical representation is associated with service on state administrative boards. Commonly connected to state executive agencies such as the Department of Planning and contrary to good administrative theory, these multimembered bodies have often been assigned substantial policy-making and appointment powers. The Maryland State Roads Commission, for example, until recently a key policy force and still with some substantive authority, has geographical requirements for its members. The Eastern Shore (Atlantic Ocean), Montgomery County, Prince Georges County, and Baltimore City (separate from the county), for instance, are all provided one seat each on this body.

Similarly, the Maryland Transportation Commission, part of the state Department of Transportation, contains direct regional or local representation, and Maryland law has even gone so far as to provide specific interest group representation on executive boards heading administrative agencies. The nature of the groups so named (farm organizations such as the state Grange and Farm Bureau) almost assures a voice for certain localities or local interests and not others. Most certainly, it guarantees the interest groups a direct voice in running the agencies. The pattern is not all that uncommon in the states, and it represents a form of syndicalism that is used in some countries abroad including Austria.

In the Maryland legislature, interest groups routinely ask for positions on state administrative commissions, not merely the advisory ones but those that make policy for the state agencies especially when the legislature is not in session, and they often get them. Both the Farm Bureau and the Maryland Municipal League asked to be named to the land-use board proposed under the 1974 legislation. Localism is thus built into the administrative fabric from the start, and local government or local interest group influence then picks up in the executive where it left off in the legislature.

It is fairly clear that the state can act only with considerable local support and that the administration and legislature in Annapolis do not roam the state systematically overruling local power structures and community governments. In fact, it is doubtful if they would try, or could succeed, given the politics of the situation. Edward Banfield's Political Influence, a study of local politics, would suggest that the state might be able to do this once or twice, but not consistently or over a long period of time.[13] The power simply is not there.

A strong possibility exists, given these circumstances, that a mere shift of land-use powers from one level to another, from the local to the state, will result in no change in the pressures brought to bear on the decisions and therefore no change in the substance of the decisions. A formal change then may not cause an informal one. If so, a transfer of power to the state may not alter development patterns, and this alteration has to be a goal of state involvement. This is true whether we are talking about urban (suburban) or rural areas, and it suggests some very real limits to state planning. The limits are not ideological or philosophical but practical and concrete. This makes them all the more important.

Protection of Local Interests
in the Proposed Legislation

The land-use bill's sponsors were obviously sensitive to the defeat of a similar measure in the 1973 session because they carefully worked local interests into the 1974 bill. For instance, the proposed state

land-use board was to consist of members appointed from specific
counties or county combinations. All the big suburban counties, where
presumably independent state influence is needed most, were guaran-
teed direct representation on the board, and this included Baltimore,
Anne Arundel, Montgomery, and Prince Georges. (This did not,
however, mean the county "government" per se, and this differed from
the California situation discussed above.) It will be recalled that the
experts cited felt that it was the suburbs that had most abused local
zoning powers, and certainly the suburbs are where the greatest
amount of open land under real development pressure exists. State
development controls could theoretically have their greatest positive
impact in areas like these, but representation arrangements called
for in the bill were almost certain to inhibit this. There was surprisingly little talk of this point, but as we shall see shortly, the suburbs
were thinking about it.

The land-use board, incidentally, was not merely to be an advisory
unit as good public administration would require, but was given the key
function of designating areas of "critical state concern." Even more
important, it was assigned the task of adopting direct development
controls for these areas (to be administered locally). Thus local
representation on the board would have real policy and political
implications.

Local interests were protected in yet other ways. The bill, for
instance, required the state to build into the statewide plan all local
plans that were consistent and compatible with state policies, including general, area, and functional plans of local agencies. The chances
are that this might well result in a state plan that was simply a com-
posite of local ones, and this is the way it is working in other states
such as Tennessee. In fact, this would seem to be the smart way for
the state to do it. Although it might not be "right," it would likely be
the most "political" way to proceed. The legislation put a premium
on this route.

In addition, the most significant part of the bill—relating to the
development of guidelines, criteria, and regulations for critical
areas—gave the local governments the administrative responsibilities
under any circumstances, and perhaps even the policy-making authority
(with state standards). Often in planning, zoning, and subdivision control, it is the administrative determinations that count. This is so
because legislative language is usually sufficiently broad that several
interpretations are possible. The interpretation selected may and
typically does have substantive implications, and it may affect such
basic matters as permitted densities, intensity of commercial development, layout patterns, specific setback and parking requirements,
and building height limitations. These are crucial factors, a point
that is no less true when the decisions are made administratively;
they have great effects on both developers' margins and the environment. If local governments end up administering state land-use
policy, the chances are they will also "make" it.

Effect of the Bill on Interest Groups and Development

The discussion so far suggests that a formal change in land-use decision-making assignments may produce little change in actual influences on decision makers—that is, while the level and particular personalities will change, the pressures will still be largely local. The language of the legislation seemed ideally designed to promote this pattern. For changes in development patterns to occur—which everyone assumed the state legislation would encourage—there would almost certainly have to be changes in interest group influence. The present decisions are made locally, and they result from a certain pattern of local interest group influence. Let us take a look at this decision-making process, in the context of interest groups, and see how these groups would be affected under the state legislation. Then we can assess the probable consequences for public policy, that is, more development, less development, more flexible land-use controls, less flexible ones, more high-density development, or less density, and so on.

As Robert Dahl's classic study of New Haven suggests, the local community rarely represents a monolith, dominated by a single interest possessing wide-ranging influence in all aspects of politics.[14] Maryland localities are no exception to the rule. Dahl's work also suggests that the participants in local politics vary by the policy area; so let us concentrate on the groups in land use (they would not be the same in education, for example).

In this policy area, communities in Maryland are typically split into two definite factions: developers, or real estate and landowning interests; and citizens' groups, or neighborhood associations composed of single-family home owners.[15] Both are usually organized into interest groups, the developers into "builders associations" and the latter into the likes of "Fox Hills" civic or citizens' association. Both are poised to advance their goals in local politics; both support candidates; both fund campaigns of local legislators; and both commonly seek a voice in land-use decision making, especially zoning. Developers used to have virtual sole control of local zoning and planning, but this has changed of late, and they now share the power with citizens' groups in some communities in the state, and in the affluent Montgomery County, the citizens are in the driver's seat, and developers are a distinct minority interest.

The two groups view planning and zoning differently, and they have different conceptions of the public interest. It would be a mistake, for analytical purposes, to characterize one as "bad" or "evil" and the other "good." This tells you nothing about basic patterns of influence and power. Developers want planning and zoning policies that promote or that at least do not inhibit growth and development, and they back plans and regulations that encourage higher densities and flexibility in the administration of zoning and subdivision controls. As an example, they support "cluster" zoning and "planned unit" development over conventional Euclidean regulations stipulating lot-size minimums and standard setbacks regardless of the particulars.

Citizens' groups, on the other hand, are status quo minded, and they want land-use policies and zoning decisions that reflect that goal. Specifically, they back rulings that limit or bar new commercial and industrial development and that restrict residential uses to single-family dwellings. Generally, the larger the minimum lot size the better, and in fact some citizens' groups would be happier with no new development at all. Many of them do not support cluster zoning and planned unit development. This is especially true if low- or moderate-income housing is part of the deal (as it often is). It is also generally correct that developers favor significant government outlays for development-inducing public works such as highways and water systems and that the citizens' groups are more inclined to favor the use of these facilities (especially sewers) as "tools" of planning and community growth policy. It is incorrect to portray developers as "antigovernment" or "antiplanning," and citizens necessarily pro these things; it is just that these images have little to do with the practical, eveyday aspects of land-use politics, and some of them, while serving political ends, are downright wrong.

How would the proposed land-use legislation affect the relative power of these groups? Without an answer to this question, we cannot know how the legislation would affect development patterns since these patterns are set largely by them. While again no one can know the answer for certain, it would appear to be the advantage of the "minority" interest to back the bill, and this will vary by the community depending on whether developers or citizens' groups are dominant. This is so because a shift of power to the state would at least give it, the minority interest, a chance to do better. Of course, it is even possible that the minority interest could lose influence with the shift, but this does not weaken the argument that it has a chance to improve its position. Our feeling is that minorities are typically so weak that they in practice would have little to lose.

So, for example, in suburban Washington's Montgomery County where citizens' groups have a clear majority on the planning and zoning bodies, it would presumably be in the developers' interest to press for the bill. By the same token, in some of the Baltimore suburbs such as Anne Arundel and most of Baltimore counties and in certain areas of Prince Georges County (a moderate-income Washington suburb) where citizens are not well organized and have only limited political influence locally, it would be in the citizens' interests to back the state law and hope they would have more leverage in Annapolis. In either case (developer or citizen), what is there to lose?

Let us digress for a minute. It is a fundamental principle of political science that government decisions are not made in a vacuum. They are made by men and women operating under the "laws" of practical politics. It cannot be otherwise, as the classics of the discipline from Aristotle onward suggest. There is no feasible way of making a political decision "nonpolitical," and land-use decisions are decidedly political, involving subjective values and a variety of different opinions, none of which is entirely scientific or factual. This does not mean that "rational" judgment or "knowledge" (Plato) plays no role in decisions, only that there are commonly two sets of "rational" judgments and "knowledge," one advanced by the developers and the other by the citizens. Which one is "right" cannot be known, and which set is accepted by public officials (and stamped "policy") depends, to a great extent, on the influence of the group backing it. It may depend entirely on this, although we know that even the thought offends most people, developers and citizens alike. What then would be the effect of this bill on the positions of citizens and developers? Whose "facts" will most likely prevail in Annapolis? These are the key questions, and without their answer, little can be known as to the effect of state critical areas legislation.[16]

Overall it is a distinct possiblity that developers would realize the net short-term political benefits, and this might even be true where they are presently in the "majority" position locally (they could do even better with the state). Developers, after all, have more economic resources than citizens do, and shifting the decision out of the community and to Annapolis (or Baltimore as Lee says) is apt to provide a short-run advantage to those groups that can best afford to hire experts to travel great distances to present their cases. This may turn into a long-term gain as well. Even where they are powerful, citizens' groups not only do not usually have much money, but they do not rely on attorneys and professional planners as much as developers do. Instead, they put a greater stress on "numbers" and try to turn out in mass for public hearings and meetings of zoning and planning boards. Can citizens' groups produce as many people in Annapolis or Baltimore as the county seat? By giving the state the power, a much greater premium is put on money as a policy influence, and much less on votes.

It is true that under the bill that was proposed, hearings were to be held by the state in the localities, but it is equally true that important decisions would be made in state agencies in Annapolis or Baltimore. Interests that are not present when the decisions are actually made will almost certainly have less influence than those who are. This is the psychology of the matter, and it has important political ramifications. In a recent example, citizens' groups in one area of Montgomery County were able to get only a handful of their members to drive to Annapolis to oppose a state road project, while they turned out nearly a thousand residents when a meeting on the matter was held in the community.

It is most likely that the important battles would be fought over the land-use provisions of the bill and not "planning," and if it passed as it was introduced, the contest would then extend to the administration. The crux of the matter is that these controls can be used either to encourage and plan ahead for new development, or to inhibit or stop it (in critical areas, since the bill limited regulation to these). In all probability, citizens' groups would press for the designation of areas as "critical" that are under strong development pressure and work for the limitation or exclusion of many or all new land uses in these areas. By the same token, developers would presumably seek to have areas designated that are presently restricted from intense commercial or high-density residential development or under a development moratorium, and highway interchanges come to mind in this respect. The present restrictions might be local zoning that calls for single-family use, possibly the large-lot variety, and developers might ask for state intervention to up-zone the interchange to higher-density residential or commercial uses. Our reading of the bill would make this strategy, or the reverse of it by citizens' groups, entirely possible.

This bill was not an invitation to stop development as it was portrayed in many quarters (this was the typical popular interpretation). In fact, it was quite possible to interpret it in exactly the opposite way, as developers of course had a tendency to do. And they were right. The bill was "neutral" as much legislation is, and its provisions could be "used" by either developers or citizens' groups to promote their separate ends. Much depends on the administration and the person or body doing the interpreting. Even if the bill was written in antidevelopment terms, if developers gained control of it in the administrative stage, it could be turned around. Land-use legislation is administered to accord with political realities in Maryland, and it is doubtful if it is any different elsewhere. But the fact was that the measure was neither anti- or pro-development.

Several studies have shown that the states are generally quite sensitive to the "business" (developer) point of view, perhaps more so than local governments, a pattern detected by such researchers as V. O. Key, Harmon Zeigler, Wayne Francis, and others; the studies were done both before and after reapportionment of state legislatures, and the one-man, one-vote decision appears to have had little effect on business influence in this context.[17] Maryland again is no exception and seems to reinforce the general pattern. The administration in Annapolis, for example, is by no means as "liberal" or "pro-citizen" as the County Council in Montgomery or the county executive in Prince Georges.

In our opinion, unless the political pressures are strongly to the contrary, administration officials in the state government are more likely to make decisions consistent with development than its limitation. The recent decision of the governor to locate a new advanced wastewater treatment plant (AWT) in Dickerson, Maryland, is a good example of this. This site was bitterly fought by citizens' groups in the area and their most vocal representatives in the Montgomery County government, on the grounds that it would open up the western part of the county to premature development. The state stepped in and overruled the citizens after the County Council deadlocked on the issue; this was something the county could not or would not do. If this reasoning holds, the bill could permit more flexibility in land-use regulations, more advance planning and funds for new public facilities, and more planning (for change) generally.

The Decision

Maryland approved a state land-use bill in 1974, the first ever, but it was much less than the blue-ribbon committee and the administration had asked for. The state was not given the right to designate and control critical areas, and no land-use board was established. A preexisting agency, the Planning Department, was given the authority to intervene in local planning and zoning decisions where the state or regional interests were affected (that is, "critical areas"), but it was provided no vote or control in these decisions. They remained in the hands of local government. This constituted a substantial watering-down of the proposed version, and it amounted to very little indeed.

WHAT CAN BE LEARNED
FROM THE MARYLAND EXPERIENCE?

Here the Maryland government sought to move on the land-use issue but could not. Everything was tried, or so it seemed, including catering to the pertinent interest groups. But it did not work. The governor set up a panel of respected citizens and officials to propose the legislation, and the bill attempted to build local government interests into the program and to protect local interests in a variety of ways. The bill could not get through the legislature.

Why? If we had to pinpoint one reason, it would be the influence of the local governments, specifically the counties and more specifically the Maryland Association of Counties. It will be recalled that some key local officials from the suburbs of Washington and Baltimore were not included on the committee that proposed the legislation. The establishment of this committee was obviously tactical on the part of the state administration, and it was set up to provide support for the legislation. The panel did not, in reality, draw up the

legislation as was said; it was given to them, by administrators.
Some important suburban figures declined to participate or were not
given the chance, and in the final analysis none of the four big suburban
counties backed the measure, that is, in terms of their major officials
being united in favor of it. The only bloc of support from the suburban
officials came from Montgomery County, and there the County Council,
but the Montgomery executive did not support it and told the legislators
so. The executive of Baltimore County, the largest jurisdiction in the
state outside Baltimore City, also worked against it, and Prince
Georges' officials were noticeably cool toward it.

Much was made of the "farm bloc" and that it defeated the bill,
but this could not have been true since they controlled no more than
a quarter of the votes in either house. This makes a nice scapegoat,
but it misses the point. It was the organized counties, in other words
the "local government" lobby. The Maryland Municipal League
seemed ambivalent on the measure (the cities fear both the counties
and the state), but their influence was minimal in any event. The
county group was far more important.

In California, Proposition 20 included the local governments in
the administration of the land-use program there, and it was approved.
What is the difference? First, the California legislation was approved
by the voters and not by the legislature. The California legislature,
in fact, never did act on the measure and apparently could not for
some reason, and maybe local governments had something to do with
it. The League of California Cities is no pushover, and it is a respected
force in the state. If the local governments had reservations about the
California coastal zone law, it is most likely thay could have had it
held up in the state legislature. Second, in practice Proposition 20
cut into local powers it is true, but it also provided for direct local
government representation on the regional commissions set up to
administer the program. One-half of the membership of these decision-making bodies was to come directly from the local governments
in the area, selected by specific local governments or associations
of them. This was not the case in Maryland, and although the counties
as geographical areas were provided representation, the county
"governments" were given none. The Maryland counties saw through
this and would have no part of it. They also had a chance to do something about it since the measure had to be approved by the state legislature (where they were strong). Appointments to the Maryland land-
use board were to be made by the governor, and although the
legislation directed him to "take into account" the interests of "local
governments" in making the appointments, it required no direct representation.

There is another important difference between the California
and Maryland measures, and this is a difference in approach. The
California law is very specific; it covers a specific area (1,000 yards
inland) and no more. Thus it is not as threatening to local government,

which currently exercises the control. "Critical areas" legislation
is something else. No one knows what it covers, not even the lieutenant governor. Why should the local governments gamble and possibly
lose many, most, or even all their planning and zoning powers? This
is the way they think, and we might as well face up to it. The state
administration said local governments had nothing to fear (it was not
"zoning," local governments were told), but they did not buy the
argument. One reason was that local officials had read the bill, and
they knew what the state said was not true; they had much to fear, and
the bill did involve zoning (although not labeled as such).

Actually, the bill was amended late in the session to provide a
5 percent area limitation, but this had little meaning once the substance
of the "critical areas" portion was eliminated (the limitation applied
both statewide and to any given county). But even that amendment was
not enough to satisfy the counties. They were given the chance to
stop the legislation, and they did.

It seems that one way of relieving local governments of some of
their fears is to couch specialized state zoning in more definitive
terms and to restrict it to particular and concrete categories of use
such as power plants and surface mining, or areas like flood plains,
wetlands, and coastal zones. These, of course, fall in the more
"traditional" class of specialized state land-use controls. In many
respects, these are just the kinds of things envisioned under the "critical areas" approach, and the only difference is that the first class
specifies the limitations and particular targets in clear terms, while
the "critical areas" approach does not. It is true that the state "gets
more" via the critical areas route, but it may also end up getting
nothing at all by that route, too. In fact, the latter seems more likely,
given the nature of politics in most states. Hawaii and Vermont are
exceptions, and neither has long traditions of local control or powerful local government interest groups. Hawaii, in fact, has a tradition
of central control, and Vermont has a history of no control. Neither
has powerful lobbies representing local government in the state legislature. In Hawaii, the state appears to have no real enemies; Vermont
seems to have conservatives as the main opponents (no control tradition); but Maryland has local governments (tradition of local control). We suggest that Maryland is the more typical.

It is almost certainly true that the least opposition is generated
by two tacks: traditional specialized controls directly under the state
and local controls with state standards. These are probably the best
routes for the states to follow, and they are the most politically
feasible. They may be the only ones that have any widespread chance
of success. The state has an important role in each and no doubt
should be more involved in both areas than it is at present. It can
take on specific land-use powers, one at a time as conditions require
and political realities permit. This is being done by many states,
and in fact up to the time it sought critical areas legislation, Maryland

had more or less followed this approach (the state had previously enacted wetlands, power plant siting, and surface mining controls). Instead of including coastal zones as one of a dozen or more "critical areas" and losing it along with everything else, would it not make more sense to push for a specific coastal zone program? Everyone understands this, and the local governments know precisely how they will be affected. Neighboring Virginia and Delaware have such programs and zone their coastal areas. Would Maryland not be well advised to do the same? The other route is too risky.

The second tack has to do with local controls. It is generally agreed that local government has not handled planning and zoning in an ideal manner, and even most local officials will probably agree with this. The state has a role here. In a way, the legislation that was approved in Maryland was a step in the right direction, for it authorized state intervention in local development decisions where "broader" interests were involved. This is just where the state has the advantage. It represents more people and a wider land area than local governments, and thus its perspectives should be different. It seems to make more sense if the state were to try to inject this "wider" vision into the local decision-making process than to "take it over." Besides, the local governments have the power, which they are not going to give up without a fight. But local governments are seriously deficient in many respects, and much of this gets back to their limited jurisdiction.

State power should be used to widen the inputs in the local planning and zoning decision-making arena and to broaden the political base of these decisions. Much of this can be accomplished through a revision of enabling legislation, particularly that in the zoning area.[18] As was pointed out in Chapter 2, much of this legislation was written in the 1920s and 1930s when conditions were different, and change is very much in order now.

We are tempted to conclude that while specialized forms of state zoning are quite likely to be workable, the "critical areas" kind is not. Ideally, we cannot oppose it, and it has much merit, but in practice it has a number of weaknesses. We think it would be a mistake to base national policy on the prospects of this sort of state action. The country's politics and administration are highly specialized and localized, and any national policy that does not recognize this cannot succeed. As good as the arguments for central control and higher-level government decision making, they do not seem to accord with the realities of the situation. Of course, if this "central" and "higher-level" power is kept limited, it will work. Washington officials should take note and provide more specialized assistance to the states for such purposes as wetlands control, power plant siting, subdivision regulation, and flood plain management. The pattern set by the coastal zone legislation in 1972 is a good one and represents a move in the right direction. Critical areas do not.

NOTES

1. At the national level, see Nader's Raiders, Report on the Federal Trade Commission (New York: Grove Press, 1969); and their The Interstate Commerce Omission (New York: Grossman, 1970).

2. Thad L. Beyle, Sureva Seligson, and Deil S. Wright, "New Directions in State Planning," in Thad L. Beyle and George T. Lathrop (eds.), Planning and Politics (New York: Odyssey Press, 1970), p. 15.

3. William H. Whyte, The Last Landscape (Garden City, N. Y.: Doubleday, 1968), p. 47.

4. David C. Ranney, Planning and Politics in the Metropolis (Columbus: Charles E. Merrill, 1969), Chap. 4. See also Scott Greer, Urban Renewal and American Cities (Indianapolis: Bobbs-Merrill Co., 1965).

5. Proceedings of the Conference on Organizing and Managing the Coastal Zone, June 13-14, 1973 (Washington, D. C.: Council of State Governments, 1973).

6. See Brett W. Hawkins, "Consequences of Reapportionment in Georgia," in Richard I. Hofferbert and Ira Sharkansky (eds.), State and Urban Politics (Boston: Little, Brown, 1971), pp. 273-298.

7. Elizabeth H. Haskell and others, Managing the Environment: Nine States Look for New Answers (Washington, D. C.: Smithsonian Institution, 1971), Chap. 6.

8. The Washington Post, December 6, 1972, p. A17.

9. National Commission on Urban Problems, Building the American City (Washington, D. C.: Government Printing Office, 1968).

10. Richard F. Babcock, The Zoning Game (Madison: University of Wisconsin Press, 1968).

11. Arthur W. Macmahon, Administering Federalism in a Democracy (New York: Oxford University Press, 1972), Chap. 5.

12. John H. Fenton, Politics in the Border States (New Orleans: Hauser Press, 1957), Chap. 8.

13. Edward C. Banfield, Political Influence (New York: Free Press, 1961).

14. See Robert A. Dahl, Who Governs? Democracy and Power in an American City (New Haven: Yale University Press, 1961). Cf. Floyd Hunter, Community Power Structure: A Study of Decision Makers (Garden City, N. Y.: Doubleday, 1953).

15. The citizens' groups are called "neighborhood improvement associations" in a recent standard text. See Thomas R. Dye, Politics in States and Communities, 2nd ed. (Englewood Cliffs, N. J.: Prentice-Hall, 1973), p. 307.

16. For a discussion of the issues in this paragraph, see Francine F. Rabinovitz, City Politics and Planning (New York: Atherton, 1969), Chap. 6.

17. See V. O. Key, Jr., American State Politics (New York: Knopf, 1956); Harmon Zeigler and Michael Baer, Lobbying: Interaction and Influence in American State Legislatures (Belmont, Calif.: Wadsworth Publishing, 1969); and Wayne L. Francis, Legislative Issues of the Fifty States: A Comparative Analysis (Chicago: Rand McNally, 1967). See also Thomas R. Dye, "State Legislative Politics," in Herbert Jacob and Kenneth N. Vines (eds.), Politics in the American States, 2nd ed. (Boston: Little, Brown, 1971), pp. 163-209.

18. Some ideas are provided in Norman Marcus and Marilyn W. Groves (eds.), The New Zoning (New York: Praeger Publishers, 1970).

6

**THE STATE AND
REGIONAL PLANNING**

SUBSTATE AND INTERSTATE PLANNING

The kind of planning treated in this chapter covers a portion of
the state broader than a single local jurisdiction but not the state as
a whole. If it covered the entire state, it would be "state planning"
pure and simple, and it would be done directly by the state and one
of its executive agencies. Of course, state planning has already been
treated in the context of statewide zoning, specifically in the chapters
on Hawaii and Vermont. Vermont has probably done the most state
planning in the country, even more than Hawaii, and may be the only
state to be on the verge of adopting a statewide land-use plan that is
independent of zoning.

This kind of planning (broader than a locality, not extending to
the state as a whole) includes metropolitan planning, or planning done
for a particular metropolitan area; substate districting, a practice
whereby the state divides its entire territory into areas again broader
than a single locality but smaller than the state, establishes planning
commissions for the areas and assigns them different comprehensive
planning and development review functions; "regional" planning or
planning that is done for a specific region in the state and not others,
normally including urban and rural populations; and rural planning,
or planning that is done for nonmetropolitan regions, again broader
than a single county or other rural jurisdiction but not extending to
the state's entire rural area. Also included is planning that takes
place in the context of an area broader than any single state, up to
two, three, or more states, although not necessarily covering any
state's entire land or population. This is called interstate or multistate planning, and it is a form of regional planning (considered in
the broader sense). Regional planning is used in two ways in this

chapter: to refer to all forms of planning treated and to refer to a specific type of planning in this category (a specific region in the state).

The state plays a key role in all these kinds of planning, through the direct creation of the agencies that do this sort of planning, through authorizing their creation by state enabling legislation, and through their direct formation by interstate compact. The state in some cases has become an important partner in these planning efforts, beyond the creation and authorization, and may supply representatives for the boards that run the regional planning agencies and may provide funds and other forms of assistance.

In some instances, the agencies have been established through the initiative of the state, while in others the state has reacted to influence from the outside and perhaps then only grudgingly authorized regional planning and granted it little or no aid. In fact, the latter has been the traditional posture of the state, but there is now much evidence suggesting that this is changing and that the states are moving along toward a positive regional planning stance. For example, as we saw in Chapter 2 (Table 3), over half the states are making "moderate" progress in stimulating, supporting, and coordinating regional planning, or planning involving substate district, metropolitan, rural, and interstate agencies.

Generally, the state has not been the dominant influence in regional planning bodies and has been satisfied to give the formal voice to local governments and others outside the capital. This approach has its advantages, and perhaps most important it can be "sold" more easily than could too much state interference. The idea is that while the state is permitting or mandating regional planning, it is handing the control over to the localities, and this should make it more palatable. Otherwise, it is possible that the state could not pass the legislation in the first place and that localities would stop it in the state legislature (see Chapter 5, and the case of Maryland).

CREATION OF REGIONAL PLANNING AGENCIES

Of course regional planning is not done in a vacuum, and it must be performed by some body or organization. The state has authorized or directed that regional planning commissions be set up for this purpose, and this is done, as the words suggest, in a variety of ways. There are three basic ones: direct establishment of the agency by state law, authorization of the agency under state enabling legislation, and direct creation of the agency by interstate compact. More generally, it boils down to "direct" and "indirect" creation, although there are two kinds of "direct," one done unilaterally by the state and the other done in cooperation with other states. The indirect route requires additional action on the part of local governments, not another state.

It would be a mistake to think that the states have done all this on their own, for they have not, and much of it has been encouraged by Washington. It is easy to become romantic about these things. The federal government provides assistance for most, if not all, forms of regional planning, and the federal stimulus has often been more direct and immediate than this suggests. For instance, Washington agencies supply the states with "model" legislation authorizing this or that kind of regional planning, and the states have generally cooperated. Sometimes, Washington works through state public interest groups in this respect, such as the Council of State Governments or the National Legislative Conference. The federal system may not be unitary as the textbooks say, but in practice there are many elements of unitarism influencing the system. The Department of Housing and Urban Development (HUD) has been particularly active in this sense, and its interests are by no means limited to urban areas in the states as its name suggests, but extend to rural or "nonmetropolitan" regions as it likes to call them.

There have been few comprehensive studies of regional planning, and what exists is a collection of largely unrelated documents and materials covering only a portion of the topic or the country. And then the works might not be too up-to-date. HUD used to do national surveys of metropolitan planning, a form of regional planning, but these have been discontinued. The Graduate School of the State University of New York at Albany has also done this sort of thing, but it is not as comprehensive as the HUD surveys were, and their work is not as widely accessible. The American Institute of Planners and the Council of State Planning Agencies have also done some work along these lines, but again the scope is limited, and it is quickly dated.

One HUD survey examined the means of creating regional planning agencies, and although the study was limited to "metropolitan planning" bodies, there is no reason to assume it would be any different if the category were broader. Specifically, the survey showed the following:[1]

Regional Agency Established By:

State enabling act	99
Special act of state legislature	17
Interstate compact	1
Joint exercise of power statute	5
Other	9

Clearly, most agencies are created under state enabling legislation, which means that local governments wishing to participate in "regional" or "metropolitan" planning act jointly to cooperate in this sort of endeavor. Generally, the local governments approve a resolution, which is likely to be a local ordinance, that authorizes

the involvement of a particular government in the regional planning
agency, perhaps providing for a means of naming a local member or
members to the board of the regional unit as well. Two or more local
governments may participate, and the number may be as high as a
dozen or more. Only in a minority of cases are regional agencies
formed directly by the state legislature–"special act"–although these
agencies may be more powerful and overshadow the others in impact.
This is suggested by the information to come.

"Joint exercise of power statute" refers to the special process
used in California, whereby councils of governments and other regional
organizations are established, and it is basically the same as "enabling legislation" in other states. Thus, the "five" in this category
can be added to the first one, making the dominant pattern even more
striking. Only one agency in the study was created by interstate
compact, and no information is provided on the "other" category,
and we do not know what it means.

The specific means by which the regional agency is established
includes the following:[2]

Local resolution or ordinance	93
Public vote	3
Mandatory state action	13
Other	16

This adds little to the first table, and why "special act of state legislature," (above), and "mandatory state action" are not the same we
cannot tell; but apparently four states provide direct legislation
making action permissive, or perhaps making it subject to a public
vote or some other comparable prerequisite. But the principal point
is that the regional agencies are, in the technical stage, established
by vote of the local governing body (city, county, township) in the
vast majority of the cases. No distinction is made in this survey
between "resolution" and "ordinance," and it probably is not necessary, although the latter is "law" and presumably more binding.
Then again, some localities use the term "resolution" in another
way, and it may also be an "ordinance" and carry the force of law.
Thus, this is confusing, and we can shed no further light on it.

The dry technical questions are raised for a purpose, and that
is to see if there are any correlations. We are interested in strong
planning and workable land-use controls, and if we can cite any legal
foundations or formation patterns that are associated with strong
planning or workable land-use controls, it is our hope and intention
to point them out. Our feeling is that all avenues must be explored,
and our suspicion is that good planning comes less from good motives
than from technical considerations like the appropriate legislative

action and the proper legal base. In any event, we shall stress whatever factors seem to promote these ends. We know that not everyone agrees with this reasoning, and if we are proved wrong, we will be happy to admit it.

The point is that the legislation and the particular means of doing things often have substantive implications, and for example a specific legal strategy may put more of a certain kind of person in command of regional planning agencies, say, "environmentalists" or "conservationists," and another may give the power to, say, developers. Whoever has the power will exercise it in a way reflecting their life styles, values, backgrounds, and interests, and the rest of us will live with it. Regional planning agencies are important in this respect, and we believe we have uncovered some links along these lines and shall report them in this chapter. As unpleasant as this sort of thing is to some people, we should not overlook it, and we think most people will agree with this.

Board members of regional agencies are named in the following manner:[3]

Members Selected By:

City or county governing body or mayor	98
Local planning commission	3
State	3
Other	34

The pattern again is clear, and nearly all members of these bodies are appointed by local-government-elected officials. This is true in 98 of the units surveyed, and local planning commissions and the state (governor, legislature) name members in a distinct minority of the cases, three each. Another finding was that commission members are usually a combination of elected and appointed officials in local government and lay citizens. However, about 40 percent of the agencies examined limit commissioners to "citizens" (only five restrict membership to "elected" and nine to "appointed" local officials).

The structure of representation can have its political and policy implications and, as we shall show shortly, it appears that elected officials have become increasingly sensitive to the "citizens' group" point of view and that planning boards (local) have retained developer loyalties. Thus, stressing elected membership on the regional agencies could have its effect on policies and might mean more restrictive growth and the use of key public facilities like sewers for "planning" and not promotional purposes. We return to these matters in detail later, but the point here is that they may have real substantive meaning.

Incidentally, regional planning agencies generally have a board and staff, with the board membership ranging from 3 to 20 or more, and with an average size of 12.^{4} The board is responsible for general policy matters and supervises the staff, which prepares the reports and does the studies. At the same time, because of the limited time most board members have to spend on regional matters, the staff in these agencies may be quite important, more so than in a comparable city or county situation, and may be the key policy force as well. This pattern has definitely been uncovered in the field work undertaken in connection with this study (it was true in Tennessee and Michigan, for example, where all portions of the state have ''regional planning commissions'').

The ''citizen'' and ''local planning commission'' membership on regional agencies is almost without question dominated by the real estate industry, a pattern that Robert Walker found at the city level somewhat earlier.^{5} Architects were represented on 69 of the agencies' boards (109 agencies were surveyed), engineers on a similar number, realtors on 72, home-builders on 31, general business interests (chamber of commerce, retail) on 94, and attorneys on 40. Farm interests were also represented on 38 of the boards, and they have to be counted among the real estate community. Other represented included housewives, retired persons, and teachers. Again, there may be a difference as to whether the state provides for ''elected official'' or ''citizen'' dominance of the boards, and these are not minor legal questions or technicalities, and they cannot be discounted.

Elected officials are subject to a variety of influences and pressures, money being only one of these, and more and more they are influenced by citizens' groups. As this suggests, ''citizen'' representation does not necessarily mean what it says or implies, and it may spell representation for particular interests and not others. It definitely is not the equivalent of ''citizens' groups.'' It is necessary to penetrate into these matters to find out what they mean in reality and what effect they have for planning. It should not be concluded, however, that if developers, builders, realtors, and their allies dominate or influence a planning agency, that agency will do no planning. This is wrong, and this is not the reason these groups normally seek representation. They seek it because planning is important to them and because they are part of a community that sees planning as needed. Planning represents the power and money of government, and builders like the rest of us are dependent on these things. They want a voice because they are concerned with the public interest, and also because they want these powers and moneys to be used in a way that promotes their goals and their conception of the public interest. Developers need public facilities like sewers and water systems to provide homes for people at the lowest possible costs. They need streets and highways to bring people to their subdivisions. They need street lighting to protect their home buyers.

They need waste treatment plants to make construction economical.
Businesses need public garages so their customers can have some-
place to park. And most important of all, they need the advance planning
that makes all these things possible and in an orderly fashion. This
means security and high returns all the way around. There is no way
you can keep developers out of planning, regardless of how they are
viewed, and almost without question they will have a major say in
the process. Their interest in planning is not fleeting or romantic,
it is real and concrete. We can never understand the politics of
planning if we do not understand this.

Our own study of the membership in three regional planning
bodies in one multistate area showed the following pattern of representation:

Real estate	18
General business	10
Local government	6
Housewife	3
Professional	2
Unknown	1
Total	40

This follows the general model and shows how important real estate
groups are. Developers are not against planning or government
involvement in land use, and quite to the contrary, they are very
active participants in the process.

TYPES OF REGIONAL PLANNING AGENCIES

Generally, this refers to the different geographical areas covered
by regional planning, and this has already been touched on (metropolitan, substate district, regional, rural, and interstate). Let us take
each in order.

Metropolitan Planning Commissions

These agencies serve the metropolitan area as a whole, and their
authority extends across local jurisdictional lines. This represents
a good deal of coordinating, for according to the latest Census of
Governments (1972), there are over 22,000 local governments in

metropolitan areas, down less than 100 over 1967. This means there
has been little change in the number of local governments per metropolitan area, and the figure remains around 90. The current distribution of these governments is as follows'

School districts	4,758
Other local governments	17,427
Counties	444
Municipalities	5,467
Townships	3,462
Special districts	8,054

Not only has there been no appreciable decline in the number of local
governments in metropolitan areas since 1967, but there has been an
absolute increase in the local governments most directly involved
in planning, and that is the nonschool variety. While the number of
school districts declined over this period from 5,421 to 4,758, the
number of other local governments increased from 16,820 to 17,427.
This represents about a 4 percent hike over 1967 (school districts
represent a 12 percent decrease), and specifically the number of cities
went up by about 3 percent, and the number of special districts jumped
by over 6 percent. With the general revenue-sharing measure approved
in 1972, the Census Bureau expects the "municipalities" category to
go up significantly.[6]
    This will not make the metropolitan planning commissions' job
any easier, and the rise in the special district area is particularly
alarming. These are agencies with key duties in the metropolitan
scheme of things, such as sewage disposal, airports, water supply,
recreation, mass transit, and others, and these are typically the
functions with the greatest impact on development (exclusive of highways
and of course direct regulation).[7] Special districts are rarely represented on metropolitan planning bodies, and this has to make their
activities all the more difficult to bring into line with regional objectives. Even if metropolitan planning bodies controlled all the elected
officials in the metropolitan area, those with general planning and
zoning powers, they may not be able to set metropolitan development
patterns because of the independence and freewheeling of the special
districts.[8] There is much to suggest that metropolitan planning cannot
be made a reality until these special districts and authorities are
brought under central direction, but saying this and doing it are two
different things. The fact is that they are often overlooked in the entire
picture in the first place, and second, they have key contacts in state
legislatures and elsewhere, and this will make any legal changes in
their relationships, power, and bases nearly impossible. Ideally, the
kind of public facilities that they control should be assigned to

metropolitan planning bodies, as key means of carrying out metropolitan planning and programming objectives. This does not mean that
all functions should be transferred to the metropolitan unit, only
those under the special districts, and these are in practice likely to
be the most important.

As this suggests, the typical metropolitan planning commission
has no implementation powers, and its authority is generally
advisory. In fact, its control over development in the metropolitan
area is considerably less than the local planning commission's (city,
county, township), since the latter at least has subdivision regulation
powers and perhaps others along these lines (subdivision regulation
was assigned local planning commissions under the model state enabling legislation of the 1920s, the one adopted by most states). The
metropolitan planning commission commonly has the authority to prepare and adopt a metropolitan plan and to make recommendations for
this plan's implementation. By and large, metropolitan planning
commissions do not enjoy the prestige or the power base of the local
planning body.

Metropolitan planning is also carried out by councils of governments or "regional councils" as they are known. The metropolitan
planning commission has a longer history than the councils of governments, and the latter never really became popular until the mid-
1960s. Metropolitan planning commissions, on the other hand, go
back much further, and according to the national surveys, the average
one was created in the mid-1950s. The first regional council was the
Supervisors' Intercounty Committee in Detroit, organized in 1954.
Also, councils of governments were not given federal planning (701)
assistance until 1966, while metropolitan planning commissions were
first given 701 grants in 1954.

Councils of governments differ from the planning commissions
in one very important respect; that is, they represent local "elected"
officials. The metropolitan planning commission tends to represent
a combination of forces, but lay citizens and local planning board
members are definitely included. Councils of governments are strictly
elected officials, being drawn chiefly from local governing bodies
such as city councils and county boards, and where the two have existed
side by side as in Washington, D. C., and Philadelphia, there has often
been conflict and struggle over the control of the planning function.

Different interests may be involved in this, as the above has
already suggested, and councils of governments appear to be more
influenced by "citizens' groups," and planning commissions more by
the developers. During most of the 1960s, the federal government
(liberal Democrats) put its weight behind councils of governments,
and much pressure was exerted to get rid of the "planning commissions" (metropolitan, not local). It was charged that the latter were
politically irresponsible and out-of-date, and since they could not
implement plans anyway, so what good were they. But likely the real

reason was to build a base for the more "liberal" way of thinking in
planning, and that was the citizen group way; also, of course, there
was a power thing, pure and simple, as local conservative Democrats
and Republicans had generally supported the metropolitan planning
commissions, and the national liberals wanted to undermine their
base. It is instructive in this regard that metropolitan planning commissions were first given assistance by a GOP administration and
the regional councils by a liberal Democratic one, with the Republicans
getting into the act 12 years before the Democrats. This again suggests
that planning is not something that has its roots outside the business
community and that business is not against it, assuming the Republicans represent business.

The Nixon administration seemed to be of two minds on the subject and supported both types of metropolitan organizations. This
was not unreasonable from a political point of view. Still, that administration did not put the same emphasis on the earlier Democratic
ones on "metropolitanwide" planning, and thus the issue was not a
major one to it; and in addition it has tended to put greater stress
on "state planning," certainly more so than the former administrations,
which served to downplay metropolitan planning in a broader sense.
State planning, of course, was the foundation of the president's land-
use strategy, as it was of other bills on the subject up to 1975, and
thus the focus shifted from the metropolitan area to the state.

According to one study, metropolitan planning agencies are most
likely to be concerned with transportation, housing, renewal, industrial development, open space and recreation, air and water pollution,
public utilities, and social development.[9] This refers to "planning"
for such matters naturally, and not too much should be made of social
development since most planning commissions have tended to avoid
any detailed involvement here. It is simply too controversial, and
even the mention of it causes a political stir. For example, in one
instance we are familiar with, an official in a local government presented the case for a regionwide public housing policy to a council
of governments, and the issue was referred to a committee of the body
and never reported or discussed since. Councils of governments (COG)
also avoid education questions, and in fact the federal legislation
providing funds to COGs (as they are called) stipulates that education
is not to be one of their concerns (this is the Demonstration Cities
and Metropolitan Development Act of 1966). It was not necessary
to put this provision in the law though, for it is not an issue since
no one will raise it; public schools are reserved for a small segment
of the community, generally the school board, the educational bureaucracy, the PTA, administrators, and a few others.[10]

While councils of governments do contain the local officials with
plan implementation powers (such as zoning), they themselves have
no implementation powers, and their local controllers may not have
any power over key development-inducing public facilities such as

sewer, water, and mass transit. Thus they are a mixed bag. It is important to make this point since their partisans imply that they have plan implementation powers, but that those who control them do, in another context, have some of these powers does not mean they have them. The argument also overlooks the crucial and perhaps decisive role of the special districts, which operate largely independently of these officials.

One review done in the 1960s was fairly critical of them and concluded that the coalition of governments represented by regional councils is the "weakest kind of alliance conceivable," providing them little leverage over either their members or metropolitan area development. The study went on to say that COGs have the best chance of succeeding where the problems are noncontroversial, where the proposed solution will not "disparage" any member government in any way, where the decision is self-executing and does not require positive action by member governments, and where the costs are little or nothing. Another investigation of regional councils in eight areas is more optimistic, and it finds that they have the potential of developing into organizations capable of running operating programs and that they may become "action" or implementation agencies, at least in some policy areas. It dismisses the notion that councils of governments have to work by consensus (as their detractors suggest) or that their decisions must be unanimous.[11]

More recent research suggests that COGs are service organizations, for the most part simply providing assistance to their members and collating plans (not doing them), and that they have not served as independent political or decision-making forces. They are in short "brokers," operating principally as catalysts, mediators, and communications links, a mode that is highly compatible with their structure and organizational capabilities. The author sees little hope that they can break out of this mold, although he indicates that stronger federal backing and a strengthening of their powers by the state legislatures would help.[12] Of course, the greatest help the states could provide along these lines would be to assign them operating programs or plan implementation functions such as sewers, water supply, airports, mass transit, and highways, and the same goes for metropolitan planning commissions. But this is unlikely and would be opposed by a variety of groups, most notably the agencies and local governments that now have the powers, and it may not get through the legislature. In fact, as we shall see shortly, even the attempt in one state to provide the regional planning agency with veto powers has run into trouble, and the units with the operating programs are working in the state legislature to deny these powers to the planners. As long as you stick to planning, there is no problem; its is when you try to make that planning real that the problems arise. There you infringe on vested interests, and the interests can fight. The state is the arena.

The federal government has helped. The Demonstration Cities and Metropolitan Development Act of 1966 provided funds to councils of governments (they were favored by the wording of the legislation) and metropolitan planning commissions; the latter already had federal aid, but they got more here. In addition, the Intergovernmental Cooperation Act of 1968 and the National Environmental Policy Act of 1969 addressed metropolitan planning, and under the Office of Management and Budget Circular A-95 (based on these three acts), metropolitan planning commissions and councils of governments are given the authority to "review and comment" on key proposed federal projects, including those assisted by federal grants. The federal regulation cites them as "metropolitan planning and development clearinghouses," and their perspectives are required before a federal agency can fund a local or state project in the metropolitan area or undertake certain activities directly that impact on development in this context.

The "review and comment" authority represents the first real political breakthrough for these agencies, and prior to this they were groping for a base. The basic responsibility for this new power rests with the staffs of the metropolitan bodies, and thus the planners are adding to their bargaining capital by tapping it. However, the new authority has also caused problems, for few metropolitan planning commissions or councils of governments have definitive plans and standards by which to make judgments. Apparently adopting a plan is too politically sensitive a matter for the regional agencies, but in any event most of them have not done it. Thus, federal projects are being assessed on an ad hoc and local planning basis, with metropolitan perspectives playing only a limited role. Under federal highway legislation approved in 1962, metropolitan transportation planning has been added as a specific duty of these agencies (it always was in general), and most of them have created special "metropolitan transportation planning boards" composed of local and state officials to consider new highway and other related matters in the metropolitan area. The state representatives are from the highway agency, the notion being to bring them under greater metropolitan pressures; of course, it could work the other way around, and much depends on the politics of the situation.[13]

Probably the most significant contribution that could be made by the states would be to expand the authority and broaden the base of metropolitan planning bodies. Greater emphasis should be put on naming local elected officials to their governing boards, via state law; this can be done through the existing metropolitan planning commissions, and it is not necessary to have "councils of governments" per se. In fact, the state of Maryland did this in the mid-1960s, when it provided for greater representation of local elected officials on the board of the Regional Planning Council, an agency it created directly to plan for the Baltimore metropolitan area. It did this to be sure the organization qualified for new federal aid and review powers under the 1966 Metropolitan Development Act, but the motives do not matter and it in the idea that counts. It would not be too much, as we have already suggested, if the states were to give the metropolitan planning agencies at least veto power over major development projects of local and state governments and ultimately to assign these functions directly to the metropolitanwide units. They are, after all, metropolitan and regionwide in authority and impact, and there is much merit in the pattern. This is a significant political task, needless to say, and it will not be easy to do. Still, it is not too early for the states to start thinking about it.

In some instances, the states might even go further. They could, as the Indiana legislature recently did, consolidate the local governments into a metropolitan government and give it both planning and implementation powers. The Indiana action merged the city of Indianapolis and Marion County, with the consolidation taking effect in 1970, and it followed the pattern used more in Canada than the United States (Toronto, Winnepeg)–that is, action of a higher level government (province) without a popular referendum or the consent of the local governments. In fact, the people often vote against it, and the local governments often oppose it.[14] Barring direct action by the state, it could at least pass legislation facilitating merger, as was done in Florida and Tennessee. Jacksonville and Duval County merged in 1968, and the Miami area now has a metropolitan government (still opposed by the Dade County League of Municipalities); in both instances there is a separate planning board that is generally responsible to the metropolitan governing body and chief executive (mayor in Jacksonville, manager in Dade). Similarly, Nashville and Davidson voted consolidation 12 years ago, this under facilitating state legislation.

The state of Washington has taken steps in this direction and has, through legislation, encouraged metropolitan planning and the assignment of programs to metropolitan planning agencies. The Municipality of Metropolitan Seattle was formed in 1958 under this procedure. It was initially given sewage disposal and water pollution control powers, and since then it has added planning. Perhaps this is the way to proceed, that is, having the substantive programs precede planning, and it was certainly the way it was done at the state level in Hawaii and Vermont, although different programs were involved. In addition, the state enabling legislation, under which the agency operates, is so broad that it can even adopt more functions as time goes on, up to six in all, and the state recently acted to expedite the process as it amended the enabling legislation to make it possible to assume new powers without a referendum; it merely requires the approval of the general-purpose local governments in the area.

Metro, as it is called, serves 270 square miles in the Seattle region, including a total of 15 cities. Its governing board is selected by and from local governments, elected officials for the most part, and it seems to be progressing well, based on discussions with its staff.

Because of its wide geographical jurisdiction, its control of key operating programs in addition to "planning," its multifunctional nature,
and its responsibility to local general-purpose government, Metro
seems ideally suited to promote regional perspectives. Indeed it
might well serve as a model for states desiring to move along these
lines.
        The action of the state, as this shows, can be mandatory or per-
missive, and both can be useful. The two approaches are reviewed at
length by Daniel Grant in The State and the Urban Crisis.[15]

Substate District Planning Commissions

        A somewhat new planning strategy has been used by the states
of late, and that is "substate districting." Much of the impetus for
this came from the work of the Appalachian Regional Commission,
an organization set up by federal law to do planning and development
in a multistate region in the Appalachian mountains. But it has caught
on independently of this now and shows great promise. Probably the
best example of substate districting is Georgia, and let us take a
look at their operation.
        The Georgia system is called by Sundquist the "most elaborate"
of the state subdistricting plans, and it includes 18 area planning and
development commissions covering all but 6 of the state's 159
counties.[16] The plan was established by direct state legislation, and
it was not merely "authorized" or "permitted" as is typically the
case with state involvement in planning. Backed by the Georgia Power
Company, the arrangement called for the creation of area commissions
comprising two or more counties each, and many of the specifics
were left to the localities to work out. Under the system, commissioners
are selected by the county and city governing bodies, and the control
is almost entirely local. At the same time, the legislation authorized
state assistance, with figures now showing the state pumping over
$1 million a year into the districts. Federal money is also involved,
largely through the Economic Development Administration of the
Department of Commerce (Public Works Act of 1965) and also HUD,
as are local funds (not much though). The state gave the district
commissions responsibility for the "total development" of the area's
resources, and thus the effort was not limited to planning or even
land-use considerations as is usually the case.
        Still, state subdistricting has an "economic development" ring
to it, and this is probably because of its origins in Appalachia and
under federal economic development legislation. In fact, the Georgia
law says that the first purpose of the district commissions is to
provide the means whereby the local governments of the area can
"collectively consider economic development problems and needs

of mutual concern." The measure also puts a strong emphasis on the development of highways, recreational facilities, tourism, and industry as the solution to these problems, and the goal seems more "promotional" than planning, a point we come back to in a moment.

A distinguishing trait of substate districting is that it covers the entire state (or nearly so as in Georgia) and not merely a section or particular region of it, and it is still not done directly by the state. Otherwise, it (per se) has no special appeal. It is a means which states can use to plan their entire territory without doing it themselves, that is, through state agencies in the capital. As we have found in the earlier chapters, there is much resistance to direct state planning if it amounts to anything, and thus the substate district approach, with a definite state role and involvement, may provide a reasonable alternative; it is especially attractive since control is exercised locally.

It appears that other states have followed Georgia's lead, and Tennessee is one of them. In that state, the entire land area is included, including Nashville and Knoxville, and if a personal visit to one of the district commissions is any indication (Cumberland), it seems that they are getting along well. Still, they suffer from a lack of implementation powers and a dependency on local power structures. Thus, a principal advantage (local support) may be the major problem (local constraint), or at least the Tennessee experience suggests this. From what can be gleaned from the six-volume report of the Advisory Commission on Intergovernmental Relations, Substate Regionalism, it seems that 14 states have substate districting plans fully in effect; this includes 273 districts organized and in operation. Let us examine one such district unit.

The organization is the Northwest Michigan Economic Development District and Regional Planning Commission, and its jurisdiction can be seen on the map in Figure 6, which also shows the other 12 subdistricts in the state (they range all the way from the southeast Michigan council of governments in the Detroit area in the lower right to one in the far western tip of the state near Wisconsin on the Upper Peninsula). Like the situation in Appalachia, the commission was originally established as part of the economic development effort of the state (state enabling legislation), in cooperation with the federal government (which provided the funds), and then reorganized into a regional planning body in 1968; this amounted to adding a new function—planning—to economic development. Nevertheless, the commission is no longer rooted in economic development enabling legislation, but state law in planning (which is also enabling legislation, in part). Although it has no plan to date, it has channeled federal and state funds into local sewer, water, recreational, and other public works projects and has served to coordinate the local input. Its jurisdiction extends to a land area of 4,761 square miles and over 100,000 people, covering 10 counties, 12 cities, 29 villages, and 139 townships.

However, it has no zoning or subdivision powers, with these being exercised mostly by the townships, and it has done very little in the way of planning, guiding, or controlling growth. Again its role is almost entirely promotional, which keeps it in good standing with the key interests in the area including the builders and developers as well as the local governments, who do the appointing (of its board). Its advisory nature works in a similar direction.

The Michigan experience shows that substate districting can build on preexisting organizations and arrangements, which has its political advantages, and both the Northwest Commission and, for example, the Detroit council of governments were already in operation. With Detroit COG, little change was needed, and with the Northwest Commission it was only necessary to expand the functions slightly, and for both it was necessary to build the structures into a statewide network. Substate districting of this kind also has the advantage of widening the perspectives of preexisting bodies, without cutting into their present powers, and this is a real service the state can provide. Actually, substate districting as practiced in Michigan combines the direct approach with the enabling legislation approach, since although state law directly sets up the districts, the specifics including the formation of the commission are left to local governments, who can tap existing organizations; thus, in Michigan substate districting is not only permitted and strongly encouraged by the state enabling legislation, but also is mandated by the state.

Regional Planning Commissions

These agencies have authority over one area of the state, broader than a single jurisdiction (city, county) but not extending to the state as a whole. Unlike substate commissions, they are not part of a state-wide scheme, and metropolitan planning commissions are also excluded from this category. Unlike the metropolitan variety, regional planning commissions generally have authority over both urban and rural areas, and with rare exceptions, they are formed directly by the state (and not through enabling legislation).

An example is the Adirondack Park Agency, created in 1971 by the New York State legislature. The regional body has the power to prepare a master plan for all public lands and to develop land-use controls for all private lands in the park, and until the plans and controls were completed, it was empowered to regulate through a "permit" system. The Master Plan for public grounds was in fact drawn up and adopted in 1972 by the agency. Having been formally approved by the governor, the plan called for the following classes of land use in the 6-million-acre park:

FIGURE 6

Area Under the Jurisdiction of the Northwest Michigan
Economic Development and Regional
Planning Commission (shaded area)

1. wilderness, in which most activities are prohibited;
2. primitive, in which limited activities are permitted;
3. canoe, where certain water and fishery management activities are
    allowed;
4. wild forest, which permits limited recreational uses of different
    kinds, such as snowmobiling;
5. intensive use, referring to such recreational uses as campgrounds,
    beaches, and ski centers;
6. wild, scenic, and recreational rivers, which covers 180 miles of
    waterways and stipulates limited permitted uses on and near them;
7. travel corridors, which includes highways and the uses permitted
    along rights of way.
This "plan" is a powerful one, and the state has the right to enforce
it; it is not advisory.
    Development controls for private land in the area were also
adopted in 1973, and they apply to six uses: hamlet, moderate use,
low-intensity use, rural use, resource management, and industrial.

For each category of use regulated, there is a description of development that is permitted without special approval along with that requiring a permit. Many other restrictions are also spelled out in the controls, including setbacks from shorelines and vegetation removal standards. This amounts to zoning pure and simple, and in fact it includes subdivision control as well.

The states are thus not constrained as much as localities are when they get into land use, and they have more freedom to combine the different powers of regulation in a single development control package. This, as we saw in Chapter 4, was true of Vermont, and there is a lot to be said for it. It is also part of the model enabling legislation as proposed by the American Law Institute; that is, zoning and subdivision powers have been combined into a single development ordinance.[17] The fact of the matter is that the states are not controlled by their own enabling statutes, and this is fortunate from their standpoint; perhaps they should give localities the same break. A single development ordinance strikes us as a great improvement over the presently highly fragmented and compartmentalized approach, and it is better from an administrative standpoint (central planning), and the citizens' standpoint (central influence). It is also helpful to the developer since it simplifies the process considerably . Instructively, not only do communities have separate ordinances for zoning and subdivision regulations, but there are two separate sets of state enabling laws on the subject, one on zoning and the other on subdivision (and planning).

The New York Agency is given land-use authority over virtually all development in its boundaries, and again following the Vermont pattern, in municipalities minor uses are exempt if the locality has a land-use program that has been approved by the agency. This has apparently given the local governments in the area a real incentive to adopt the full range of land-use controls, and from all indications it is working well. The state agency does review the regulations to determine consistency with regional policy, but once approved the controls are in the hands of local government and not the state. The similarities to Vermont are remarkable. Still perhaps the prospects of state impact are even greater under the New York approach since it seems to be less of an interference with local powers (the chief difference being that it is limited to one section of the state).

Other examples of regional planning agencies, in each case created directly by the state legislature, are the San Francisco Bay Conservation and Development Commission, the Twin Cities Metropolitan Council, the Hackensack Meadowlands Development Commission, and the Maryland-National Capital Park and Planning Commission. All serve a particular section of the state and both urban and rural areas.

Set up by California legislation in 1969, the San Francisco Bay Conservation and Development Commission was given the power to

plan and regulate uses in the bay area so as to preserve and promote
its value as a port as well as recreational, fish, and wildlife complex.
This power extends to an area 100 feet back from the shoreline and
to certain other lands such as creeks and diked areas adjoining the
bay and its wetlands, and it applies both to government and private
uses; specifically, "permits" are required for all development. Of
course, federal cooperation is voluntary since it cannot be compelled
by the state to submit to land controls, but so far at least the Corps
of Engineers has chosen to be guided by the regulations.

Again, this power is not advisory, and in fact the body has turned
down a number of proposals, including a major one to develop 23 miles
of the bay area for commercial and industrial uses. This proposal
was found to be inconsistent with the San Francisco Bay Plan, which
is provided for in the legislation and which has apparently been
adopted, and it is useful to note that this plan by law cannot be overriden by state agencies including the highway department. This again
suggests an advantage the state has in getting into land-use control
in this way, for it is not subject to the same constraints and limitations as local governments are, or that they subject them to. The
commission's board, incidentally, is composed of government officials,
mostly named by state and local agencies with interests and responsibilities in the bay.

The Twin Cities Metropolitan Council represents more central
direction on the part of the state, and the agency, created in 1967 by
the state legislature, has a 15-member board, nearly all appointed
by the governor. The chief executive is required by law to "consult"
with all members of the assembly from the Two Cities area before
making the selections, but they are his alone. The Twin Cities, of
course, refers to Minneapolis and St. Paul. The state acted decisively
in this case, and while it did not assign it any operating programs, the
council is given the veto power over key projects of local government
in the area. Its decisions are virtually final, although an appeals
process is provided for outside the courts, and the council has exercised this power. In at least one instance, the action prompted the
supporters of the agency whose program was vetoed to seek amendments to the state law curbing the council's authority. Those affected
by the council's review are largely the special-purpose authorities
who have the responsibility for the public facilities and services with
the greatest impact on regional development, and they include the
Metropolitan Sewer Board, the Metropolitan Park Board, and the
Metropolitan Airports Commission. In addition, the council has the
planning powers for the region, which it shares with local governments,
and presumably it is the regional plan that serves as the basis for its
review decisions.[18]

In a move that was widely noted in urban planning circles, the
New Jersey legislature formed the Hackensack Meadowlands Development Commission in 1969 and gave it planning and regulatory powers

over a 28-square-mile area of marshland in the northern part of the
state. The land has been used mostly as a dump by the some 128
communities in the area, and the chief job has been reclamation. The
specific area being regulated by the agency contains some 15 cities
and counties, which are represented on the board, and it is described
by one observer as "one of the most unsightly areas on earth."[19]

The panel's powers include master planning, setting construction
standards, reviewing the reclamation, redeveloping the land itself,
issuing revenue bonds to finance its undertakings, and assessing property for the public improvements; both the state and, as mentioned,
local governments are represented on the board, with the local officials
being given the veto power by majority vote. The state has already
poured several million dollars into the project, constituting but another
way state government can participate in regional planning.

The New Jersey experience represents another version of state-
local cooperation in controlling development in a particular region,
and although we have no feedback on how it is working, it seems ideal
in theory. That the state has pitched in financially is also to be
commended. The state moved into an area that local governments
could not or would not, gave the agency real powers, backed it with
its own resources, and provided the localities a strong voice in the
administration. This looks like a fine model to us.

Similarly, the Maryland legislature formed the Maryland-National
Capital Park and Planning Commission to serve the Washington suburbs in that state. This agency, one of the most powerful and effective
of its kind, has full planning authority over a 1,000-square-mile area
containing more than 1 million residents, an area that is both urban
and rural, and, as important, has direct subdivision control powers
over the same region. The subdivision power is final, and appeals
from the planning commission go directly to the court and not the
governing bodies of the counties; it is worth noting that this power
was given it directly by the state legislature. It also serves in an
advisory capacity to the councils of the two counties in the region,
mostly on zoning matters. The commission adopted a general plan
(wedges and corridors) in 1964 and draws on it as a basis for development decisions. Again we can see what the state can do in urban
areas or at least mixed urban-rural areas, and the state role in
planning is by no means limited to rural regions.

Rural Planning Commissions

Rural planning has only recently gotten underway in this country,
and it lags considerably behind urban planning. Rural planning also,
like substate districting, differs from urban planning in that it is
largely directed to economic development, and while urban planning

includes this, it has not been the principal thrust. Further, unlike the situation in urban areas, no single organizational form (or two) exists that typifies the planning function. Another point along these same lines is that it has been the federal government rather than the state that has been chiefly responsible for stimulating rural planning, most notably the Department of Commerce (recently) and the Department of Agriculture (traditionally).

The major rural planning bodies are the economic development districts that blanket most of the underdeveloped sections of the country, including much of the South, the Appalachian states and counties, rural Ohio, northern Michigan and Wisconsin, and the Ozarks. The economic development districts are not considered governments in and of themselves, and they were set up largely in conjunction with the federal regional commissions for the Coastal Plains (southeastern states), Upper Great Lakes (Michigan, Wisconsin, Minnesota), Appalachia (as noted), the Ozarks (Oklahoma, Arkansas, Missouri), and Four Corners (Colorado, Utah, Arizona, New Mexico). The federal regional commissions were established under the provisions of the Public Works and Economic Development Act of 1965 or a special act for Appalachia (Appalachian Regional Development Act of 1965). This shows the federal roots to the districts. The national government, in funding the development districts, requires a wide range of representatives on their boards and by no means is this limited to local elected or planning commission officials; priority, for example, is put on minority interests (Indians, blacks), industrial representatives and the general business community along with labor, but little emphasis is placed on planning officials. Other rural planning groups include the rural areas development committees of the U. S. Department of Agriculture and soil and water conservation districts (sponsored by the Department of Agriculture, but theoretically separate governments).

Pierre Clavel says we would make a mistake if we tried to judge the rural planning efforts by the experience in urban areas. He argues that, in the first place, the rural areas are unaccustomed to planning, and they do not see it as the solution many of us do elsewhere, and in fact, he writes, they do not particularly see the government as a legitimate controller of private activity including land use, economic development, and industrial enterprise. In short, he notes that the major stress there is on "stimulus" and not "regulation of public and private economic activity."[20] Clearly, the idea is that we have to take into account the different political and social contexts in which rural planning must exist and grow.

While we have said that the state role is not limited to rural areas, perhaps it can make the greatest contribution there. Certainly it would make more political sense for the states to concentrate on them than the urban areas where local governments are strong and have great influence in the state legislatures; besides, few planning bureaucracies exist in the countryside, and there would be less opposition

to the state stepping in. In addition, more of a service can be provided
there. It also seems that the state can participate more directly in
rural planning, and this can be done in a variety of ways including
enabling legislation, direct laws, funding, and technical assistance.
No doubt in many areas the state and it development agencies should
be represented on the boards of rural planning commissions—directly
that is.

Interstate Planning Commissions

The last but by no means the least important of the various kinds
of regional planning involving the state is interstate planning, or the
planning done by agencies created by interstate compact. An interstate compact is set up by joint action of two or more state legislatures
and with the permission of Congress. Congress may provide this
permission in advance, as it has done in several functional areas
outside of planning per se (education, for example), but in any event
it is generally no problem (they are willing to do it; it is not a political
issue, in other words). The state action amounts to state law, but it
does not take effect until all the states have acted and Congress has
approved.

Generally, interstate compacts have been used in such matters
as river basin development, pollution control, soil erosion, education,
fisheries, parks, and public safety. Planning is new here. An example of an
planning agency created across state boundaries is the Tahoe Regional
Planning Agency, formed in 1971 by acts of the Nevada and California
legislatures; in fact, it may be the only such unit to be created to date.
The organization has powers over all land-use decisions in the Tahoe
basin and has already adopted both a regional plan and an implementing
ordinance. It is interesting to note that the regional agency, however,
was provided no authority over casinos and related hotels as long as
they were constructed in accordance with the zoning and planning on
the books through 1968; ostensibly to close this loophole, Nevada
recently set up the Nevada Tahoe Regional Planning Agency and
gave it authority over any development not subject to the interstate
agency's controls. Reports on lakes containing treated sewage and
adjacent land uses subject to its regulations indicate that it is doing
a fine job.

A STATE STRATEGY

The states will play a significant part in regional planning,
whether we (or they) like it or not. They set the ground rules

regardless, because they have the police power. Besides, even though
Washington can do much in the way of funding and stimulating, the
basic patterns of power authorizations and state/local bureaucracies
and interrelationships have been set, this under state law. This law
can be direct, or it can be of the enabling variety.

We think that the states can do much here. They can promote
metropolitan centralization by directly creating metropolitan planning
bodies (Twin Cities, Baltimore), by directly creating a metropolitanwide government (Indianapolis), by facilitating metropolitan government
(Jacksonville, Miami, Nashville), and by permitting metropolitan
planning agencies to run operating programs (Seattle). They can
promote regional centralization by directly forming planning and
development commissions for a single area (Hackensack Meadowlands, Adirondack Park, San Francisco Bay Commission, Maryland-
National Capital Park and Planning Commission), by cooperating with
other states for the same purpose (Lake Tahoe), by subdistricting
their entire territories (Georgia, Tennessee, Michigan), or by authorizing local government actions in this area (economic development
districts). Significantly, they are not constrained by their own enabling
legislation, and they have full powers over state and local agencies
(unlike the federal or local governments). This has a number of advantages as we have seen throughout this chapter.

All indications are that state action in regional planning has
worked. In any event, the regional planning is working, and it works
best when substantive power (veto) and operating programs (sewers)
are provided. The states, in fact, may well hold the key to the future
of regional planning. It seems to be a far more profitable route to
follow than direct zoning, if for not other reason than the fact that it
has a better chance of being done.

NOTES

1. National Survey of Metropolitan Planning, prepared for the
U. S. Senate Committee on Government Operations (Washington, D. C.:
Government Printing Office, 1963), p. 4. A more recent survey, done
in 1972, shows similar results with another kind of regional agency,
councils of governments. Sixty-eight percent of the councils were
formed under state enabling legislation, and another 20 percent under
a special act of the state legislature or some variety of joint exercise
of power statute. Advisory Commission on Intergovernmental Relations, Regional Decision Making: New Strategies for Substate Districts
(Washington, D. C.: Government Printing Office, 1973), p. 79.

2. National Survey of Metropolitan Planning, p. 4.

3. 1964 National Survey of Metropolitan Planning, prepared for
the U.S. Senate Committee on Government Operations (Washington, D.C.:
Government Printing Office, 1965), p. 5.

    4. Ibid., p. 5.
    5. Robert A. Walker, The Planning Function in Urban Govern-
ment (Chicago: University of Chicago Press, 1950).
    6. Information in the paragraph comes from U. S. Bureau of the
Census, Census of Governments 1972, Vol. 1 (Washington, D. C.:
Government Printing Office, 1973), p. 10.
    7. Special districts are sharply criticized in the literature,
mostly because of their lack of political responsibility. See Advisory
Commission on Intergovernmental Relations, The Problem of Special
Districts in American Government (Washington, D. C.: Government
Printing Office, 1964).
    8. See James Ridgeway, The Politics of Ecology (New York:
Dutton, 1971), Chap. 4.
    9. Joint Center for Urban Studies of the Massachusetts Institute
of Technology and Harvard University, The Effectiveness of Metro-
politan Planning (Washington, D. C.: Government Printing Office, 1964),
p. 122.
    10. Roscoe C. Martin, Government and the Suburban School (Syra-
cuse: Syracuse University Press, 1962).
    11. See Roscoe C. Martin, Metropolis in Transition (Washington,
D. C.: Government Printing Office, 1963), pp. 49-50: and Royce
Hanson, Councils of Governments (Washington, D. C.: Government
Printing Office, 1966), pp. 30-33.
    12. Melvin B. Mogulof, Governing Metropolitan Areas (Washington,
D.C.: Urban Institute, 1971), pp. 85-91, 124-126.
    13. See David E. Boyce and others, Metropolitan Plan Evaluation
Methodology (Philadelphia: University of Pennsylvania, 1969). This
report was prepared by the Institute of Environmental Studies of the
university, and it was done for the U.S. Department of Transportation.
    14. Advisory Commission on Intergovernmental Relations,
Factors Affecting Voter Reaction to Governmental Reorganization
in Metropolitan Areas (Washington, D. C.: Government Printing
Office, 1962).
    15. Daniel R. Grant, "Urban Needs and State Response: Local
Government Reorganization," in Alan K. Campbell, (ed.), The States
and the Urban Crisis (Englewood Cliffs, N. J.: Prentice-Hall, 1970),
pp. 59-84.
    16. James L. Sundquist, Making Federalism Work (Washington,
D. C.: Brookings, 1969), p. 159.
    17. American Law Institute, A Model Land Development Code,
April 15, 1974, Philadelphia, p. 33.
    18. For a somewhat earlier description of planning in this area,
see Alan Altshuler, The City Planning Process (Ithaca, N. Y.:
Cornell University Press, 1965).
    19. John N. Kolesar, "The States and Urban Planning and Devel-
opment," in Campbell (ed.), op. cit., p. 125.

20. Pierre Clavel, "The Politics of Planning: The Case of Non-metropolitan Regions," in Thad L. Beyle and George T. Lathrop (eds.), Planning and Politics (New York: Odyssey, 1971), p. 193.

7

IMPORTANCE OF LOCAL PLANNING

This may be the most important chapter in the book, for it deals with local government and their planning powers. It is at the local level that land regulation powers are currently exercised, and this is likely to be the case into the indefinite future. What is done here will determine not only the nature of planning and zoning in the United States but the character of development as well. It is here where the basic land-use patterns will be set.

Unlike Chapter 6, this one is not limited to planning. This is because while regional agencies rarely have implementation powers, local governments do. They have zoning, subdivision regulation, official map, and perhaps other powers in addition to planning. Zoning refers to the designation of different districts for certain uses such as commercial, residential, industrial, and specific stipulations in each; subdivision regulation to the control of layout patterns and the provision of streets and other public facilities,within the context of zoning; the official map to the means of reserving land needed for future roads and other public purposes; and planning to the master plan process providing the future dimension to community development.

Of course, as we have seen, zoning, subdivision controls, and the rest do not have to be "tools" of planning or enforcement powers. Only in the ideal sense is this true, and in practice they may become more important and even precede planning. That more communities in the metropolitan area have zoning than planning suggests the point, and we have noted instances in the states where zoning is put on the books first and planning later if at all. Thus the tools may become the tail that wags the dog. This has been a central theme of this book. Let us now turn to some of the key principles of local planning and land regulation and then consider changes needed in state enabling legislation.

THE GROUND RULES ARE SET BY THE STATE

The first and most important principle of local planning is that it is structured by the states. This applies to controls as well, and as we have pointed out in Chapter 2, the states have the police power, which includes land regulation. Under our system, the localities are not free to do as they please, and to the contrary, they are significantly constrained by state action.

Specifically we are talking about state enabling legislation or measures that were typically adopted in the 1920s or 1930s and which have been changed very little since. It is true that some municipalities developed land-use controls before the first state provided enabling legislation, but now all states have this legislation on the books, and no locality can adopt planning and other land-use powers unless this is provided for by state law. And then it is required to follow what are commonly rather detailed procedures and restrictions. If the state does not stipulate that a particular class or category of local government is permitted to plan and zone or otherwise provide for the power, municipalities or others in this class do not have this authority and cannot exercise it. There are sometimes ways around this, and the locality may adopt what amount to land controls through some other authority it has (building codes) and regulate in this manner, but this is difficult, time-consuming, and perhaps somewhat deceptive. Thus the states not only tell the localities how they must do it, but also whether they can.

In some states it has been only recently that counties have been authorized to plan and zone, and for years small municipalities in a few states were denied these powers. Now only a few states do not have zoning enabling legislation for counties, and these include some states in New England and others like Idaho. All states but Hawaii authorize their cities to plan and zone, meaning that 49 states have provided these powers to their cities.

The reasons for some of the exceptions are obvious. In the New England states of Connecticut and Maine, which do not authorize county zoning, all or most the county governments have been "deorganized" and do not exist (previously they performed limited judicial powers), and in Hawaii there are no "city governments" in the legal sense, only counties (four of them); Honolulu, for instance, is a "county" under state law. These data are taken from our own survey of the matter, and they are as of mid-1974.

In all, nearly 11,000 communities have planning boards, and this represents over half of the local governments that might be expected to have them.[1] Of this number, nearly all large cities (50,000 or more population) have them; 90 percent of the municipalities in the 5,000 to 50,000 range also have them. In a typical metropolitan area (central city of 50,000 minimum plus surrounding suburbs), there will be dozens of local planning commissions, usually one for each unit of general local government. About the same number of localities have zoning ordinances, and about 8,000 have subdivision regulations.

It is possible that local governments are assigned planning and zoning powers directly by the state and not through enabling legislation. Enabling legislation means that the states authorize local planning or land-use control, but do not require it. Direct state legislation may require it. For example, the Maryland legislature years ago enacted direct legislation requiring planning, zoning, and subdivision controls for the Washington suburbs and assigning the planning and subdivision authority to the bicounty Maryland-National Capital Park and Planning Commission and the zoning power to the governing bodies of the two counties. It is also possible, although we know of no cases of it, that the state could pass legislation applying directly to a particular locality and "permitting" and not requiring planning and zoning.[2] Generally, when the state gets involved directly, it mandates the action. But the broad pattern is clear; that is, cities and counties are typically authorized to plan and zone through state enabling legislation, which permits but does not require the localities to act.

STATE ENABLING LEGISLATION IS FRAGMENTED

State enabling legislation in land regulation and development does not come in a single package. It is divided; zoning enabling legislation is separate from planning enabling legislation, and both are separate from community redevelopment enabling legislation and that in public housing. The zoning and planning enabling laws, in fact, may have been approved in different years and perhaps virtually different eras. In practice there was commonly a six- to eight-year gap in the states' actions on the two, since this represents the period in between the federal issuance of the two models on the topics.

Most states approved their zoning enabling legislation years before doing anything about planning. This took place in the 1920s, and the action was based largely on the Standard State Zoning Enabling Act provided by the U. S. Department of Commerce.[3] It was not until the 1930s or later that most states authorized planning through enabling legislation, and again this was based on the Department of Commerce model, A Standard City Planning Enabling Act.[4] The city planning act covered not only planning per se but subdivision controls, the official map, and regional planning agencies, making it somewhat broader than the former which dealt solely with zoning. Still, it was the zoning measure that the experts wanted to get out first and that communities were anxious to get on their law books.

Clearly the states have not seen planning, zoning, subdivision
controls, and the official map as part of the same thrust, but as independent matters to be taken up as the need arises. The same goes
for urban renewal and public housing, and they are also provided
independently of each other and of broader land-use controls and
planning. At the same time, most states put planning and zoning
enabling legislation in the same section of their codes (codified laws),
and it does not show. This approach does not provide for a unified
land-use and development policy in the communities, and it will almost
certainly have to be modified for a more coherent policy to emerge.

STATE ENABLING LEGISLATION IS OUT-OF-DATE

State enabling laws have been approved for the most part years
ago, going back into the 1920s. This has been discussed in Chapter 2,
and the reader is familiar with it and the chief criticisms of the
practice, but in sum the legislation generally reflects conditions
and problems of a different age and not those of the present.[5] For
example, the model legislation provides that planning is to be assigned
an independent commission that is free of politics and outside the
mainstream of municipal decision making. Whatever the reasons, the
concept is now considered dated and reflective of the somewhat pecu-
liar political conditions of an earlier day. Now the notion is to put
planning directly into the hands of central decision makers and to
integrate it with the other functions of local government that have an
impact on community development.[6] Yet until the state law is changed,
communities must retain the independent planning commission whether
it works or not.

FRAGMENTED DECISION MAKING IN THE COMMUNITY

Most community governments have less than a unified and comprehensive strategy in land development, and much of this can be attributed to state enabling legislation. Perhaps if the state legislation
were different, this would be different, and there would be a more
cohesive land-use policy. But the fact of the matter is that local
governments have one ordinance for planning, another for zoning, a
third for subdivision, and perhaps others for other land-use powers
such as the official map. This has to have its substantive implications
and policy effects, and a fragmented legal base must spell a fragmented
administration and decision-making process.

In fact, the agency that administers the local planning function
is usually not the same as that administering the zoning ordinance,

and neither typically has zoning adjustment powers or makes the final
land-use decisions. The only functions that are in reality combined
are planning and subdivision control, and both are under the planning
commission. Normally the master plan is done by the local planning
commission; zoning is administered by the department of licenses
and inspections or buildings; zoning adjustment powers rest with the
board of zoning appeals; and the governing body makes the final zoning
decisions. Most of this pattern can be traced to the state enabling
legislation. For instance, the model zoning statute provides for the
establishment of a board of adjustment to consider zoning variances
and special exceptions, and nearly every state has followed suit and
required their localities to set up such a board for this purpose.
Fragmentation is the norm, and the root is the state.

Probably the most serious problem in this respect is that the
model legislation made planning independent of the general political
processes of local government. This, of course, refers to the independent planning commission. We have talked about the need for planning
to be independent of zoning (Vermont, Hawaii), but at the local level,
there is often so much independence that planning loses much of its
meaning. It is ideal, abstract, and like an ivory tower and does not
form the base of land-use decision making. The answer is not for
planning to be absorbed by zoning (as in Hawaii) and thus to completely
lose any semblance of independence, but to have just the right degree
of it so that it can have some independent effect on implementation
decisions. The pattern cannot be changed until state enabling legislation is changed.

Furthermore, there are another series of agencies that administer
controls that have an impact on planning and zoning, and they include
public works, housing (private) and community development, health,
urban renewal, and public housing departments and authorities; these
units are responsible for such matters as building, housing, fire,
electric, plumbing, sanitary, public housing, urban renewal, and similar codes and ordinances.[7]

This raises the general question of the relationship between
administrative patterns and policy output, and no one knows the answer
for sure. The research literature is divided on the subject, and while
some of it has found that the specifics of planning organization and
bureaucracy have their influence on the effectiveness of planning,
other work has concluded that there are few, if any, links. One study,
in fact, found that the planning bureaucracy was the chief obstacle to
successful planning, while another found no correlations.[8] We can only
report these findings and add that many practitioners believe that a
change in administrative organization can produce desired policy
results, and specifically that a more centralized decision-making
process would produce a more cohesive and unified planning and
land-use policy.

STATE ENABLING LAWS ARE DETAILED

State enabling laws are quite detailed and impose rather strict
requirements on local governments. They are probably overly concerned with minor planning and zoning considerations, and there appears
to be no need to have this kind of specificity. There is a special preoccupation with procedural and administrative matters, things that
are probably best left to the judgment of the locality.

As illustrations, they deal with such things as the number of
members on the planning commission (no less than so many, no more
than so many), the length of terms of planning commission members,
when each should be appointed (staggered terms), who should do the
appointing, how often the planning commission should meet and when
(such as January, April, July, and October), and where. One state
gives them a choice of meeting in either the offices of the board of
public works or county commissioners and no others! Out-of-date
provisions are common, and the Indiana statute sets a maximum of
$5.00 a planning commissioner can get for attending a single meeting
and conditions even this on the "availability of appropriations."
Specific duties are spelled out, and they concentrate on such matters
as record keeping, budgets, supervision techniques, and custodial
practices.

Much of the problem comes from the standard planning and zoning
enabling acts, and they were very detailed in these respects. Would it
not be sufficient for the state to set up some widely accepted standards
of due process and fair procedures and drop it at that? Some common
notions exist of equitable administrative and decision-making practices,
and these could be put in the state law. It is important that they be
covered in the eanbling legislation, but it is not necessary that excessive detail be provided. This does not mean that citizens' and private
groups are not protected, and the broader approach may well afford
more protection. It is also wise for the state legislation to set forth
the general purposes of planning and zoning and to tie them into the
police power—and this refers to the promotion of the health, safety,
and general welfare of the public (most states add "morals," but this
is not needed). Yet this can be stated once at the beginning of the
legislation, and it need not be repeated throughout as often as it is.
Undue repetition means more confusion and complexity, and there will
be enough of this without it.

In another example, one state law defines a master plan, and the
definition goes on for pages getting into such particulars as refuse
sites, "neighborhood units," "history," bridges, and so on. It seems
clear that as good as the minds of some state legislators may be,
they cannot anticipate everything that might be included in a master
plan for every community in the state. Besides, these things change

over time. What legislator could have anticipated even ten years ago
the need to put bike paths and trails in master plans? Should the
community not be given the freedom to make its own determinations
in this regard? Perhaps the general state guidelines could be something like "all those factors impacting on community development."

As it works out in practice, the state restrictions and requirements
are negative. If the state were to follow up on the legislation and provide administrative guidance, funds, and technical expertise, it might
be a different story. But as we saw in Chapter 2, this is not the way
it works, and the state gets quickly out of it after passing the legislation.

ENABLING LEGISLATION VIEWS
ZONING IN NEGATIVE TERMS

Zoning as reflected in the enabling laws is negative. Zoning was
to be adopted by communities, and the means were to be provided by
the state to assure that certain uses would not be permitted in certain
districts. Zoning was prohibitive, and the emphasis was on what was
not permitted. It did not even have to be related to planning in these
laws, and planning could have provided some positive guides. Zoning
was king, and it was negative.[9] The stress was on how communities
could keep certain uses from happening, and the good community was
defined in terms of what it was not, and not what it was. Put more
simply, zoning was seen as the tool of keeping commercial uses out
of residential neighborhoods.

Today zoning is viewed differently. The fact is that the whole
nature of zoning has changed since the 1920s when the states approved
their enabling laws. At that time, it was seen almost exclusively in
terms of "use districts," with the idea that each city should be given
the authority to divide its land into three basic districts: residential,
commercial, and industrial, and to keep the latter two from spreading
into the former. Planning was at best an afterthought, and if it was to
be used at all, it would be for the purpose of justifying these zoning
patterns and providing them the necessary legitimacy.

Now zoning is typically seen in more positive terms, and both
planning and zoning are seen in terms of how they can produce a better
community. Certainly planning is now related to zoning, and the two
tied together, with planning setting the objectives and zoning carrying
them out. The idea is no longer to stop builders and developers from
doing this or that, but to put them more firmly in the public harness.
Government's role is more positive as is that of planning and zoning,
and this takes the public officials out of their traditional "reactive"
posture and puts them more in the driver's seat. It is not as though
it works this way everyplace, but that this is the new thinking. Current

state enabling laws and local operating procedures based on them will have to be altered for the new view to be accommodated in its entirety, and there is already some evidence that it is making headway in Oregon and California where the state legislation is being changed.[10]

One of the main obstacles has been that government in this country has seldom been seen as the coordinator of private activities, except perhaps in times of emergency. This philosophy stems from Jeffersonian, Jacksonian, and Social Darwinist logic, which elevated the private sector and spun elaborate ideologies and theories to back up the position. It was not drawn from the views of the founders who saw government in a different light and believed it could, in cooperation with business, direct the economy and industrial activity. The founding fathers were not fearful of using the power of government to regulate private property, a concept reflected in the Federalist Papers and in the actions of the Federalist administrations under Washington and Adams.[11] Yet the founders were not to have their day until the New Deal.[12]

Free enterprise was the dominant philosophy in the 1920s when zoning enabling legislation was first considered, and perhaps the most that the drafters could pull out of the situation was a kind of "negative" power for government. This may have been especially true in the light of the conservative Hoover's sponsorship of the model, but the reading here is mixed because it appears that Hoover did not oppose government involvement per se but wanted interest groups to do the administering, a position not far from that of the founders. Hoover seemed to be an early supporter of the "NRA concept" (for National Industrial Recovery Act), whereby government would step in and do the regulating but the pertinent interest groups would make most of the decisions; at least this is suggested from the evidence presented in Chapter 2. Whatever the reasons, zoning was negative, and it was structured as such in the standard enabling legislation.

ENABLING LEGISLATION
EXCLUDES REGIONAL FACTORS

Under state enabling legislation, the context of local planning and zoning decision making is drastically limited and this is seen in practice in the narrowest of respects, and again the standard state law is partly to blame. Section 1 of the 1922 model granted the zoning power to the "municipality" for the purpose of promoting the health, safety, morals, and general welfare "of the community" (underlining supplied). Most states put language to this effect in their laws, and this gave the localities the perfect out; that is, by state law they are required to consider only the interests of the community and not of the area or region of which they are a part. Isolation is legally

sanctioned and given the institutional blessing of the state legislature.
This fit in nicely with the anticity feelings of the emerging suburbs,
and they were happy to comply. [13]

It is even conceivable under this provision that if the local governing
body took "metropolitan" or "regional" considerations into account,
it could be taken to court and its decisions overturned. The enabling
legislation makes this possible, and it is not in reality all that farfetched. The point was touched on in Chapter 2, where we pointed
out an instance of the local ordinance, based on state legislation,
permitting the consideration of only "local" need in a zoning decision,
and even though the applicant could cite need arising from the interstate character of the area, only local factors were allowed in the
record. This was by local and state law, and broader factors were
ruled out. The case involved an application for a zoning exception
for a gas station, and although the site was on a country road with
only a few hundred cars a day, it was next to an interstate highway
interchange (40,000 cars a day). The vehicle count on the interstate
could not be considered by the zoning board since an interstate highway is not "local."

Clearly this practice cannot be substantiated in this day and age,
and yet it is being challenged on very few fronts. Although it is sometimes easier to talk theoretically of our problems, it is changing the
"minor" matters like this ordinance's definition of need, which can
reshape development and alter dozens of social and economic patterns
based on it. Communities all over the country are systematically
thumbing their noses at the metropolitan area, the region, the state,
and the nation, and they are getting away with it through zoning. Can
we afford to continue in this direction? The job is done (on us) by
zoning and legitimated by planning, and we have the state legislation
to blame.

Does this mean that state legislatures can change people's attitudes? Surely it does not. People believe what they want, and laws
have little to do with it. It only means that zoning should not be used
as the means of enforcing specialized ideologies and restrictive
practices on the rest of the country. The problem is particularly
noticeable in the suburbs, and they are zoning us out. That is the
long and short of it, and the citations have been provided. The point
is that people will have their exclusionary desires whether or not the
law gives vent to these desires, but if the legal base for them is eliminated, they will have a much harder time of it. If the suburbs continue
to exclude uses needed to serve metropolitanwide and regionwide ends,
they can be taken to court if the enabling legislation is changed.

In sum, the enabling legislation poses two problems here: It gives
the zoning power to local governments and not units covering a wider
area; second, it restricts the base of the decisions to a single community and not a broader context. That there are 90 units of local
government per metropolitan area gives you an indication of the extent

of the problem. Although not all of these have zoning powers, many
of them do, and they are typically using them in exclusionary fashion.

ENABLING LEGISLATION OVERLOOKS HOUSING NEEDS

The needs of housing are almost entirely neglected in the state
enabling laws. Of course, layout and provisions protecting residential
areas from incompatible uses are covered, and this is not what we
are talking about here. The problem is one of land-use controls limiting
the supply of housing, pushing the costs up, and failing to deal with the
housing needs of lower socioeconomic groups. In all probability, it
was not a lack of concern on the part of the drafters of the model
legislation that caused the problem but unforeseen and unexpected
consequences. Somehow zoning has cut into the supply of housing
and raised housing prices, and clearly this was not planned.

Babcock and Bosselman have done a whole book on the subject,
and they have shown in one city and state after another how land
regulations have caused housing problems, especially for minorities
and blacks.[14] Controls restrict the supply of land available for housing,
and this forces prices of existing housing upward, and the toll is particularly heavy in the lower-income ranges. Research of the National
Commission on Urban Problems has shown pretty much the same
thing, and heavy votes against zoning in black and poor white precincts
suggest that they may be sensitive to the matter.[15] This means that
zoning and other land-use controls have not been particularly good
tools for providing the needed housing for any except those in the
more affluent classes, and the reverse may be more nearly the truth.

There is little question that changes are needed in this regard.
Generally, the legislation is silent on the point, and the omission may
be important. The idea is that unless housing needs are specifically
stipulated as a goal of zoning, the controls will most likely work
against them. That is the natural way, and this refers to the automatic
effects of restrictive and exclusionary zoning practices. Since zoning
tends to be restrictive by its very nature, some specific mention of
housing is needed. Zoning can clearly be tailored to provide housing
for all income groups, and this can be done through providing density
bonuses to developers willing to build it in their subdivisions and by
requiring local zoning bodies to consider regionwide housing needs
in their decisions. The "density bonus" plan is already in effect in
some communities, and in return for zoning exceptions permitting
more housing, developers are to provide a certain percentage of it
to lower-income groups, and regional criteria can be easily inserted
in state enabling legislation governing local land-use decision making.
Again, communities can provide zoning categories that induce developers to build for low- and moderate-income families, and the details
are found in our The Politics of Land Use (Praeger, 1973).

ENABLING LEGISLATION
OVERLOOKS PUBLIC FACILITIES

    The model enabling legislation is aimed at private uses and pri-
vate property, and public uses and facilities are virtually overlooked.
The idea was that you could have the kind of community you wanted
if you controlled private land, for this was where the uses most feared
were likely to take place. Again the target was commercial and industrial development. However, it is silent on the regulation of public
uses and public facilities, and this refers to institutional uses like
government office buildings and more important to the development-
setting facilities like highways, mass transit, sewer lines, water
systems, and recreational networks. The emphasis on private uses
also reflected the negative character of zoning and land-use control,
and it has only been relatively recently that the development effects
of the different public services have been at all widely recognized.
Most of the discussion in this section relates to zoning enabling
legislation and not planning. It is zoning that does the actual regulating
of land uses, and while planning may take into account public facilities,
the enabling legislation does not require that zoning apply to public
facilities and services like highways and the rest. Put another way,
it does not subject these public matters to local zoning.
    It has been a "law" of land use that if you get the public facilities,
the zoning will follow. We are not saying way it works this way, only
that it does, and if you can get the highways, the mass transit, the
water system, and, last but by no means least, the sewers, you can
get the zoning. Thus regulation of private property may not be enough,
and it may be missing the point. It is the public facilities that most
basically structure growth and land use, and private development
generally follows them; therefore if you control the public facilities,
you control development. Focusing on zoning private land may be
dealing with a manifestation rather than the cause, and it may have
less meaning; certainly a good case can be built for having the enabling
legislation stipulate that all things affecting development should be
included.
    State highway agencies, for example, do not normally have to pay
any attention to local zoning. This goes for the actual location of the
right-of-way—and it cannot be stopped by local zoning (for example,
putting the right-of-way in a residential zone)—and more important
the impact of the road on adjoining and nearby uses. Once the road
goes in, the local zoning must be altered to accord with the road.
This represents the facts of the situation, and it does not work the
other way around. For years, no one questioned even the right of the
highway agency to put the road wherever it was "needed," and if subdivisions or other areas had to give way, they did. This is exclusive
of the question of zoning.

It is obvious that putting a major highway through a neighborhood can drastically alter the character of the area, and the state builds most of the major roads in communities (the others are built by local highway agencies who are also exempt). Yet the state highway department is not subject to local regulations. The state legislation does not require this, and the state roads agencies are not about to restrict their options voluntarily in this respect—their job is not building good communities but good roads. Much research suggests that the two may be in conflict, and this says nothing about the motives or efficiency of the highway departments; they are simply doing their job.[16]

Why could the state not, in the enabling legislation, subject the state highway bureaucracy to local zoning and planning? We know of no place where they are currently subject to zoning, although some states like California do require a local review of proposed roads, including a possible veto; however, this is not zoning per se, and that is what we are discussing. This would take real courage on the part of the state legislators, who usually take their cues from the highway agency and not vice versa.

The same goes for sewer and water agencies, the kind that lay the lines and construct the sewage—"advanced wastewater treatment facilities"—and water plants (both functions have important consequences for development patterns), for mass transit authorities (rail transit lines have set development trends—for example, witness the development following the Mainline of the Pennsylvania Railroad out of Philadelphia), for airport authorities (important, but not as much as the sewer, water, and other transportation agencies), for park and recreation agencies (key in terms of providing buffers and thus shaping development), for public works departments of local government (local streets and perhaps other public facilities powers), and all other state and local agencies with any authority over any function having an impact on development, land use, and physical growth.

In some communities it may make sense for the more significant and development-shaping functions to be assigned directly to the planning agency, and this would provide it an operating "tool" for carrying out plans. This would provide a useful addition to the present purely regulatory powers, but this should be merely permitted on the part of the state and not mandated as we suggested in connection with regional and metropolitan planning agencies (Chapter 6).

It would even be desirable to have federal agencies brought under local planning and zoning, but this would have to be done by federal law and could not be accomplished solely by state action. We have already shown that it is being done voluntarily by at least one federal agency with programs in the San Francisco Bay Area, but we are suggesting that it become a matter of law. One way of doing this would be for Congress to pass legislation requiring federal agencies to abide by local planning and zoning, where the state requires its own agencies and those of local government to do the same. This would require

supplemental state legislation of course, specifying that local land
regulations apply to federal projects (as well as state and local ones).
Congress has this power, although again it would take some courage
on the part of the legislators, and some agencies would no doubt resist
the action. Even if federal legislation was approved along these lines,
its enforcement would by no means be automatic, and much experience
of the National Capital Planning Commission suggests this; the commission has review authority over all federal programs planned for
the National Capital Region, but perhaps as many as half of the agencies
fail to conform to the requirement.

Short of this Congress could pass legislation requiring federal
agencies to check with local planning and zoning authorities before
proceeding on any construction or funding of any local or state development project. This is done now under a federal administrative
regulation (A-95), but it does not extend to all projects affecting development, and the ''checking'' is done with metropolitanwide and regionwide agencies. The idea is to subject all federal activities to local
controls and to provide a ''local'' review, or one with the agencies
and bodies with the actual land development powers. The fact of the
matter is that regional agencies do not work all that closely with
local units; besides, the additional review would not hurt. Perhaps
this could be done through another executive order, possibly based
on the Intergovernmental Cooperation Act of 1968 or the Environmental
Policy Act of 1969. The simpler the process the better, but some action
is in order.

ENABLING LEGISLATION DOES NOT RELATE ZONING
TO THE PROVISION OF PUBLIC FACILITIES

Present state enabling legislation does not require that planning
or zoning be related directly to the provision of public facilities. To
a certain extent, it does this with subdivision regulations which deal
with this sort of thing, but this amounts to a major omission in the
legislation insofar as zoning is concerned. In our opinion, there should
be a clearer link between the most important of the land-use controls
and the provision of public facilities serving new development. This
applies mostly to facilities or services outside a new subdivision or
development but serving it.

Generally, the government has been seen as the vehicle to provide these facilities, and if they are not there when the development
is needed, the community should pick up the tab. There are some
variations to this, and this would include the situation where new
property owners are required to pay special assessments for improvements of principal benefit to them or where the developer pays for
facilities through the subdivision process, but generally it has meant

that the preexisting community foots the bill. Of course, in time the
development may pay for itself, and over again, but this is not true
immediately. The enabling legislation is silent on the point, and it
provides no means by which zoning can be used to finance the facilities
or is to be related to them at all. Yet this can be done.

There are some new ways that the controls and the facilities can
be linked, and the enabling legislation can address itself to the question.
This is in addition to subdivision regulations which can and do provide
for developers' financing of some public improvements like streets,
sidewalks, water and sewer lines, and land for certain public purposes
in subdivisions.[17] For example, developers can be given density
bonuses for providing certain facilities that are presently not part of
their responsibility. They could also be given the right to develop
only if the facilities are provided by them or if the facilities are already
available, although the bonus approach is better. These are not minor
suggestions, and they can have a great effect on development, on
developers' proposals and their solvency, and on the whole concept
of land use. The point is that the controls and the facilities should
be more closely and creatively related than they are at present.

Some communities now require that developers prove the existence
of "adequate public facilities" to serve new subdivisions before being
given final permission to go ahead with development, and this is tied
to the subdivision ordinance and covers such things as sewers, water,
police, schools, libraries, streets, fire, health, and other services.
Such a measure was put into effect in Montgomery County, Maryland,
in 1973, and no subdivision plan can be approved unless the county
determines that the facilities in the "service area" of the proposed
development are adequate to support it. In the case of roads, for
example, the county has to decide if existing roads in the area can
accommodate traffic to be generated from the subdivision, that is,
in addition to the present volume, and if not whether the necessary
roads are proposed on an adopted master plan and in the county or
state's five-year programs.

Other communities, such as Loudoun County in the Hunt Country
of Virginia, require the existence of the necessary facilities before
the zoning (prior to subdivision) is granted, and in their absence the
developer must provide them if he wants the zoning. This approach
has already had its impact, and the giant Levitt firm has been turned
down twice on this basis. Levitt proposed a massive subdivision in
the countryside on the scale of a "new town," and the wealthy residents of the country clearly do not want it and do not want to pay for
it. The firm is appealing the decision.

Ramapo, New York, has probably gone the furthest with the idea,
requiring developers to "score" a certain number of points before
getting the permission to develop, and the system allocates the largest
number of points for proposed developments with the required public
facilities already in existence and the lowest number of points for

those without them. The Ramapo plan, incidentally, has been upheld
in the state's highest court, and it is being watched closely by observers all over the country. Another similar plan is under consideration
in the California courts, and only time will tell its feasibility. Of
course, these cases are being decided on the basis of enabling legislation that does not address the question in the first place, which makes
the question blurry and based mostly on private property rights and
the proper extent of government regulatory power (does the Ramapo
plan involve a "taking" of private property without compensation,
barred under most state and the national constitutions?)

Probably some solution, whereby existing property owners do
not have to pay for new development and where the developers do not
have to provide funds of their own(which is passed on to the home
buyer), is the best way to proceed. The way this can be done is to
allow higher densities in situations where the facilities are not available and where the community wants them, charge the developer for
the additional facilities, and have the developer absorb the costs in
the higher land values (following the change in densities) and pass them
off to no one. This can be done without anyone paying since the developer buys land at its current zoning (lower density, lower values);
the local government changes the zoning to allow higher densities
(the value thus goes up); and the developer does not pass on the costs
for the facilities but absorbs them in the higher land values and the
greater number of sales with the greater densities.

We are not saying that this is the only way, but it does have the
advantage of catering to all the interests involved and to their pocket-
bookd—the citizens who do not want to pay for the facilities in taxes;
the developers who do not want to use their own funds for the facilities
and who do not in reality want to charge the home buyers since housing
prices will be higher and less competitive; and the new home owners
who are not charged for the facilities through higher home prices or
special assessments. It is a situation where everyone wins and no
one loses. The one catch, of course, would be the higher densities,
and the citizens' groups may oppose this. The argument also assumes
that the local government is not anxious to burden itself with new costs
and programs, an assumption that might not be true (they may want
the new power that goes with this).

In all likelihood, no change is needed in most states' enabling
legislation to build the "adequate public facilities" principle into the
subdivision process. The present legislation permits the localities
to provide for the orderly development of subdivisions, and this
includes requiring the developer to put in (and pay for) such improvements as streets, curbs, gutters, sidewalks, sewer and water lines,
and to set aside land for, say, schools, parks, open space, or other
public purposes. It is not much of a stretch of the law to require
that the developer prove that the existing public facilities in the area
are adequate to accommodate his subdivision, and that if he cannot

prove this, he cannot develop. To repeat, these facilities (as opposed
to the improvements in the subdivision) generally refer to those not
in the subdivision per se but nearby and serving it; a feeder road
(into and out of the subdivision) would be an example, and so would a
public school in the neighborhood.

The way it works in the communities that have it is that the
developer must obtain in writing a statement from the public roads
agency saying that the streets or highways serving the proposed subdivision can accommodate the additional traffic generated by the subdivision, or a statement from the school board that the elementary,
junior high, and high schools in the area have enough classroom space
to serve the children from the proposed subdivision. If the developer
cannot produce such statements or otherwise prove that the public
facilities are adequate (through his own research, for example), he is
turned down. In fact, in Montgomery County, the local government has
denied the right to subdivide on these grounds, and it is not just a
theoretical matter. It might be well to extend the principle in this
section to development outside of residential subdivisions as well—
that is, to apartment, commercial, industrial, and other comparable
proposed uses—for they all impact on public facilities. The residential
subdivider should not be the only one involved.

PLANNING AND ZONING ARE PERMISSIVE

Planning and zoning in the United States are permissive, meaning
that they are not required or mandated by state law. The point is that
the state permits them and does not require them of localities; nor
does the national goverment, which generally is not involved one way
or another. It is, of course, "required" on the part of landowners in
a community that has it, but we do not mean it in this sense. Put
more specifically, state enabling laws do not require planning, zoning,
and subdivision controls but "permit" them, and this is important in
and of itself. It tells you much about the states and the localities and
the general approach toward land use in this country, and it is also
a problem as we shall see shortly.

There are a couple of exceptions, however, and they appear to
be growing. We thereof see this as an entirely unhealthy trend. For
example, the states of Oregon, Washington, and California have revised
their enabling legislation to mandate local land-use controls.[10] In
these states they are not optional or permissive but required. Oregon
recently passed legislation making local planning and zoning compul-
sory. If the local government has no controls and is not making satis-
factory progress toward development then, the law says, the state can
step in and take over. Specifically, it gives the power to the state
Land Conservation and Development Commission, a new agency, and

it is authorized to go into the community and develop and administer the plans and regulations; this can be done without the participation of the city or county government. At the same time, if at a later date the locality decides to opt for land-use controls, it preempts direct state regulation—this again by state law (the state can preempt itself if it wants). As shown in Chapter 4, it appears that nearly all cities and counties in Oregon either already have the regulations or are in the process of developing them, and thus state action may not be necessary. But the principle is important, and it will have its effects.

It is not too much, we think, that the states consider mandating local land-use regulations. We do not make too much of the point, but only show several arguments for this. In the first place, it is realistic. Planning and zoning are popular in this county, and there is little likelihood of this changing, and Siegan (who opposes zoning) will almost certainly not prevail. Thus, if most areas are going to get the controls anyway in time, why not now? This eliminates a lot of confusion and bitterness as we saw in the Charlevoix case in an earlier chapter. Second, planning and zoning can help. They can improve land-use and development patterns and eliminate hazards and problems that might arise without them, and this is especially true in remote rural areas where unplanned development, overflowing septic tanks, despoilage of the environment, overnight resorts, indiscriminate removal of trees and other vegetation, and local indifference are common.

Third, we may have little choice in the long run whether we shall have planning and zoning; our choice may be only over who will do it. We now have a chance of giving the power to localities, and this, with proper state guidance, is where it belongs. If localities do not adopt the ordinances, they are inviting state and possibly even federal controls, and this is true whether they know it or believe it or not, or whether they think planning and zoning are infringements of private property rights. Certainly planning and zoning affect these rights, but we are going to have them anyway; so let us make the best of it. This is not necessarily our thinking, but the point has to be made. The issue is not really as ideological as it is frequently made (witness the interchange, much of it heated and most of it ideological, between the proponents and opponents of federal land-use planning legislation[*]) but practical, and it is the practical facts that will prevail, largely

---

[*]Congressmen and witnesses, in hearings on the Land-Use Planning Act of 1974, sought to make the issue planning versus no planning, land-use controls versus no land-use controls, government control versus no government control, and federal planning versus no planning. These are not the issues, but whether the federal government is going to assist subnational planning and zoning and how. We have the controls now, and we will have them in the future regardless of what the federal government does.

independent of any ideology or theory. We now have the chance to
develop and shape the controls the way we want them. Later we may
not be given the chance, and the federal government may not be as
generous as Oregon (and allow itself to be preempted). Once it gets
in, it may never leave.

Fourth, we are concerned that land-use decisions reflect, to the
extent possible, rationality, due process, and fairness to all involved.
The absence of a plan and zoning ordinance can mean, and often does
mean, control by some private power structure and even social pressure, factors that are hard to get at in the courts of law. There may
be more equity for developers (presumably the ones opposed to the
controls) in open land-use controls, which are written policy and are
made law and subject to public hearings, than the absence of these.
Developers, like the rest of us, can deal with law and written policy,
but the unwritten and invisible variety can be more arbitrary, emo-
tional, blatantly political, socially rooted, prejudiced, and downright
unfair.

Fifth and along the same lines, planning and zoning force communities to think in advance what they want and where they are going.
They are not really as much of an infringement on property rights as
they appear, once you get into them and see how they work (private
property owners can influence the public regulations), and, as noted,
the absence of either can represent greater infringements. The idea
is that planning and zoning make things more predictable, with everyone knowing what to expect. This has to increase personal security
for the citizens and promote financial stability for developers, and it
also means a heightened role for public officials, who are engaged
(under the controls) in truly important work. The payoffs are great
all the way around.

Finally, even if communities succeed in blocking zoning (the
greatest fear), they will probably get the controls in some other way.
For example, Houston, which has no zoning, has virtually the same
control through a detailed subdivision ordinance (covering many things
zoning does elsewhere including setbacks and applying both in the
city and five miles beyond it), site plan review, general plans, a
"major street plan" (that has guided most newly platted subdivisions
over the 40 years it has been in existence), and widespread deed
restrictions (the latter are common, deal with the same kind of things
zoning does such as permitted uses and lot size minimums, and can
be enforced by public authority).[10] And in Charlevoix, where they
turned down county zoning in 1974, groups are already busily at work
getting the twonships to adopt zoning, and most of them have cooperated.

NEEDED REVISIONS IN STATE ENABLING LEGISLATION

Virtually all states should revise and update their enabling legislation relating to local planning, zoning, subdivision controls, and official maps. Specifically, the folowing five ideas are proposed.

First, state enabling legislation should stipulate a single development ordinance. This means that the state law itself would cover all matters of community development including planning, zoning, subdivision control, and official map as well as building and housing codes, urban renewal and redevelopment, and public housing. This would require a single state law treating all these matters that are now treated separately and enacted at one time.

It is high time that the legislation be centralized at both the state and local levels, that a single enabling statute be provided for all programs regulating community development, and that a single local ordinance be required by the state statute for these programs. In the community this could be called a "development" ordinance or code, and it would cover all the areas mentioned in the first paragraph, ranging from zoning through public housing. This means that local governments would be compelled by state law to consolidate all their presently independent ordinances, codes, controls, and regulations in these areas such as the zoning ordinance, the subdivision ordinance, and the others. This will not be easy, for existing bureaucracies are found in each area (one in zoning, another in subdivision, and so on), and they will be threatened by the legal consolidation. They will assume, although they will not admit it publicly, that it will have substantive implications and that it may cut down on their powers or require staff reductions, and they will lobby against it in the state legislature and locally. The pressure against state action thus will not be so much in the state itself but from the localities.

Normal reform theory refuses to take these realities into account and argues that the attack should be directed at the "farmers" and "special interests" in the state legislatures, and this is why it has failed in the past. The states have been unwilling to act in this area because local interests and local governments do not want them to, and it cannot be attributed to the sinister forces from the rural areas and corporations. This is especially true since reapportionment has been ordered and implemented for state legislatures. * Now urban groups control most states, and we should be able to get the changes, or at least we shall no longer be able to blame the farmers.

---

*The Supreme Court decision applying the one-man one-vote principle to both houses of the state legislature was Reynolds v. Sims, 377 U.S. 533 (1964). This was based on the general finding of the Court that legislative apportionment plans based on other principles (areas, for example) were unconstituitonal. See Baker v. Carr, 369 U.S. 186 (1962).

The advantages of this approach are obvious, and it means greater coordination in the planning and developing of our communities. It provides more control for central elected and appointed officials, more central influence for citizens' groups, a single check point for developers, and easier comprehension and simpler communications for all of us. There will still be elements of decentralization, for a legal merger does not necessarily mean a practical, political, or policy one—but it is a step in the right direction.

The code should be broad enough to accommodate new types of land-use controls and to permit experimentation in this regard. It should encompass, for example, transferable development rights, a new concept whereby developers can acquire "development rights" from others and apply them to property where the market requires high-density uses (all landowners get a minimum of development rights, and they can buy, sell, and exchange these as market conditions dictate); various forms of "permit" systems (Chapters 4 and 6); government-backed private covenants and deed restrictions; and land trusts.*

Second, state legislation should provide flexibility to communities in the administration of their planning and land-use controls. State legislation is too detailed in this respect, and it should be simplified. It is important that the state provide for strict rules of due process and fairness in policy making and administration, but it is not necessary for the enabling law to spell out how often the planning commission should meet, where it should meet, how many years the members should serve, whether it should be independent of the governing body, or even whether it should exist. These matters should be left up to the localities.

Third, state enabling legislation should require local decisions to consider metropolitan, regional, and statewide factors. The present stipulations in this regard should be eliminated and new constraints added, and the most important of the present ones is that which restricts the "health, safety, and general welfare" requirement to the local community. New legislation should require a broader context, or, in other words, local government should be required to take into account factors and needs on a wider scale in making land-use decisions. Local considerations are certainly relevant, but they should not be the exclusive or sole concern as they are now. This would mean that local governments would have to consider the impact and the relationship of their planning, zoning, and other land-use decisions to such questions as regionwide sewage treatment plant, commercial center, gas station, pollution control, and low-income housing needs. Some of these things are presently covered by zoning, and others are

---

*We know of no place where the transferable development rights plan is in effect (exclusive of zoning that is), but it is very widely discussed in planning circles.

not but are, at the same time, affected by it; under a later proposal, all development would be covered. All are affected by planning and relate to it in some way.

We know of a case where a community governing body denied a sewage treatment plant in an area where technical studies showed it was needed, causing it to be located 15 miles from the population needing it. A local consideration prevailed over a "regional" one since the plant was to serve an area wider than a single jurisdiction; such a process is encouraged by current state enabling legislation. In the meantime, not only did this mean a delay in the opening of the plant with the associated higher costs of construction, but sewage overflows in the existing lines and plants for a longer period of time. The fact of the matter is that the governing body turned it down because of pressures of the neighbors who did not want it. We have also pointed to a situation above and in Chapter 2, where a community zoning ordinance does not permit consideration of factors other than "local" ones in land-use decisions (gas station case).

Although supplying no concrete examples, Richard Babcock cites potential situations where "broader" regional and metropolitan matters whould be considered by localities in land-use decisions. These are taken from the areas of transportation—land near major intersections or adjacent to "vehicular arteries," near water and water pollution—concerning zoning of land near lakes and rivers and the possible pollution of the water that flows into other communities; housing, requiring local zoning to consider "variation" and "inter-mixing" of densities and dwelling types (low-cost housing); and density, or the impact of density on regional transportation, recreation, and other public facilities, taking into account the effect of local decisions on a possible overburdening of these facilities and on the quality of services.[20] All of this should be built into the state enabling legislation according to Babcock, and local governments held to it.

Fourth, state enabling legislation should require that all community planning, zoning, and other land-use control ordinances apply to all uses, public and private alike. This follows the experiences of Hawaii and Vermont (statewide zoning) and New York (regional zoning), and it is something the states, and only the states, can do (it will take federal cooperation in regard to federal agencies). The states should mandate by law that, specifically, the state highway department, the state transportation agency (if separate from highways),[21] the state natural resources department,[22] the state education department (particularly if it funds local school construction), and other state agencies abide by local zoning and other local controls and be required to go through the same process as private property owners are in seeking to use or change the use of land. The law should apply to direct projects of these agencies (state highways) and the ones funded by them but carried out, say, by local governments (sewers). The state enabling legislation should also cover all local agencies and units

including special districts and authorities, especially those with
operating programs impacting on development. This is similar to the
way it is handled under federal regulations (A-95) although much
stronger. The federal orders require only "review and comment." 23

Highways, sewer plants and lines, water supply facilities, mass
transit line extensions, new airports and additions to existing ones,
new parks, and institutional facilities proposed by state and local
public agencies should fit into the local planning and zoning process
and be approved formally in that context. We should get away from the
idea of this or that specific approval and move toward simply "getting
approval for development." This is a goal of the single development
code concept, and the impact of development in general and in a
variety of particulars should by considered, matters now covered in
a series of ordinances and codes or sometimes not covered at all.
This follows the practice in the states and in Great Britain, and it
works. We also feel that the federal government should take steps on
its own to compel conformance of all federal projects (including grants)
to local planning, zoning, and subdivision requirements.

Fifth, state enabling legislation should concentrate on the positive
and on facilitating desirable development, not on the negative and
prohibiting undesirable development. The state legislation should not
even hint that localities divide all their land into "use districts" to
be applied city or countywide. They should drop "special exceptions,"
"variances," and the like and concentrate on good development and
land use. The communities should be given flexibility in other words
and be encouraged to set up a program whereby desired land uses are
stressed but not made too specific and whereby development is seen
as a cooperative venture between the local government and the private
developer.

The emphasis should be on what should be done and not what should
not; plans should be required as a matter of course; and planning
should be independent of zoning but not too independent (following the
states' and not local experiences). The state legislation should put
a premium on experimentation and innovation and should do nothing
to inhibit this. It should, in fact, suggest the use of new techniques
of development, and these might include

- planned unit development, or zoning providing a mixture of residential and commercial uses and administration with flexible legislative guidelines;
- cluster zoning, which concentrates housing in one portion of a
  subdivision and preserves the area saved in smaller lots in open
  space for use of the residents in common;24
- floating zone, or a provision of the zoning text that is applied only
  under special conditions and not put on the map at the time of the
  original zoning—and useful in transitional areas between residential
  and commercial development, or areas likely to change over time
  and which cannot be easily planned for over the long run;

- site plans, or a means by which final layout patterns can be determined under flexible standards by administrators, citizens, and
developers and facilitating decisions based on current needs and
not earlier concepts which stipulate rigid setbacks, height limits,
densities, open space, and the like—and useful in mixed commercial/
residential areas but applicable to all uses;
- vertical zoning, or a device allowing for different uses in the same
structure or, for example, shops on the bottom floors, offices
immediately above them, and apartments on the top floors;
- new town zoning, or special controls, flexible and general in nature,
applying to large residential subdivisions such as Columbia, Reston,
and Irvine Ranch and permitting all kinds of uses including commercial and industrial but leaving the specifics to later determination;
- unzoned or reserved areas, or specific areas set aside for experimentation and innovative techniques and including conventional
sites that might be used for residential, commercial, and industrial
purposes, and other sites such as historical, cultural, recreational,
or scenic areas.

There is plenty of room for innovation in planning and zoning, although
we have done little of it with our district, setback, lot size, and similar
requirements, and the state legislation can facilitate it or retard it.
In the past it has been the latter, and in the future it can be the former.

WHAT THE FEDERAL GOVERNMENT CAN DO

Finally, the federal government should enact a national land-use
policy, but the emphasis should be changed. It should require states
to broaden and alter their planning and zoning enabling legislation
along the lines suggested in this book, as a condition of receiving
federal planning grants, and to take up programs of specialized
(traditional) zoning for areas and uses like wetlands, coasts, flood
plains, power plants, and strip mining. It should also provide inducements to the states to create regional and metropolitan planning
agencies and state subdistricts (this should be done directly and not
through enabling legislation) and to give them wide planning powers
and perhaps some operating programs in the development area (see
Chapter 6). In fact, the federal government may well be the key here,
as some states will be reluctant to move otherwise; the federal grants
may move them.
Last, the federal land-use policy should provide assistance to the
states and bolster their statewide planning programs, but this should
be limited to planning and not cover statewide zoning or other direct
statewide regulation or "critical areas" control. These are the
avenues that are most promising, and the federal government can be

an enormous help. The federal government should also require its own agencies to follow local planning and zoning, and this could be done through the land use policy.

NOTES

1. Allen D. Manvel, Local Land and Building Regulation (Washington, D.C.: Government Printing Office, 1968).

2. Apparently this has happened at the metropolitan level (Chapter 5). See National Survey of Metropolitan Planning, prepared for the U.S. Senate Committee on Government Operations (Washington, D. C.: Government Printing Office, 1963), p. 4.

3. U. S. Advisory Committee on Zoning, Department of Commerce, A Standard State Zoning Enabling Act under Which Municipalities May Adopt Zoning Regulations, rev. ed. (Washington, D. C.: Government Printing Office, 1926). The document was first released in 1922.

4. U. S. Advisory Committee on City Planning and Zoning, Department, A Standard City Planning Enabling Act (Washington, D. C.: Government Printing Office, 1928).

5. See David C. Ranney, Planning and Politics in the Metropolis (Columbus, Ohio: Charles E. Merrill, 1969), Chap. 3.

6. See, for example, T. J. Kent, Jr., The Urban General Plan (San Francisco: Chandler, 1964), Chap. 1.

7. Barnet Lieberman, Local Administration and Enforcement of Housing Codes: A Survey of 39 Cities (Washington, D. C.: National Association of Housing and Redevelopment Officials, 1969).

8. The first study is Thad L. Beyle, Sureva Seligson, and Deil S. Wright, ''New Directions in State Planning,'' in Thad L. Beyle and George T. Lathrop (eds.), Planning and Politics (New York: Odyssey Press, 1970), pp. 14-35; and the second is Francine F. Rabinowitz and J. Stanley Pottinger, ''Organization for Local Planning: The Attitudes of Directors,'' Journal of the American Institute of Planners (January 1967): pp. 27-32.

9. R. Robert Linowes and Don T. Allensworth, The Politics of Land Use: Planning, Zoning, and the Private Developer (New York: Praeger Publishers, 1973), Chap. 3 (Zoning is King).

10. See the sections on Oregon and California in U. S. Senate, Committee on Interior and Insular Affairs, State Land-Use Programs (Washington, D. C.: Government Printing Office, 1974), pp. 7-17, 55-64.

11. Alexander Hamilton, James Madison, and John Jay, The Federalist Papers (New York: Mentor, 1961).

12. Richard Hofstadter, Social Darwinism in American Thought (Boston: Beacon, 1955), especially the Introduction.

13. See Scott Greer, Governing the Metropolis (New York: Wiley, 1962), especially Chap. 5.

14. Richard F. Babcock and Fred P. Bosselman, Exclusionary Zoning: Land Regulation and Housing in the 1970s (New York: Praeger Publishers, 1973).

15. It may show other things as well such as a lack of understanding of the issue, a desire to convert their homes to nonresidential uses if the need or opportunity arises, a lack of concern for aesthetic or environmental factors, a preference for mixed residential/commercial living, the absence of cars to travel distances for shopping or work, and a desire to sell their property for nonresidential uses. Figures presented by Siegan show lower-income, Democratic, and black precincts voting against zoning and higher-income, Republican, and white areas voting for it, and they are taken from Houston (1962) and other cities in Texas. Siegan says the strongest support for zoning comes from "middle-middle- to upper-middle-income homeowners" in areas with the newest houses. See Bernard H. Siegan, Land Use Without Zoning (Lexington, Mass.: D. C. Heath, 1972), pp. 25-29 (quote p. 26).

16. Helen Leavitt, Superhighway-Superhoax (Garden City, N. Y.: Doubleday, 1970).

17. For a survey of which facilities are paid for by the developer in localities in three states, see Ruth L. Mace and Warren J. Wicker, Do Single-Family Homes Pay Their Way? (Washington, D. C.: Urban Land Institute, 1968), Research Monograph 15.

18. American Law Institute, A Model Land Development Code, Philadelphia, April 15, 1974, pp. xx, 37.

19. David L. Stirton, "Deed Restrictions in the City of Houston," 3 pp. (mimeographed), May 10, 1968. See also Land Use Without Zoning.

20. Richard F. Babcock, The Zoning Game (Madison: University of Wisconsin Press, 1966), Chap. 10.

21. State Transportation organization is treated in Richard G. RuBino, A Quest for Integrated and Balanced Transportation Systems in State Government (Tallahassee: Florida State University, 1971).

22. State administrative organization in this area is covered in Elizabeth H. Haskell and others, Managing the Environment (Washington, D. C.: Smithsonian Institution, 1971).

23. See "Areawide Review of Federal Grant Applications: Implications for Urban Management," Urban Data Service Report (February 1972), International City Management Association.

24. The technique is discussed in detail in William H. Whyte, The Last Landscape (Garden City, N. Y.: Doubleday, 1968), Chap. 12.

8

ZONING, STATES, AND
THE COURTS

To attempt to show trends in judicial decisions on zoning and land-use regulation is risky at best, and this is the task of this chapter. The book is on state planning and zoning, and our emphasis in this chapter will be much the same, in the sense that we treat state zoning first. But the states are also involved in local land-use controls, and we seek to examine recent court cases in this area as well. We shall be particularly interested in pointing to any links that the states may have to local cases, especially in terms of enabling legislation, and of course the cases are heard in state courts, which suggests a rather strong state involvement.

STATE COURTS

Most of the case law in zoning and land-use control can be traced to the state courts, and most of it, quantitatively, deals with local zoning decisions. State zoning and regulation are rarely involved, largely because of the limited incidence of these activities, and planning at either the state or local level is seldom the issue because of the typical advisory nature of this function (thus it is not as often contested). By and large, the federal courts are not involved in zoning cases, the Supreme Court of the United States almost never. There is no particular reason for this other than that most parties to disputes have preferred to use the state courts since frequently the issues involve a federal constitutional question, and thus the federal courts could be tapped but are not. This suggests a strategic choice, and of course a decision of the state courts can always be appealed to the federal courts (with cause); perhaps this explains why the state courts are used as much as they are, with local options being exhausted first.

The United States Supreme Court has considered very few zoning cases, and since its famous Euclid decision, it has ruled on the subject only four times, in 1927, 1928, 1962, and 1974 (see the cases below). All had to do with local zoning and land regulation and not planning or state zoning. What this has meant is that most of the litigation in land-use regulation has been left within the province of the state courts, and it has been an important part of their workload.[1] Some State supreme courts, in fact, consider over 30 zoning cases a year, which has to cut into their other work.

The state judiciary is unitary in structure, with two or three levels depending on the state:

1. trial courts such as district, circuit, superior, and county courts (the names vary by the state);
2. intermediate appellate courts, found in a minority of states;
3. the highest court or court of last resort, also an appellate body, and named variously supreme court, supreme court of appeals or court of appeals (it is important that not all the states' highest court is called "supreme court").

Cases are generally brought in the trial court and may be appealed all the way up through the intermediate court to the highest court in the state, and after this, if a federal question is involved, they may be taken to the United States courts.

Most states elect their judges, some on a partisan ballot, which distinguishes them from federal courts, and state courts are subject to a variety of pressures from a variety of sources. Although the pressures are less direct than in the other two branches, judges seem especially influenced by the values of their social class, their personal background, group identities, and the philosophical outlook which all of this more or less compels.[2] The influence of parties and interest groups is evident, but is probably more indirect than direct and reflected more in general attachments of the judges and their early environment than specific contacts and "lobbying." We know of no studies along these lines on zoning decisions per se, although some research has shown Republican, Anglo-Saxon, and Protestant judges more sympathetic to the claims of the private sector than Democratic, ethnic group, and Catholic judges.[3] We should say, however, that this may have little bearing on zoning and land-use cases since they commonly involve more than a simple contenst between the government on the one hand and private interests on the other, a point that will become clearer as we proceed.

STATE LAND-USE REGULATION

It appears that the state courts have been more than tolerant of
state land-use regulation than local controls although comparisons
are difficult since there are so few cases on state zoning. Fred
Bosselman and his associates have suggested that "local land-use
regulations have not been treated by the courts with the same deference
shown . . . state regulations," and this may be attributed to the wider
area covered by these regulations and the higher level of government
involved (which may make them easier to sustain).[4] Still the record
here is far from perfect, and there are instances of the courts ruling
that the state has gone too far and overstepped its bounds. Much
depends on the specifics, the particular state, and the extent and impact
of the regulations, and much of it cannot be traced to anything concrete.

The courts have typically been sympathetic to a wide construction
of state powers in this area and have tended to side with public over
private rights—and this covers such matters as state zoning of shorelines and coastal areas, state regulation of wetlands, direct state
control of flood plains, regional planning set up by the state, airport
zoning under state powers, and general state zoning (very limited,
and fewer cases). General state zoning is obviously the most important
of these, but it has been listed last since it is so uncommon and since
there are so few cases dealing with it. The state specialization in this
field is zoning in particular areas such as wetlands and flood plains
(Chapter 5) and most of the cases are found here.

In a recent one in Wisconsin, for example, Just v. Marinette County
(1972), a state court upheld the Wisconsin Shoreland Zoning Law of
1970, which regulates land 1,000 feet back from all lakes and 300
feet from river basins.[5] The court ruled that the measure does not
represent an unreasonable exercise of the police power and that the
state is perfectly justified in limiting the use of private property to
its largely natural state to prevent harm to public rights. The plaintiff (Just, the landowner, or the party suing) had argued that the law's
restrictions on his land (nonresidential use, nonpermanent buildings)
were a "taking without compensation," which is barred under the
state and federal constitutions, specifically in the latter the Fifth and
Fourteenth Amendments. The court disagreed. Incidentally, the
county was listed in this suit because local governments in the state
have the authority to do the actual regulating under the Shoreland
Zoning Law, with the state stepping in only if the county fails to exercise
the power.

A Maryland court decided similarly on a state wetlands enactment.
In Potomac Sand and Gravel Co. v. Governor of Maryland, the Maryland
Court of Appeals, the state's highest court, sustained the legislature's
wetlands act, which prohibits the dredging of tidal waters or marsh-

lands in certain areas.[6] Ruling that the law represented a valid use
of the state's police powers, the court held that it was not a taking as
the plaintiff argued, but merely a limitation on the use of property
requiring no compensation. (The Fourteenth Amendment to the Constitution requires the states to guarantee due process, and included
in this protection, as interpreted by the courts, is the Fifth Amendment prohibition against government taking private property "without
just compensation.") In upholding the decision of the trial court, the
higher body described the ecological values coming from the prohibi-
tions on sand, gravel, and other forms of dredging and said that its
views were consistent with current trends considering the preservation
of natural resources as within the police powers.

Along these same lines, the Connecticut Supreme Court approved
a state law regulating development in flood plains and, in Vartelas v.
Water Resources Commission, denied a landowner's claim that the
legislation amounted to a taking without compensation; it ruled that
the law was a proper exercise of the police power and that it was
applied reasonably.[7] The statute that was sustained authorized the
state Water Resources Commission to set a line beyond which no
structure or encroachment could be placed without special permission.

The position of the judiciary on regional planning appears particularly favorable, and this refers to regional planning established directly
by state law and not to that authorized under state enabling legislation
(see Chapter 6). For instance, the California Supreme Court, in a
wide-ranging decision on the merits of regional planning, affirmed
the constitutionality of the Tahoe Regional Planning Agency (established
in 1970–Chapter 6). In People ex rel Younger v. County of El Dorado,
the justices turned back the appeal of local governments that had
challenged the legality of the regional organization.[8] The localities
argued that the legislation violated the "home rule" provisions of the
California constitution and asked that it be invalidated on these grounds.
The agency, which was formed by the states of California and Nevada
through interstate compact, has the power to plan and develop controls
for the Tahoe Basin, and it has done both. It is instructive that local
governments rarely object to state "planning" so long as it does not
involve implementation (regulation), and if they cannot stop the latter
in the state legislature, it is clear that they are prepared to go to the
courts. The courts are, in this sense, a sort of the last tactic available
in the political struggle and are resorted to when all else fails.

In a similar development, the California Court of Appeals upheld
the San Francisco Bay Conservation and Development Commission's
power to prevent filling of the bay and, in Candlestick Properties Inc.
v. San Francisco Bay Conservation and Development Commission,
ruled that the agency's authority was part of the police power of the
state and that its exercise did not involve an infringement on the rights
of the plaintiff (or a taking without compensation).[9] In the decision,
the court made a distinction between eminent domain or direct

acquisition of private property requiring compensation and police power involving regulation, and it held that the commission's controls were within the regulatory sphere and thus did not involve the taking issue.

Established by state law in 1969, the conservation agency was given the power to plan and regulate uses in the bay area, including the authority to issue "permits" for all development and filling (filling was the issue in Candlestick); in reasoning like that used in Potomac Sand, the court in Candlestick said that the definition of "police power" changes over time and that as the state develops politically and socially so does the police power. This suggests an ever-widening focus in the courts, and it seems to be evident in terms of local controls as well, as we shall see shortly. It also shows that the state's police power can be altered in much the same way the Constitution of the United States has been over the years, to conform with present realities and the demands of a changing society.

There is very little to go on in the area of general state zoning, and we have no details on the cases from Hawaii, the only state to have it in the comprehensive sense. In fact, in their review of Hawaii's land-use legislation, lawyers Bosselman and Callies report little litigation, although one important case on state zoning is currently pending.[10] Apparently Vermont's recent legislation setting up a state-wide land planning and regulation system has been approved in the courts (see In re Barker Sargent Corporation), and Maine's Site Location Law has also passed a key judicial test in a recent ruling (In the Matter of Spring Valley Development).[11] The 1970 Vermont measure required state permits for most residential, commercial, and industrial development, and while the Maine law was aimed mostly at industrial and commercial uses, the court in Spring Valley ruled that the legislation also covered residential development, arguing that subdivisions sold for a profit were in effect "commercial" offerings and thus subject to the controls. Also in Spring Valley the court said that the state law was designed to protect the public health and welfare and that it was therefore within the scope of the police power delegated by the state legislature. In this light, it is entirely reasonable, the court held, that limits be put on the use of private property.

On the other side of the ledger, some state regulatory controls have been struck down by the courts, mostly on the grounds that they went beyond the limits of reasonableness and the proper bounds of the police power. Of course, an element of judgment almost has to be involved here, and where a given court or judge may view a set of regulations constitutional, another may not.

An Ohio Appellate Court, for instance, ruled against a series of regulations issued by a special airport zoning board set up by state law to control land-use around Wright Patterson Air Force Base near Dayton, and a Maine court found that the state's Wetlands Act left property owners with commercially valueless land and therefore, as applied, could not be sustained.[12] In both situations, steps are being taken in an attempt to salvage the general powers for the state, and in both cases it was the specifics that were found unacceptable and not the principle of regulation per se.

In a case more important to the "taking issue" (Bosselman and associates) than state land regulation, the Supreme Court in Pennsylvania Coal v. Mahon (1922) invalidated a state law regulating certain coal mining practices on the grounds that it was beyond the police power and constituted a "taking" without compensation.[13] Although an old case without much bearing on current state controls, the decision was pertinent to later land-use case law in that it established the principle that if regulation goes too far, it will be recognized as a taking without compensation. This, as noted, is prohibited under the Fourteenth Amendment provision requiring the states to guarantee due process of law to all the citizens and under the Fifth Amendment stipulation requiring compensation for the deprivation of property (applies to the states through the Fourteenth Amendment).

In all, the record of state zoning in the courts has been a good one. It is clear that the states have been successful in drawing up legislation that can meet constitutional and legal standards and in applying it in a fair and reasonable manner. And the courts in the main seem willing to follow the state legislatures' opening new vistas and expanding the application of the "police power" as new conditions arise. One especially notable trend is the willingness of the judiciary to incorporate new concepts within the subjects to be regulated and the considerations to be taken into account in the regulation—or at least the Potomac Sand, Just, Candlestick Properties, and Spring Valley cases suggest this. Let us now turn to local zoning with a special view toward identifying those areas of local controls most susceptible to state legislation and guidelines.

LOCAL ZONING CASES

Supreme Court

Zoning was found to be constitutional in the first case on the matter ever to reach the Supreme Court of the United States, Village of Euclid v. Ambler Realty Co., and it was the Euclid decision that sustained zoning as the proper exercise of the police power of the states.[14] The Court did not mean by this to put no limits on zoning or its exercise in particular situations, and in fact set up some important standards to determine the validity of particular zoning provisions or applications. In other words, after Euclid, zoning was to be decided on a case-by-case basis, and whether it was to be accepted in any given community depended on the particular facts and specifics of the situation.

184 THE STATES AND LAND-USE CONTROLS

The Euclid ruling also established the "presumption of validity" principle, under which as long as the legislative action (zoning) is "fairly debatable," the (legislative) judgment is to be allowed to control, and the courts are not to substitute their judgment for it. This doctrine was also to put the burden of proof on the party aggrieved by the municipal action (developer, landowner)—to show that the zoning was not in the public interest—and it clearly related to the whole idea of separation of powers (the courts, in general, would stay out of the legislative sphere). We come back to this point later in the chapter.

The Court quickly took up another zoning case, in 1927, and in Zahn v. Board of Public Works upheld a second ordinance on grounds that the city decided the controls promoted the general welfare and that the Court had found no reason to substitute its judgment for the city's.[15] However, in a slight reversal, the Supreme Court ruled in Nectow v. Cambridge (1928) that a particular zoning classification was invalid in that it conflicted with the due process clause of the Fourteenth Amendment.[16] Specifically, it held that the landowner had been deprived of his property without due process and compensation since the regulation amounted to a "taking." It is important to note, however, that this action did not hold zoning unconstitutional, only its application in this particular case with these particular circumstances. In fact, the landowner was in an ideal position to prove his point because he had a signed contract showing what his land was worth without the new zoning classification (his land was put in the residential category, and the contract was based on its previous industrial use).

In the "post-Nectow" period as Babcock and Bosselman call it, the Court rarely looked at a zoning case, and it was not until 1962 and then until 1974 that it again considered the matter.[17] In the 1962 case, Goldblatt v. Town of Hempstead, the Court upheld a city regulation barring the operation of a gravel pit and said that the owner had not proved the municipal action unreasonable under the police power (presumption of validity).[18] The owner, a sand and gravel mining concern, was contesting a city ordinance limiting excavating below the local water table (25 feet down), and the firm charged that the regulation was a confiscation of the entire mining utility of the property for which no compensation was provided. The Court was not impressed.

And in Village of Belle Terre et al., Appellants v. Bruce Borass et al., the latest case the Court has taken (1974), the justices sustained a local zoning ordinance limiting development to single-family homes and occupancy to families or groups of not more than two unrelated individuals.[19] The village ordinance was challenged on several grounds, one of the most important of which was the constitutional right to travel that has been interpreted (in other cases) to include the right to "enter and abide."[20] Actually the case involved more than two unrelated persons living in the same house, including both male and female and unmarried, and thus another element came into the picture (and may have had something to do with the decision).

The reading on Belle Terre is unclear since no basic zoning question was involved and since it does not relate too directly to any of the major zoning issues of the day such as exclusionary or racially restrictive practices. At the same time, the case does suggest that the present Court is not willing to tamper with local zoning ordinances which are becoming more restrictive by the day, and in fact there was an aspect of restrictiveness in this situation. In other words, the decision hints that the Court (in this case, Justice Douglas plus the conservatives) will line up on the side of the suburbs and not minorities, newcomers, or property owners; Douglas can be considered an "environmentalist liberal" (see below), and the more conservative members might be expected to support the suburban approach to zoning. The ruling also tells us nothing about the Court's position on regional zoning, metropolitan planning, or statewide land-use controls, even though it does (in a footnote) recognize the work of Congress in promoting state zoning and the progress of Vermont in this respect.

In an important dissent to Belle Terre, Justice Marshall argued that the ordinance violated the constitutional rights of the appellees including the rights of association, privacy, and equal protection of the laws under the First and Fourteenth Amendments, and he disagreed with the Court majority that the ordinance bore a rational relationship to the fulfillment of legitimate government objectives (or the police power). It is worth pointing out that Marshall is the Court's only black, and he and Justice Brennan, also a dissenter in the case, might be described as "minority group" liberals and distinguished from Douglas in this respect.

Another decision should be mentioned before leaving the Supreme Court, Berman v. Parker (1954), and although it had nothing to do with zoning per se, it has probably influenced the thinking of some judges on the subject, and it has a bearing on the theme of this chapter.[21] The case concerned urban renewal in the District of Columbia, and it has been widely read as upholding these powers even though it dealt with a federal instrumentality and not a city operating under state legislation (the latter is the one with the urban renewal powers in this country). Its link to zoning is its wide definition of the police power.

Justice Douglas, writing for the majority, held that the police power cannot be limited to such specifics as sanitation, health, and public safety and encompasses broader considerations such as "aesthetics" and beauty as well. If applied to zoning, this could have a major effect and lead to the sustaining of all sorts of controls that were unclear (legally) under traditional concepts, and it appears to have had its influence in this regard. The ruling also broadened the purposes for which private property could be taken by government to include, in addition to that needed for direct government use (highways, sewage plant), that which served a "public benefit." Traditionally, with few exceptions such as private utilities and railroads, it had been assumed that land could be taken by government only for "government" use; the Constitution uses the term "public use," and so do many state constitutions, to designate the purpose for government taking of property. In urban renewal, private land is condemned by local government and then sold, at a markdown, to private developers who use it largely for private purposes.[22]

State and Federal Cases on Regionalism

The Supreme Court in Euclid did not say that the municipality must prevail in all instances, that is, when conflicts with wider interests are involved, and in fact it suggested that there would be some situations in which municipal interests would have to give way to broader ones. Of course, these things are difficult to determine, and it amounts to a judgment as to whether the municipal or broader interests should prevail in any case or even what they are, but at least the Court was setting up some limits to municipal exclusivity. We noted in Chapter 7 that state enabling legislation may restrict municipal zoning decisions to "local" considerations, and this makes it even harder for the courts to rule against localities on these grounds. But let us take a look at the record.

An early decision in this area was Edwards v. California, and in it the Supreme Court justices voided state action barring the migration of "Okies" to California unless certain conditions were met in that it obstructed the "right to travel"; the case is important because it had an influence on later interpretations of local zoning ordinances excluding certain groups of residents.[23] A Michigan court likewise invalidated a local ordinance under which a landowner had been denied the permission to build a large manufacturing facility on the grounds that the operation would be of great benefit to the residents of the state as a whole.[24] The court also held that the facility was in the interests of the local residents, but the point is that it was broader interests and not purely local ones that governed the judge's determination of what zoning action was in the "general welfare." The police power and the public interest, in other words, were not seen strictly in terms of the welfare of a single municipality.

New Jersey courts seem to have taken the lead in considering regional criteria in local zoning decisions, and the Pennsylvania courts are not far behind. In Oakwood at Madison, Inc. v. Township of Madison, a superior (lower) court in New Jersey found a local zoning ordinance void in its entirety because it neglected "regional" factors.[25] Specifically, the court held that the ordinance was not consistent with the state "general welfare" requirements and that the municipality could not ignore the housing needs of the region nor, indeed, those of its own less fortunate residents. The township ordinance had zoned most of the vacant land in the community into one- and two-acre residential minimums with high floor space requirements, and local officials argued that this would provide balanced housing (the township was not wealthy), encourage the in-migration of higher-income people, and protect drainage systems where greater densities might result in floods and dangers to underground water resources. In a similar ruling in 1972, a New Jersey court struck down another zoning ordinance and launched a strong verbal attack on the common practice of equating the "general welfare" with the narrowest and most prejudiced of local desires.[26] In a somewhat earlier decision in the same state, Kunzler v. Hoffman (1966), the court rejected the notion that the general welfare was simply the welfare of the locality in question and mandated a zoning permit for a facility of regionwide benefit (the township had denied it).[27]

Finding regional housing needs to be pertinent, a Michigan court in 1971 held that there was a need for the reformulation of the "general welfare" as it applied to zoning and refused to grant a local zoning action the traditional "presumption of validity."[28] This case raises a broader legal question, which, although dealt with in Euclid, is apparently still subject to a variety of interpretations, and presumption of validity was denied because the locality had clearly overlooked a nationwide and state housing shortage. The decision was issued by the Michigan Court of Appeals, an intermediate body, which overturned local zoning banning a mobile home park (on grounds that the principal purpose was the exclusion of a certain class of residential dwellers). The court also noted that the "general welfare" had become the means by which communities can avoid responsibility for land uses of substantial benefit to wider areas and populations.

In perhaps one of the most far-reaching decisions ever handed down by a state court, Pennsylvania's highest tribunal held an ordinance with a four-acre minimum lot size unconstitutional on grounds that it violated the rights of newcomers, this in National Land and Investment Co. v. Easttown Township Board of Adjustment (1965).[29] As Bernard Siegan has suggested, this may be one of the first times that the public was put on both sides of a land dispute—for in the past the issue was between the property owner and the municipality.[30] Now the "public interest" figured in both. This is not a minor point, and we treat it in greater detail later. It is instructive that Babcock, Bosselman, Callies, et al. seem to consider the zoning struggle as pitting the government against private interests, while Siegan and our Politics of Land Use lean more to the position that it is one between citizens' associations and developers; the latter view sees government (municipalities) acting in the interests of one or the other and not apart from these interests.

In the National Land case, the court also said that the municipality, an exclusive Mainline township near Philadelphia, was seeking to use zoning to head off future burdens implicit in metropolitan living and that in the process it infringed on the rights of property owners as well. Although the decision applied to a specific provision of a specific ordinance as applied to a specific parcel, it has stimulated a good deal of interest and has had a bearing on other cases. For instance, the head of a suburban real estate group applauded the ruling and told the Philadelphia papers that had the four-acre zoning gone unchallenged, "sociology would have triumphed once more over traditional values."[31] It is true that the chief justice of the Pennsylvania Supreme Court in 1965, John C. Bell, Jr., has been an outspoken critic of government intrusions in the private sphere (wills, property), a point stressed in the Philadelphia papers and thus "made" an issue in the press, but it would be a mistake to assume this court and others like it are moved solely or even principally by this concern. The point is that a variety of groups without these conservative views support this position as well, and this would include liberals interested in housing for blacks and poor whites ("minority group" liberals), blacks seeking better living and educational opportunities, civil rights organizations like the National Association for the Advancement of Colored People (NAACP) and low-income whites who have suffered under restrictive zoning practices. The U. S. Civil Rights Commission, for example, recently asked for legislation requiring states assisted under federal community development programs to set up new metropolitan agencies with the power to override local zoning ordinances that stand in the way of low-income housing and integration.[32]

Thus you may have a line-up something like this:[33]

> . . . a public hearing on 5-acre zoning [in one of the two communities studied] held in June 1973 produced the following alignment: opposed—large landowners, developers, speculators, working class whites, farmers, blacks, and open-housing and civil rights groups; favored—middle and upper-middle economic level citizens' groups, wealthy estate owners, and environmental organizations. This represents a change in the typical, or expected, pattern.

In another somewhat similar case, the Pennsylvania Supreme Court again held large-lot zoning void, in this situation two- and three-acre minimums, and suggested that one acre may be the maximum size permissible under the police power. This was in In re Mt. Builders, Inc. v. Township of Concord, and although again it would be impossible to apply the ruling to all other cases with large-lot zoning or similar restrictions (the specifics of this case must be taken into account), it certainly has some relevance to the broader questions of exclusionary zoning and regionalism.[34] The recent Pennsylvania and New Jersey cases, incidentally, seem remarkably like the dissent of Justice Frederick Hall in Vickers v. Township Committee of Gloucester Township (1962),in which the New Jersey judge unleashed a virtual barrage against municipalities that use zoning to build walls around themselves.[35] Arguing that the general welfare transcends the "artificial" boundaries of any locality, he also got into the unintended but real consequences of zoning as well as the unstated but intended purposes, hinting perhaps at racial, class, social, and ethnic factors. He additionally raised some intriguing questions about the court's acceptance of the validity of municipal actions on the face of it and proposed a much wider judicial role. The case involved had to do with a municipal zoning ordinance that excluded all trailer parks from its borders (the majority upheld it), clearly a major concern of suburban residents.

In probably the most recent case on the subject, Construction Industry Association of Sonoma County v. City of Petaluma (1974), a federal court ruled in favor of "regionalism" over and against a strict municipal zoning regulation calling for specific growth controls.* Petaluma is a small town in northern California that, by law, strictly limited new housing and adopted a plan to do this in 1972. The plan permits the addition of a maximum of 2,500 new housing units over a five-year period, or 500 a year, and it was appealed by the builders in the area. Located on the outer fringes of the San Francisco metropolitan area and under some urban pressures, the city has sought to put a lid on development on two principle grounds: remaining within the existing water and sewer facility capacities and preserving its "small-town" character. More particularly, the federal court for the Northern District of California held that the zoning legislation violated the Constitution's provisions guaranteeing the "right to travel," and it appears that the builders took the case to the federal courts to improve their chances; the California courts have been notably prone to approve municipal zoning and wide interpretations of the police power, and some California builders also charge that the state courts ignore other states' cases invalidating restrictive zoning ordinances. The city in any event is planning to appeal, and this is no doubt one to watch.

Another pattern is evident here, and that is deciding one way and talking another. In a case heard not too long ago, Valley View Village, Inc. v. Proffett, a federal court spoke the language of regionalism, but came down on the side of the municipality.[36] While finding that Valley View, Ohio (near Cleveland), was not a self-contained community but only a fragment of the metropolitan region, the U. S. Court of Appeals nevertheless declined to overrule zoning in which the locality had placed its entire land area in a residential zone. It said only that the community should not have to close its eyes to development needs beyond its borders (perhaps as required by state enabling legislation).

---

*Oral Decision, January 17, 1974; Written Opinion, April 26, 1974. Supreme Court Justice William O. Douglas recently issued a stay of decision, pending appeal.

However, as Richard Babcock alertly pointed out, the court did not require the municipality to "open its eyes" to such factors.[37]

Cases Upholding Wide Local Powers

The courts appear to be increasingly upholding wider zoning and land-use control powers on the part of local governments and their agencies. There seems to be a clear tendency for the courts to take a broader view of the police power in this respect, and they have in recent years ruled in favor of the municipalities in such areas as historic zoning, down-zoning (decrease in densities), stronger subdivision and flood plain controls, zoning based on aesthetic considerations, plans restricting development to the capacities of existing public facilities, and others. At the same time, there is another conflicting pattern, and that is a trend toward judicial invalidation of some zoning and land-use ordinances, especially, it appears, the exclusionary variety. The two patterns are mutually exclusive no matter how you cut it, and they move on simultaneously. There is probably no way they can be compatible (some have tried) or placed on the same side of the continuum, and we shall not attempt to do so. We do not, in other words, see any rational pattern—that is, the judges are consistent from one state or court to the next, and a single standard is involved—and this comes after an examination of many of the cases on the subject. The fact of the matter is that the courts simply do not see the same or similar circumstances in the same way, and they decide differently; it is also no doubt true that the judges are under different pressures depending on the circumstances and the time frame.

The courts have been somewhat more inclined to uphold zoning for historic purposes lately, and this should provide an indication of their willingness to take the broader view of the police power and the general welfare. This is all the more important with the spread of historic zoning, once used almost exclusively in a few cities like Charlestown, Alexandria (Va.), and New Orleans, and by no means has the question been a settled one among legal experts.

In Owen E. Hall v. Village of Franklin, et al., a Michigan Circuit Court judge sustained zoning creating a historical district and reclassifying land from commercial to historical residential, and denying the plaintiff's claims that the zoning was a confiscation without just compensation, the court upheld the municipal action as a proper exercise of the police power.[38] In another ruling on the subject, an Illinois court approved historical zoning as falling within the general welfare. The court in Rebman v. City of Springfield held that a city ordinance putting property around Lincoln's home in a special class was not confiscatory or unreasonable, notwithstanding that property values were diminished as a result or that they would be higher without the particular regulation.[39]

Similarly, a California decision left standing a local ordinance designed to preserve "Old Town," a historic district in San Diego, and declared that the measure contributed to the "general welfare" and was compatible with the police power.[40] Courts in New Mexico, by the same token, have upheld detailed provisions of local zoning relating to the size of windows in the historic areas of Santa Fe, in New York have sustained the city landmarks ordinance, and in Rhode Island have approved the regulation of design in historic districts.[41] There seem to be few exceptions to the pattern, and it tells us much about pushing back the limits of the police power in zoning,

The courts are not of one mind on down-zoning, however, or on a decrease in residential densities or shift from commercial or industrial to residential use (rezonings), although they are in the main, it seems, inclined to uphold it. This may become clearer in the future. One court recently made a distinction between down-zoning in an essentially rural area as opposed to the suburbs, suggesting that the action might be more reasonable in the former where the need for higher-density uses and housing is not as great. But whether this distinction has general applicability cannot be known, and the ruling also conveniently served the court's purposes at the moment (it upheld the zoning in a rural environment and was not faced with the sticky problem of deciding in a more explosive suburban scene). In Steel Hill Development, Inc. v. Town of Sanbornton, a federal court okayed a significant down-zoning in New Hampshire, involving a rezoning from a higher-density residential use permitting "cluster" (allowing concentration and deviation from normal lot sizes) to a "forest conservation" zone with a six-acre minimum lot size requirement and a prohibition against clustering.[42] (Developers nearly always favor cluster since it means lower building, lower improvement and public facilities costs and better margins.)[43]

The builder, Steel Hill Development, charged in a sharply worded suit that the down-zoning bore no relationship to the health, safety, morals, or general welfare as required by New Hampshire enabling legislation and told the court that it substantially reduced the value of its property. In an agonizing decision, the court denied that the action was a taking without compensation but called the rezoning "severely restrictive" and said that its position should not be taken as a general approval of six-acre zoning. This point is important because this was a federal court, and the decision could have been widely interpreted as a precedent for large-lot zoning with high minimums. Yet the political balancing act of the court was nothing short of a stroke of brilliance and is reminiscent of Justice Marshall's in Marbury v. Madison (1803).[44] It is also worth noting that New Hampshire's enabling legislation is broad and provides few specifics and guidelines, and this may make it easier for the courts to sustain actions under it (it could also have the opposite effect if the specifics were too traditional or constraining, and much depends on the particular nature of the "specifics").

With more gusto, the Maryland Court of Appeals recently upheld a
down-zoning in the city of Rockville on the outskirts of the District
of Columbia. In Mayor and Council of Rockville v. Raymond E. Stone
et al., the court sustained the city's changing the zoning from industrial to single-family residential on the grounds that all use of the
property was not denied and that the land (therefore) had not been
unconstitutionally confiscated.[45] The higher body reversed the trial
court ruling that since two-thirds or the greater part of the value of
the property was lost through the change in classification, the rezoning
was a "taking" and thus illegal, and rejected the property holders'
arguments of financial "hardship" and "disaster." Some legal scholars
have suggested that the dividing line between a taking and legitimate
regulation may be a two-thirds reduction, but this is not necessarily
accepted by the courts, and besides, it is almost impossible to determine the precise effects of down-zonings (without a written contract
as in Nectow).[46]

Two recent cases on flood plain zoning suggest a similar pattern.
A California Appellate Court, in Turner v. County of Del Norte, upheld
a flood plain regulation and ruled that it did not involve a taking and
merely formalized the natural qualities of the land.[47] And in Turnpike
Realty v. Town of Dedham, the Massachusetts Supreme Judicial Court
sustained a particularly strict set of flood plain controls.[48] The plaintiff in the Massachusetts case owned about 70 acres of land, most of
which was in low swamp, and argued that the regulations caused an
88-percent reduction in the value of his property. Citing a United
States Supreme Court decision where a 90-percent diminution in value
was held not to be a taking, the Massachusetts court said that the
controls fell within the scope of the police power and were not an
exercise of eminent domain without compensation.

The question of aesthetics has long been an uncertain one in zoning
law, and it was not clear for years that perhaps outside certain well-
defined historic districts, it could be used as a base of zoning actions.
Even in these areas it was not an entirely established fact as to just
how far they could go. Presumably if the courts were willing to consider aesthetics as being within the police power and the general
welfare (as the Supreme Court argued in Berman v. Parker, an urban
renewal case), there would be few obstacles to zoning of almost any
kind. Aesthetics represent the outer limits of zoning powers and are
less concrete and definitive than more technical factors like sanitation
and flood control. It is a long way from using the most restrictive
form of zoning such as large-lot zoning to protect river basins and
watersheds than to promote a more livable environment or a more
beautiful community. At least from a legal standpoint, the two are
poles apart, and municipalities have tended to base their actions on
the former and not the latter (whether this constrains them or not is
another matter, and the actions may in reality be motivated by the
latter and justified by the former).

Although not involving a zoning ordinance per se, a recent New York case gives us an indication of the trends here. In People v. Goodman (1972), the New York Court of Appeals, the state's highest court, decided that aesthetics was a proper subject of legislative concern.[49] The test was that there be a substantial relationship between the regulation and the economic, social, and cultural patterns of the community, and detecting this link the court approved a village sign control ordinance. In a case cited above, Gamble-Skogmo, a New Mexico court upheld a municipal control that stipulated the permissible size of windows in historic districts, and while the case involved historic zoning (the courts have been more lenient here), it concerned a narrow aesthetic factor and may provide some indication of the judiciary's general attitudes in this area. Of course, the New Mexico case involved zoning per se and has direct relevance in this respect.

The same pattern is reflected in the latest cases on subdivision regulations, and that again is a tendency toward a broader construction of municipal powers by the courts. At the outer reaches of subdivision controls is open-space dedication on the part of the developer and the power of the municipality to require this. While requirements relating to streets, sidewalks, curbs, and essential capital facilities such as sewer or water lines are fairly well settled (see Brous v. Smith, 1952), open space is different, and it is a more uncertain category.[50] Also, few states' enabling laws stipulate this as one of the contributions that can be required of the subdivider (there is no specific stipulation, that is).

Two cases shed some light on the matter. The first was decided by the California Supreme Court, Associated Home Builders v. City of Walnut Creek (1971), and the second by a Connecticut court, Aunt Hack Ridge Estates, Inc. v. Planning Commission of the City of Danbury (1970), and both suggest that wide municipal powers will be upheld in this area.[51] In Associated Home Builders, the court ruled that the provision of a park was a reasonable condition of approving a subdivision plat so long as the standards were acceptable. These included the existence of the park on the general plan and the use of an appropriate ratio in determining the extent of the required dedication (which in this situation was two and a half acres of parkland for each 1,000 subdivision residents); such dedications, the court held, were in the public interest as well as that of future lot owners. Finding that the dedications were consistent with the state law authorizing municipal subdivision control, the justices turned back the argument of the builders that the requirement was an exercise of eminent domain for which compensation was due.

In the Connecticut case, the court sustained a local planning board stipulation making the dedication of open space a condition of subdivision approval. It held that the new residents will increase the demand for park and recreation land, and this makes the need for additional open space a public one. Determining that the public welfare must be

paramount, the court also ruled that the open space would be more
healthful than the full complement of housing and noted some standards
that have to be met, including a limit on the maximum dedication
(4 percent of the land area of the subdivision) and the presence of a
citywide recreation plan.

In another case on the same subject and on a matter directly pertinent to the book, a California court approved a state enabling law
authorizing cities and counties to mandate the dedication of land for
recreational purposes. The Supreme Court of California reasoned in
Associated Home Builders of Greater East Bay, Inc. v. City of Walnut
Creek (1971) that the dedication of open space or the payment of fees
in lieu thereof are justified and in the general welfare.[52] This is so,
the court said, because of the recreation needs generated by the new
subdivisions, and the principle applies even where the development
borders on an existing park or recreational facility (there is still an
addition to the overall open-space demands of the community).

An earlier case treated a broader point, and that is the benefit of
developer dedications to residents outside the subdivision. In Ayres
v. City Council of City of Los Angeles (1962), a California court ruled
against a developer's claim that his improvements to the streets would
also benefit the city as a whole and that they therefore represent a
contribution for which he should be compensated.[53] The court called
this "no defense" against the municipal requirements, although the
courts have generally held that developers cannot be required to make
dedications of streets whose principal users are outside the subdivision
or major thoroughfares, whose need springs from the activity of the
community at large and not the subdivision. Still, in general, the trend
has been toward a wide construction of municipal powers and state
enabling legislation in this area, and the future likely holds more of
the same in store.

In perhaps one of the most important zoning cases ever decided,
the New York Court of Appeals recently upheld a strong "phased-
development" ordinance in Ramapo, New York, in suburban Rockland
County. In Golden v. Planning Board of Town of Ramapo (1972), the
state's highest court sustained Ramapo's planning system, which links
development permissions to the community's public facilities (see
Chapter 7).[54] Under this arrangement, proposed land uses are carefully scrutinized and assigned points on the basis of the availability
of public facilities such as sewers, water, streets, schools, and others;
developers must "score" 15 points to qualify. The city has a current
six-year capital program projecting these facilities and their accessi-
bility to different areas and two more (six-year programs) in reserve,
which means that a development could wait for as long as 18 years for
approval.

In upholding the ordinance, the court ruled that phased development
that is founded on a community capital budget or plan can be legal

because it deals with a specific time frame. The court also said that
the determinations in the Ramapo plan were based on fact and were not
arbitrary and that the restrictions in the ordinance, although substantial, were "not absolute"; thus they did not violate the federal or state
constitutions. The court was in effect saying that where the present
resources of the community are not adequate to serve development,
regulations limiting and timing development to accord with the facilities'
availability are entirely appropriate since this provides a "rational
basis" to the action. Unlike Petaluma (see Construction Industry
Association of Sonoma County above), Ramapo is under more direct
urban growth pressures, and this makes the decision all the more
important.

In a somewhat similar but earlier case, a Michigan court approved
a town ordinance channeling development to minimize the burden on
schools and other public facilities.[55] At the same time, the court held
that there must be a rational relationship between the controls, the
existence of the facilities, and the public welfare. Again, we are back
to the police power, and it must all be related to it, and perhaps the
typically general nature of the treatment of the subject (substantively)
in the enabling legislation has permitted the courts more latitude in
upholding municipal actions (see also the above qualifications on this
point). It would also seem that the Supreme Court's Belle Terre decision would reinforce the wider conception of local zoning powers and
therefore promote this general pattern.

It is important to note, before leaving this section, that the municipality's hand in zoning has been strengthened by a reconfirmation of
the "presumption of validity" principle, established in Euclid. Recent
cases such as Mill v. City of Manhattan Beach (1971) and Turner v.
County of Del Norte (1972) clearly demonstrate that the burden of
proof is still on the developer to show that the municipality is not
acting in the general welfare and that the courts will not substitute
their judgment for the city's where the question is reasonably debatable.[56]

Cases Restricting Local Powers

There are many fewer of these cases (one study of 25 recent cases
found the ratio 19 to 6 in favor of the municipality), and they deal more
with the outer limits of zoning than with more basic matters such as
the appropriateness of zoning per se. The legality of the general
concept is set, and the only question remaining is how far the controls
may go in restricting private or other public rights.

As this suggests, the issue is no longer simply a matter of profit
versus the public interest, or private rights versus public ones. It
appears in fact that the issue has shifted to a struggle between two

sets of "public rights," or between local and regional, existing resi-
dent and newcomer, and municipal versus metropolitan, state or interstate interests. This is a better way of putting it, and it reflects the
emerging realities. Public interests are involved on both sides, and
the property owner will likely come out well or poorly depending on
which set of public rights prevails. And developers will probably be
more advantaged by backing one or another of these "public interests"
than their own. Put another way, it will be more to their advantage
to back one set of public interests over and against another than to back
their own directly. This means in practice (developers) lining up with
metropolitan, regional, and statewide interests as well as minority
groups, blacks, newcomers, and lower-income whites, and this is the
way it will work, with the minorities out in front, since profit motives
are in such wide disrepute. The developers' role will be indirect,
serving to back the claims of others with better images and more acceptable motives. The developers will also be involved directly of course
as this chapter shows, as litigants in land-use suits (see Associated
Home Builders v. City of Walnut Creek (1971) and Construction Industry Association of Sonoma County v. City of Petaluma (1974) above).

Examples of court rulings restricting municipal land-use powers
follow, and they are largely or exclusively outside of California. A
1973 Oregon Supreme Court decision overruled a county board
up-zoning of a property from a traditional category to planned residential use, or to a less restrictive class.[57] The crucial point of this
case, however, is that the zoning voided by the court involved a change
from a lower- to a higher-density use and therefore does not fit the
typical pattern. In the substantive sense in fact, it belongs in the preceding section, although the opponents of restrictive zoning can "use"
it procedurally to advance their cause. The court refused the action
the full presumption of validity and declined to shield it from judicial
scrutiny. The ruling also questioned "local and small-group" processes and argued that they could not be equated with those of broader
bodies such as state legislatures and Congress. Still the decision
cannot be taken as a precedent for the courts taking a closer look at
restrictive practices, and the reverse may be closer to the truth
(scrutiny may be applied only when zoning is made less restrictive).
There is the possibility of a double standard here.

In Morris County Land Improvement Company v. Parsippany-Troy
Hills Township, the New Jersey Supreme Court reversed the trial
court and overruled a municipal ordinance that required a landowner
to retain his property in its more or less natural state (it was a
swampy area with limited development potential); in a similar ruling,
the Massachusetts Supreme Judicial Court held a local ordinance
invalid that prevented the owner (the court said) from using the land
in any practical way at all.[58] In the Massachusetts case, the ordinance
was aimed at preserving land in its undeveloped state for the benefit
of the public, but it was not acquired (eminent domain) only regulated

for this end. These two decisions and the ones to follow fit the more common pattern (compared to the Oregon ruling).

In a case decided in the early 1960s, the Illinois Supreme Court held that a developer's property had been "taken" without compensation through a municipal regulation.[59] The city's subdivision controls required that he dedicate land for recreational and educational purposes, and the developer appealed to the courts arguing that the facilities were not uniquely attributable to his subdivision. The court ruled that the action indeed amounted to an exercise of eminent domain and was therefore void. In a similar case before the California courts, a builder is challenging what may be the nation's largest lot-size minimum (40 acres) on the grounds that it is a taking without compensation.[60] The subdivision planned by the company in California is a large one and would accommodate 33,000 people, but with the new zoning it would be much smaller; clearly, here we have a classic situation with the interests of the existing residents pitted against those of newcomers.

The Pennsylvania and New Jersey cases cited above in connection with "regionalism," particularly National Land, bear out the same point, and they generally reflect a good deal of tension between the rights of the existing residents and their tax, aesthetic, public facility, and growth limitation interests on the one hand, and the rights of newcomers to housing and more pleasant living on the other. The regulations of the municipalities in Pennsylvania and New Jersey around Philadelphia and of those near New York City typically involved large-lot or other forms of restrictive zoning, which not only limits the number of residents but pushes up the costs of housing so that only the affluent can get in. Again the interests of one segment of the public are aligned against those of another, and both are organized and prepared to defend their views in the courts. In many respects it is not necessary for the municipalities (largely townships) in the two states to have specifically organized citizens' groups since the local government serves both a "municipal" and "interest group" function; in other words, the localities are commonly so small, perhaps 1 to 10 square miles, that only one interest is present, and formal pressure groups are not necessary. The municipal government becomes, in effect, an interest group. The Kit Mar case, also like National Land decided by the Pennsylvania Supreme Court, is equally pertinent here.

CONCLUSION

In sum, these are the trends reflected in land-use case law:

1. The courts are willing to uphold state zoning and regionally exercised powers, perhaps more so than in the past and probably more so than local zoning and other locally exercised land-use powers.

2. The courts are apparently increasingly inclined to approve broader interpretations of state enabling legislation (especially where it is general) and local land-use controls, although perhaps not quite as much so as with state controls.

Actually the courts have always been more likely to uphold than invalidate land-use controls at both levels, at least since Euclid; so it is not clear as to what extent the tendency is more evident now than in the past. Still, the scope of power typically being upheld now is broader than before, and this is a distinct pattern.

There is some evidence that the courts are overruling some restrictive and exclusionary local land-use practices, and while this is a "minority" pattern, it cannot be discounted and it could pick up steam in the future. Much depends on the degree to which different interest groups representing "outsiders" become active in zoning litigation and the extent to which the developers and large landowners back them.[61] Some zoning is also being voided on grounds of property rights, but this appears to be a "minority" trend within a "minority" pattern, and the major struggles in the future will be between two sets of public interests and not over property rights. At least this is what our crystal ball shows.

NOTES

1. See, for example, Kenneth M. Dolbeare, "Who Uses the State Trial Courts," in James R. Klonoski and Robert I. Mendelsohn (eds.), The Politics of Local Justice (Boston: Little, Brown, 1970), pp. 64-74.

2. One study concludes that the "influences of . . . socioeconomic environment can be discerned at every level of judicial activity [in the states] ." Kenneth N. Vines and Herbert Jacob, "State Courts," in Herbert Jacob and Kenneth N. Vines (eds.), Politics in the American States, 2nd ed. (Boston: Little, Brown, 1971), p. 310.

3. See, for example, Stuart Nagel, "Political Party Affiliation and Judges' Decisions," American Political Science Review 55 (1961): 843-851; and Nagel's "Ethnic Affiliation and Judicial Propensities," Journal of Politics 24 (1962): 92-110.

4. Fred Bosselman, David Callies, and John Banta, The Taking Issue (Washington, D. C.: Government Printing Office, 1973), p. 229.

5. 56 Wis. 2d 7, 201 N. W. 2d 761 (1972).

6. 266 Md. 358, 292 A. 2d 241 (1972).

7. 146 Conn. 650, 153 A. 2d 822 (1959).

8. 5 Cal. 3d 480, 487 P2d. 1193, 96 Cal. Rptr. 553 (1971).

9. 11 Cal. App. 3d 557, 89 Cal. Rptr. 897 (1970).

10. Fred Bosselman and David Callies, The Quiet Revolution in Land-Use Control (Washington, D. C.: Government Printing Office, 1971).

11. 313 A. 2d 669 (Vt. 1973); 300 A. 2d 736 (Me. 1973).

12. Hageman v. Trustees of Wayne Township, 20 Ohio App. 2d 13, 251 N. E. 2d 507 (1969); State v. Johnson, 265 A. 2d 711 (Me. 1970).

13. 269 U. S. 393 (1922).

14. 272 U. S. 365 (1926).

15. 274 U. S. 325 (1927).

16. 277 U. S. 183 (1928).

17. Richard F. Babcock and Fred P. Bosselman, Exclusionary Zoning: Land-Use Regulation and Housing in the 1970s (New York: Praeger Publishers, 1973), Chap. 2.

18. 369 U. S. 590 (1962).

19. N. 73-191, April 1, 1974.

20. See Griffin v. Breckenridge, 29 L. Ed. 338, 350-351 (1971); Shapiro v. Thompson, 394 U. S. 618 (1968); U. S. v. Guest, 383 U. S. 745 (1966); and Graham v. Richardson, 91 S. Ct. 1848, 1854 (1971).

21. 348 U. S. 26 (1954).

22. See Scott Greer, Urban Renewal and American Cities (Indianapolis: Bobbs-Merrill, 1965).

23. 314 U. S. 160 (1941).

24. Certain-Teed Products Corp. v. Paris Township, 351 Mich. 434, 88 N. W. 2d 705 (1958).

25. No. L-7502-70 P. W. (N. J. Super. Ct. Opinion filed Oct. 27, 1971).

26. Southern Burlington County NAACP v. Township of Mount Laurel, No. L-25741-70 P. W. (N. J. Super. Ct. Opinion filed May 1, 1972).

27. 48 N. J. 277, 225 A. 2d 321 (1966).

28. Bristow v. City of Woodhaven, 35 Mich. App. 205, 192 N. W. 2d 322 (1971).

29. 419 Pa. 504, 215 A. 2d 597 (1965).

30. Bernard H. Siegan, Land Use Without Zoning (Lexington, Mass.: Heath, 1972), p. 214.

31. Philadelphia Evening Bulletin, November 20, 1965, p. 6.

32. Washington Post, August 13, 1974, p. A4.

33. Don T. Allensworth, "Planning and Land-Use Decisions," in Urban Data Service Reports, International City Management Association, 5 no. 9, (September 1973): 3.

34. 439 Pa. 466, 268 A. 2d 765 (1970).

35. 181 A. 2d 129, 140 (N. J. 1962)-

36. 221 F. 2d 412, 418 (C. A. 1955).

37. Richard F. Babcock, The Zoning Game (Madison: University of Wisconsin Press, 1966), p. 178.

200 THE STATES AND LAND-USE CONTROLS

38. No. 69-52580; Circuit Court for the County of Oakland, Michigan unpublished opinion of Clark J Adams, Jr., February 10, 1972.

39. 111 Ill., App. 2d 430, 250 N. E. 2d 282 (1969).

40. Bohannan v. City of San Diego, 30 Cal. App. 3d 416, 106 Cal. Rptr. 333 (1973).

41. City of Santa Fe v. Gamble-Skogmo, 73 N. M. 410, 389 P. 2d 13 (1964); Trustees of Sailors' Snug Harbor in City of New York v. Platt, 29 App. Div. 2d 376, 288 N. Y. S. 2d 314 (1968); Ragone v. Landmarks Preservation Commission, 22 App. Div. 2d 1105, 308 N. Y. S. 2d 293 (1970); Hayes v. Smith, 92 R. I. 173, 167 A. 2d 546.

42. 469 F. 2d 956 (1st Cir. 1972).

43. See William H. Whyte, The Last Landscape (Garden City, N.Y.: Doubleday, 1968), Chap. 12.

44. 1 Cranch 137 (1803).

45. Written Opinion of the Court of Appeals of Maryland, No. 198 (September term, 1973), filed May 22, 1974.

46. See Jan Krasnowiecki and Ann Louise Strong, "Compensable Regulations for Open Space," Journal of the American Institute of Planners (1963): 87, 89.

47. 24 Cal. App. 3d 311, 101 Cal. Rptr. 93 (1972).

48. 284 N. E. 2d 891 (Mass. 1972), U. S. App. Pend.

49. 31 N. Y. 2d 262, 338 N. Y. S. 2d 97 (1972).

50. 304 N. Y. 164, 106 N. E. 2d 503 (1952).

51. 4 Cal. 2d 633, 94 Cal. Rptr. 630, 484 P. 2d 606 (1971); 160 Conn. 109, 273 A. 2d 880 (1970).

52. 4 Cal. 3d 633, 94 Cal. Rptr. 630, 484 P. 2d 606 (1971) App. Dis. 404 U. S. 878 (1972).

53. 34 Cal. 2d 31, 207 P. 2d 1 (1962).

54. 39 N. Y. 2d 359, 334 N.Y.S. 2d 138, 285 N. E. 2d 359 (1972).

55. Padover v. Township of Farmington, 132 N. W. 2d 687 (Mich. 1965).

56. 98 Cal. Rptr. 785 (1971); 101 Cal. Rptr. 93 (App. 1972).

57. Fasano v. Board of County Commissioners, 507 P. 2d 23 (Ore. 1973).

58. 40 N. J. 539, 193 A. 2d 232 (1963); MacGibbon v. Board of Appeals of Duxbury, 356 Mass. 696, 255 N. E. 2d 347 (1970).

59. Pioneer Trust & Savings Bank v. Village of Mount Prospect, 22 Ill. 2d 375, 176 N. E. 2d 799 (1961).

60. Morold Investment Company Limited v. the County of Santa Cruz, No. 48607, Superior Court, Santa Cruz County, California, filed September 12, 1972.

61. The "outsiders are most likely going to be civil rights groups (especially the NAACP), and their involvement in zoning is relatively recent. See Clement E. Vose, "Interest Groups, Judicial Review, and Local Government," in H. R. Mahood (ed.), Pressure Groups in American Politics (New York: Scribner's, 1967), pp. 268-291.

9

**PLANNING AND
THE REALITIES OF
STATE POLITICS**

PLANNING IN THE STATE POLITICAL SYSTEM

Planning, of course, does not take place in a vacuum. It will operate within a setting over which it will have little or no control, and
what happens to it will be determined to a large extent by general pressures and conditions not created by it and having little to do with it
originally. This goes for both direct planning and zoning conducted
by the state itself and its agencies and the enabling legislation it will
approve for localities in the future.

State planning will be constrained by the general political processes
in the states, and these processes will direct much of the broad pattern
and many of the specifics in planning and land-use control. It is for
this reason that we provide this chapter. We cannot say simply that
the states should do this or that in planning without taking into account
their general organization, their other functions, their present capacities in other fields, and their probable future potential in a broader
(than planning) sense. We turn to these matters now.

STATE OF THE STATES—1974

The State of the States in 1974 report of the state chief executives
says:[1]

> States stand today at the front and center of intergovernmental
> action. They constitute the important middle tier of the federal
> system composed of the nation, the states, and local govern-
> ments. State governments are the pivotal, fiscal, functional,

legal, and political mechanisms participating in the planning
of domestic policy and implementing it

The report indicates that conditions in the states have changed in the
last ten to twenty years and that the states are now strong and prepared
to undertake new challenges. For example, the report goes on, the
number of states with governors serving only two-year terms has been
reduced substantially; one state after another is reorganizing and
"streamlining" its executive structure, cutting back the number of
agencies reporting to the governor and instituting the "cabinet" form;
most state legislatures now meet annually, a sharp rise over the past
two decades where most of them met only once each two years; and
the states are making considerable progress in "modernizing" their
judicial systems and removing them from "politics."

The specifics are important: Since 1960 the number of states
restricting their governors to two-year terms was cut from 16 to 7;
since 1965 nearly 20 states have embarked on comprehensive reorganization of their executive branches; since 1960 some 14 additional
states have provided for annual legislative sessions, raising the total
number of states now requiring their legislatures to meet once a year
to 33; and by 1974 most states had "major elements" of an "integrated"
judiciary.

Other measures of state success can be seen in the fiscal and
program areas, according to the governors. Now the states are spending
close to $100 billion a year including state funds, federal aid, and state
aid to localities. Most of this money goes for education and welfare
as can be seen in Figure 7, and highways account for another large
chunk, 15 percent of the total. In fact, the states foot most of the bill
in highways (55 percent of the total, with the federal government
contributing 26 percent and local governments 18 percent) and health
(about 50 percent, with most of the rest coming from Washington).

The state chiefs are particularly proud of state accomplishments
in the past several years in housing, community development, land use,
and planning. They point out, for example, that 33 states now have
housing finance agencies, 39 have departments of community affairs
(to help local governments), and "virtually every state" by 1973 had
some form of land-use planning. Of course, it is the latter that concerns us most since it is the topic of this book, although the general
structures and status of the states are important as well since they
will determine pretty much the frame that new planning and zoning
programs will work once they get underway.

But this is all very general, and it tells us little about what the
states are really doing and what they are capable of doing. It is the
specifics of present operations that count and that explain the real
potential of the states, not the generalities. What they are doing now,
in the practical sense, will tell us much not only about the present and
the realities behind the governors' claims, but what the states can do

FIGURE 7

Where State Dollars Go
(Includes state funds from own sources,
aid to state from federal government, and
aid from state to local government)

Total expenditures: $98.8 billion

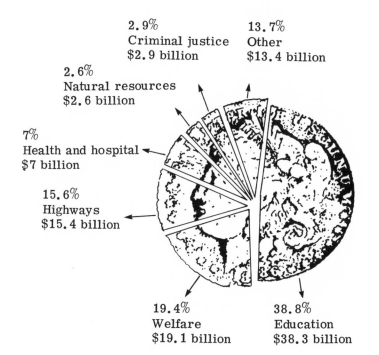

2.9%
Criminal justice
$2.9 billion

13.7%
Other
$13.4 billion

2.6%
Natural resources
$2.6 billion

7%
Health and hospital
$7 billion

15.6%
Highways
$15.4 billion

19.4%
Welfare
$19.1 billion

38.8%
Education
$38.3 billion

Source: The State of the States in 1974: Responsive Government
for the Seventies (Washington, D. C.: National Governors' Conference,
1974), p. 26.

in the future. This is the subject of this chapter, and the future of the states cannot be known without a somewhat more detailed examination of the presentation that the governors give us.

WHAT DO THE STATES DO?

We know that the states are but one of three levels of government, and they have certain functions. But what are they? What do the states do? Specifically? The latest <u>Book of the States</u> (1972-73) lists the following major state service areas:[2]

1. education
2. transportation
3. health and welfare
4. law enforcement and public protection
5. planning, housing, and development
6. natural resources
7. labor and industrial relations
8. public utility regulation

Let us describe each briefly—the general decision-making process in each and the relation of each to planning and land-use control.

State educational functions refer to programs dealing mostly with primary and secondary schools and include assisting, supervising, and setting standards for local school systems. The state provides substantial financial assistance to local schools, the biggest single item in the states' budgets, and about half of this money goes to local school boards usually in the form of grants (the remainder is used largely for higher public education, generally a state—and not local—responsibility).

The state school operations are typically handled by a department of education or public instruction, headed by a superintendent or commissioner who is known among professional schoolmen as the "chief state school officer." State education agencies work closely with key school interest groups, and together they constitute probably the strongest single force on state education matters, promoting new interest appropriations among other things.[3]

State highway agencies may be the most powerful of the various state bureaucracies, partly because of the enormous resources they command (over $20 billion a year) and partly because of the strength they have built in state politics over the years. Counting federal aid (over $5 billion a year), state highway departments may have more funds at their administrative discretion than any other state agency, and this has significant political implications as research has shown.[4] At the same time, state roads chiefs are under increasing pressure from citizens' and conservation groups, forces with whom highway bureaucracies have had little experience and less understanding. And the diversion of currently protected (in trust) federal and state highway funds to other transportation uses, a move backed by environmental and city groups, could markedly alter the position of the roads agency in state government. Road safety is usually under an agency separate from the highway bureaucracy—such as highway safety, traffic safety, motor vehicles, or public works department or commission.

Both education and highway programs under the state have an impact on planning and land use—education less so, unless as in some states, like Maryland, the state funds local school construction. The location of public schools can be important to planning, and there is no evidence suggesting that the states (where they fund construction) follow local plans any better than the local school boards. There is also no evidence showing that state education policy is part and parcel of overall comprehensive planning policy, and much of the reason is the typically independent styles of the education policy makers; in other words, these policy makers are more or less immune from the broader political processes including comprehensive planning.

The story is much the same in highways. Highway departments have been noted for their independence in the state hierarchy, and the new moves toward integrated transportation departments (20 states now have them, the little "DOTs") cannot change the pattern basically. The reason is that although the governors and the new transportation secretaries (typically old highway chiefs) allege their support of "balanced transportation" and the need to curtail the state emphasis on highways as state transportation policy, the highway "divisions" often become the tail that wags the dog; they are like zoning and planning, in other words. At least much research suggests this.[5]

The point is that the states cannot be changed overnight, especially through administrative reorganization, and there is no way they can become strong backers of mass transit ("balanced transportation") without a change in transportation funding patterns and more basically in the general political structures and pressures in the states themselves. It is instructive in this regard that the governors (organized through the National Governors' Conference) lobby in Washington for a single transportation trust fund, with highway (much) and mass transit (little) funds combined, and yet in the states they cannot get their own legislatures to do the same (most of them have not tried, and the National Legislative Conference, or the state legislators' lobby in Washington, and the American Association of State Highway Officials, or the state highway bureaucracies' political arm in Congress, oppose the national combination). The fact is that only one state—Maryland—has combined highway-mass transit-airport transportation funding, and until this is done elsewhere (at least) no change in policy can be made. Mass transit and other forms of nonhighway transportation account for a fraction of state transportation spending at present.

In addition, state highway agencies do not have to follow local plans and zoning (Chapter 7), and most of them do not. A few states like California require local approval of major highway projects, but even there the stipulation does not require consistency with a master plan, only local approval. It does not appear that the agencies are doing any better at the metropolitan or statewide level, although recent federal legislation (1962 Highway Act, at the metropolitan level) and regulations (Office of Management and Budget Circular A-95, at both the metropolitan and state levels) require highways to be reviewed by central bodies, composed at most only in part of highway interests. The highway agencies are not bound by this review, but it does help bring pressure on them where broader local or state groups do not want particular roads.[6] Highways by and large go where the state highway planners want them and not where local or state comprehensive plans call for them. Since most states do not have such plans, it is obvious why they do not at this level. But even if they did, it would be quite likely that the highway bureaucracies would determine the roads portion of the plans (which they do now sometimes at the local level); as a political reality, it would be hard for it to be otherwise. Still, a number of cities have been able to block unwanted state highways, and this includes Washington, D. C., San Antonio, New Orleans, Philadelphia, and Boston.

The states perform important health and welfare functions, and most of their major health and welfare categories are assisted by federal grants. The functions are typically administered independently, however, with the former in a board or department of health and the latter in a public welfare, social services, or social welfare agency. State health programs are directed to a wide variety of disease areas, hospitals, nursing homes, and health planning among others; the state welfare effort, called for the most part "public assistance," include at least until recently such activities as aid to families with dependent children, old-age assistance, aid to the permanently and totally disabled, aid to the blind, and general assistance (relief). Under legislation enacted in 1973, some state welfare programs were "federalized." Washington now picks up the full tab and administers the programs directly (previously they were under the states and federally assisted). Health and welfare in the substantive sense have only limited effects on land use, although the planning and location of public health facilities are important in this regard, and this is a function mostly of local and metropolitan health organizations and not the state. Most of the direct health services in this country are provided at the local level.

State law enforcement and public protection are administered by such agencies as the office of attorney general, highway patrol, department of public safety, state police, department of corrections, and department of public institutions. The state claim to have made significant progress in expanding the perspectives and increasing the effectiveness of their law enforcement programs with the passage of the

federal Omnibus Crime Control and Safe Streets Act of 1968, a key
measure which for the first time provided block grants to the states
to improve their systems of criminal justice ("block" grants are to
be distinguished from "categorical" grants, which are more restrictive and contain more federal strings).[7] This area has only a limited
relationship to comprehensive planning and zoning at the local level
and broader planning in the states, but it, of course, would be included
in the theoretical sense. The states do run public institutions such
as prisons, which could have an effect on land-use patterns and should
be part of comprehensive planning programs at both the state and local
levels.

As this book has already shown in part, planning, housing, and
community development is a relatively new concentration of state
governments. Still the states are not doing all that much in this area,
and what they do in the future may depend on directions Washington
sets. We have made a number of recommendations along these lines,
and we feel in general that Washington should turn away from its
emphasis on "critical areas" controls for the states and toward
specialized forms of state zoning, land-use planning but not zoning
for the state as a whole, and new state enabling legislation in planning,
zoning, subdivision, and other areas.

Prodded by the federal government and home-builder lobbies,
some states have moved decisively in the field of housing and urban
development, which takes us beyond planning. Some of them have
established and funded statewide housing agencies, a traditionally
local concern, and New York's Urban Development Corporation (UDC)
has been notable in this respect. UDC has several projects underway
including low- and moderate-income housing programs, but it has
not overridden any local government even though it has the authority;
nor will it go into a community unless invited.[8] Approaching the matter
from a slightly different angle, Massachusetts has empowered an
administrative unit in the state executive to reverse city and suburban
governments that bar housing for disadvantaged groups; yet not a
single house has been built under the legislation to our knowledge.[9]

Other states including Indiana and Florida have passed laws facilitating the development of industrialized or factory housing, which is
not uncommonly blocked by local building and construction codes.
The Florida measure—the Factory-Built Housing Act of 1971—permits
the state to disregard local codes in order to allow builders to provide
industrialized housing for low-income and other groups.[10] The legislation is administered by the state Department of Community Affairs,
which represents a relatively new organizational pattern in state
governments (see governors') report above).[11] In Ohio, a comparable
agency is the Department of Economic and Community Development,
which hails itself as the developer's "ombudsman." In addition, state
housing and community development agencies may assist local governments in such areas as model cities, urban renewal, and public housing,

and in some instances in fact the state bureaucracy is now the chief
force behind the creation of new local housing agencies, especially in
outlying suburban and rural regions.

Of course, housing and urban development clearly relate to planning,
and the links have been described to some extent in Chapter 7. There
is no evidence that current state legislation in the housing and community development field (per se, not including planning and zoning)
is designed to encourage comprehensive planning and land-use control
at the local level, and in reality the reverse is true (the state law
encourages or requires the establishment of separate bureaucracies
for each function—one for urban renewal, one for public housing, and
so on—and provides assistance on this basis, rather than through comprehensive planning agencies or channels). In the future, the states
should combine their housing, urban development and redevelopment,
and community affairs legislation and programs into a single effort,
and there should be a single enabling law covering not only these
functions but urban planning, zoning, and subdivision control as well
(see Chapter 7). Whether the political base for this reform is in
existence is doubtful, however, and new coalitions will probably have
to be forged before any change can be expected.

Natural resources include the age-old state functions like forests,
parks, fish and wildlife, water resources, soil and water conservation,
recreation, and agriculture. (The states have taken the lead in some
of these areas, although often with federal assistance and guidance.)
They also include the somewhat recently emphasized air and water
pollution control and environmental quality programs including, in a
couple of states, land use. State bureaucracies responsible for these
functions include natural resources departments (as such), health
boards, conservation commissions, and agricultural agencies, and in
general the pattern in this area has been toward considerable dispersion of administrative powers.

However, in the past several years some states have sought to
consolidate their various natural resources, environmental, pollution
control, and related functions into a single agency. An example is
Washington State's Department of Ecology (DOE), created in 1970 and
given authority over some natural resources, air and water pollution
control, and solid waste management.[12] This represents a trend away
from the assignment of environmental and pollution control programs
to departments or boards of health, still a common practice in the
states, and toward uniting traditional natural resources and pollution
control programs under an "environmental" umbrella. Recent federal
legislation and administrative reorganization in the pollution control
field have significantly affected state programs and bureaucracies
including organizational patterns, and the creation of the federal
Environmental Protection Agency (EPA) triggered similar moves
in the states (although in most cases a different agency title has been
used).

Natural resource and pollution control programs are obviously related to planning and zoning, and this includes state parks, recreation centers, forests, fish and wildlife preserves, and other land uses which help shape growth and serve other planning ends such as the dispersion of pollution. Environmental quality is also of concern to planning and zoning, and one of the most recently discussed links is that between emission standards (air pollution) and particular patterns of development. In this respect, air pollution control programs could end up dictating many land-use and development patterns, for if permitted pollution levels are established, this could govern at least future permitted land uses. The idea is that proposed uses and development that push the pollution levels above the maximum allowed will be turned down, and this raises a whole series of jurisdictional questions for different bureaucracies and governments.

The states, in fact, are moving in this direction, toward the use of air pollution standards to control development, with EPA encouragement. For a while EPA thought of doing the job more directly, through setting the standards itself and requiring local and state governments to regulate land use accordingly, but it has backed down, or has been forced to try a denial of funds in Congress. The politics are important, and EPA was generally supported in this effort by Senator Muskie and his environmental subcommittee and opposed by Senator Jackson, chairman of the Senate Interior Committee, the House Interior panel, the Department of the Interior, and the city and county lobby which feared an EPA takeover of local land-use powers. Apparently those latter groups were responsible for EPA's denial of funds for this purpose.

There has been some talk of integrating state land-use planning and control programs into the more broadly based natural resource or environmental quality and conservation departments. New York State has done this to some extent, through its Department of Environmental Conservation. In our opinion, while a link is definitely needed, it would probably be better to keep land-use and comprehensive planning in a separate department and put it directly under the governor; there is no reason why planning should be put in the environmental control department any more than it should be put in the highway commission or any comparable operating agency with development-influencing functions. And it cannot be put everyplace.

So far, escaping contemporary political movements and recent shifts in public opinion for the most part has been labor/industrial relations and public utility regulation administrative organization and decision making in the states. Both are key duties of state governments, and the first area includes such matters as occupational safety, child labor, minimum-wage levels, working conditions, regulation of private employment concerns, employment discrimination, employment security, and workmen's compensation. There has been a discernable tendency toward the creation of a single state department of labor to handle employment programs, although many states still contain a host of separate agencies responsible for different labor and industrial relations activities. Existing interest groups aligned with the present separate agencies typically resist the consolidation and lobby against it in the administrative sphere and may seek to overturn it in the legislature if approved in the administration. Incidentally, workmen's compensation, normally under a board independent of other agencies, is one of the rare examples of an almost exclusively state undertaking (this is changing now with the enactment of a recent occupational safety law in Washington). This requires a slight modification of the "shared powers" thesis of Grodzins and others, which holds that the powers of American governments are shared up and down the line in the federal system.[13]

State labor programs usually do not relate too directly to comprehensive land-use planning and zoning at either the state or local levels, and probably the strongest link is in the building and construction codes area. This is nearly always a local responsibility, and only a few states (four in all) have statewide building codes on the books. These codes, regardless of where administered, can affect construction costs and therefore influence development patterns, and for example they can mean more expensive housing, the barring of mobile homes, and the virtual absence of low- and moderate-income dwellings, all planning concerns. Of course, Florida is attempting to do something about this as we have noted.

Public utility services in the states include regulation and promotional activities in such areas as intrastate communications, electricity, gas, water supply, air carriers, railroads, and urban transit. Most states administer this function through a public utilities or public services commission composed of three to seven members, and a few states have "corporation" or "railroad" commissions (Virginia, Texas) for this purpose (see Chapter 6). Although public administration experts have generally recommended against plural executives of this sort, only one state runs its public utilities agency in this matter—and that is Oregon whose bureaucracy is headed by a single director and not a board. Instructively, promotion as well as regulation of utilities is involved.

As environmentalists begin to concentrate more attention on power plants and other industries governed by state public utility commission regulations, these agencies can be expected to gain increasing prominence and come under greater public scrutiny; already power plant siting has become an important issue in some states especially in the Northwest. Our own guess is that conservationists and liberals are going to have a tough time cracking these units, and there is going to be little help from labor. The fact is that development is very dependent on public utilities, and if there is a lot of controversy over each siting decision, this will slow down the whole process and have its impact on land use. Too many people and interests are dependent on these utilities to let this happen, and this includes construction workers, builders, developers, bankers, the unions and their lawyers, architects, planners, and other representatives. In general, it will be easier for new groups to gain control of zoning/planning than the growth-inducing facilities; at least the latter are going to be "given up" by old power structures with more resistance. We have completed an examination of specific functions of the states and some of the political processes associated with them, and we now turn to broader patterns of decision making in the states.

GENERAL PATTERNS OF DECISION MAKING IN THE STATES

All the states have three branches—the executive, legislative, and judicial, and in fact power in the executive is significantly divided among the governor, other elected officials, and the bureaucracies. Probably most of the important decisions in the states are made in the executive, due in part to the infrequent meetings of most state legislatures (even those meeting each year generally stay in session only two or a few months). Let us take a brief look at the chief actors.

State Legislatures

Nearly all the states have bicameral legislatures, the only exception being Nebraska which has a unicameral body, and this follows the reasoning of the founders that both wealth and people should be represented in government. Of course today, especially with the Supreme Court one-man one-vote decisions, both houses are apportioned on the basis of population, and we can point to other advantages of the system. The upper body may perform more of a deliberative function and represent "wider" points of view; this may be due to its smaller size plus the larger areas and constituencies per member and to longer terms, higher minimum ages, and longer minimum residency requirements than in the lower house. In fact, there appear to be some differences in voting behavior in the two houses of state legislatures, and some research has suggested that the senate tends to reflect broader interests and more liberal positions on public policy; it seems clearly to be less influenced by "local" factors.[14]

Separate leadership exists for each house, although it may be linked by party ties, the governor, or other means, and the influence of the majority party is particularly striking in two-party states; it may be less in one-party states where the majority party is split into many factions and may exist only on paper. Each lower chamber has a speaker, who is usually elected by the full membership and typically among his more important powers are those over committee members on the floor and interpretation and application of house rules. This formal authority may provide the speaker with important political influence, and it is clear that some leaders draw on it more fully than others. Upper houses are often headed by the lieutenant governor, and other leadership groups in each chamber include "policy committees" and caucuses of both parties, but they are probably more instruments of the leadership than vice versa.

In all likelihood the most important decisions in state legislatures are made by the leadership in cooperation with the legislative committees, that is, the formal and internal decisions. Unlike Congress, however, where the key policy is typically made by the committees and not the leadership, the edge is with the leadership.[15] Most state senates have from 10 to 25 committees, and most lower houses from 10 to 30 such units; this refers to "standing committees" or those with ongoing powers over substantive programs of the state and the state budget. They include natural resources committees with authority over park, forest, fish and wildlife, water resources, and perhaps other programs, and housing and urban affairs committees with authority over community development bills. As in Congress, there is commonly one bureaucracy that corresponds with the legislative committee, and the agency may influence it greatly and, along with the committee and allied interest groups, may form a triangle of power which Douglass Cater termed "subgovernments" in Washington.[16] In reality, these three do make much of the policy in state government, and the agencies and interest groups are probably the strongest members. In the states the legislative leadership has to be included as well. We come back to this later.

The range of membership in state legislative committees is wide indeed, in senates running from a few to 36 members and in lower houses from 3 to 63; this may make them somewhat unwieldy policy instruments, and the pattern probably contributes to the chairman's power. State legislators usually do not make much, and some states pay their legislators as little as $100 a year. Others like California pay more, perhaps as high as $25,000 per annum.

Generally the legislators have limited staff and professional assistance, and surprisingly in terms of their images they are drawn from the better-educated segments of the population and have higher status occupations than the public at large. They tend to be more representative of their constituencies in religious, ethnic, and racial terms. Businessmen and lawyers are the most common occupation represented in the assemblies, and farmers are not far behind.

State legislative policy has been recently traced in the literature of political science to socioeconomic factors. One study done a few years ago shows that expenditures in certain fields were closely linked with levels of social and economic development. State education and welfare outlays were importantly related to the degree of urbaniization, industrialization, wealth, and education in the state, and the greater the urbanization, and so on, the higher the expenditures, proportionately.[17] More recent data suggest a broader base to state legislative policy, encompassing political in addition to socioeconomic factors including the degree of interparty competition, the extent of party cohesion, the level of interest group activity, and the character of the legislature's relations with the executive. For instance, the governor has a strong influence over legislative policy, it appears, when there is competition between the two parties, and both houses are under the control of the governor's party.[18] These findings, pointing to the ''political'' foundations of state legislative policy instructively, reinforce some earlier studies of the matter done by V. O. Key, Duane Lockard, and others of Key's students.[19] The ''socioeconomic'' findings came in between the two in date.

Another factor that may affect legislative policy in the states is historical tradition. In other words, a history of high state spending in general or in particular fields may be linked to continuing high outlays and thus account for present policy. Ira Sharkansky, for instance, reports a marked correlation between the rankings of the states in the early 1900s and a recent time span in terms of spending per capita for public services, and in general states high on the list in the first period were the same as those in the top spots later.[20] This sort of explanation has been termed incrementalism, which holds that present spending levels must be based on something, and previous levels may provide that guide.

''Regionalism'' may be involved as well. Some evidence suggests the existence of similarities in state legislative outlays and expenditure emphases and in other policies within particular geographical areas embracing several states.[21] Thus states in the Great Lakes region such as Michigan, Wisconsin, Ohio, and others can be expected to support certain policies that distinguish them from other states. For example, the New England states collectively score ''low'' on education and roads outlays, and the southeastern ''high'' on sales and excise tax. Yet the basic reason for regional similarities may be historical, political, or economic realities, which are simply reflected on a regional basis. Also most state government interests like legislators, governors, and bureaucracies are organized into national associations with regional branches—the Southern Legislative Conference is an example—and this might account for the regional similarities.[22]

Before leaving this section, it is worth noting that the Citizens' Conference on State Legislatures in 1971 published a survey it conducted of state legislative bodies. There is little scientific evidence, however, that its proposals such as higher pay and more frequent meetings will lead to the desired goals, and they are based on traditional municipal reform notions applied to state legislatures.[23] We suggest the implication of legislative patterns for state planning in the concluding portion of the chapter.

Executive

   The governors are not alone in the executive branches of the states,
and in practice they share power with others including independently
elected officials such as treasurer (40 states), attorney general (42
states), secretary of state (39), auditor (27), school chief (21), and
perhaps others, and the many state agencies. By no means is it
correct to say that the governor has all policy-making power and that
he controls the other officials or the bureaucracies in the executive;
they have much legal and political independence in many cases. His
major resources are probably persuasion and "politics" and not the
formal powers, although the formal powers are in some states very
impressive (including New York, Hawaii, and Illinois).[24]
   Governors are elected for either two- or four-year terms and
they may or may not be able to succeed themselves (by law, that is).
All state chiefs but one have at least some veto power over bills of
the legislature, power that may be strong or limited (strong powers
would include the item veto, or the veto over particular lines in the
legislative budget, and a special majority such as three-fourths
required to override the veto). It would appear that strong veto powers
have their effects and serve to strengthen the governor's influence
not only over the legislature but administrative policy as well; at least
a recent scientific study shows the two linked.[25] However, other
research found no significant relationship between a wider range of
formal gubernatorial powers (collectively) and the governor's influence
over legislative policy.[26] Again formal powers may not tell the entire
story, and the skills plus the personal and political abilities of the
incumbent may come into play. Governors may also have important
budget, appointment, and administrative powers.
   Governors have other roles as well, and these may include mediator
among interst groups (not reserved to the legislature, but an important
function of it), chief intergovernmental negotiator (up to 25 percent
of the state's money may come from Washington, and this means plenty
of lobbying on the part of the governor), chief party spokesman (state
party leader), and ceremonial chief (dedication of dams, cutting the
ribbon for new highways). It might be noted that a strong governor is
not necessarily a liberal governor as many people seem to assume,
and Ronald Reagan of the GOP and George Wallace of the Democrats
(Populists?) suggest this.[27] Thus calls for strengthening the hand of
governors may be calls for strengthening the policies of George
Wallace.[28]
   Likely the single most permanent force in the state government
is the bureaucracy. It is not merely a tool of the governor or the state
legislature as theory would have it, but an independent influence in
and of itself. In fact, the reverse may be closer to the truth, and the

governor and legislature may be more subject to its will than vice versa.[29] We know that this is offensive to many people, and we apologize, but remember that the administrators are on the job all the time, and there are thousands of them. The governor is one person, and his staff is small; his powers over the bureaucracy will depend, as much as on anything, on his willingness to go to the public to defend his programs and bring pressure on the agencies. This may be more effective than any "direct" order he may issue. The pattern is similar to the situation nationally as the work of Neustadt has shown.[30] Actually the governors do not have the powers the president has (formally), and they are probably more reliant on "political" moves and strategies to reinforce their authority over the bureaucracies than the president is.

One of the key features of the state executives is the extent to which they are dominated by boards and commissions. This, in turn, leads to administrative decentralization and makes it even harder for the governor to control, and it means in practice that important policy-making powers are concentrated in administrative agencies. There is no reason why it had to work out this way theoretically but it did, and it is probably the best illustration of what Lowi calls "interest group liberalism" in American government and administration; the pattern is one of the real powers being delegated to bureaucracies and the agencies and interest groups making the decisions.[31] Lowi blames much of this on the absence of specificity in legislation and calls for more precise and definitive standards at the beginning.

Typically the key powers in the states have been given to particular executive branch boards and commissions. These panels have the authority to make major administrative and policy decisions on a year-round basis, and legislators are sometimes represented on these units, perhaps constituting the most important legislative input into the function (even more important than the law setting up the agency or prescribing the program). These boards are perched atop state bureaucracies and are an integral part of the bureaucracies.

Probably the average state administrative agency is headed by a board or commission, a reality often obscured by insufficiently detailed organization charts and officially generated impressions suggesting a more streamlined structure. This board may be appointed by the governor (most common), sometimes with legislative confirmation, the legislature, by some other state body or official, or by a combination of appointing officers or units. Appointments are usually overlapping and on a fixed-term basis, normally extending beyond or not coinciding with that of the governor. Boards range in size from three to nine or more members, and they may exercise both policy and administrative authority over agency staffs; they may, for instance, name key administrators in the bureaucracy like the agency director and his chief subordinates (meaning that members of the governor's cabinet may or may not be selected by him).

Their decision-making authority may be wide indeed, and examples include the following: adoption of statewide regulations such as sani-tary or mountain kinds of building codes, which have the force of law and clearly affect political fortunes up and down the line; determination of agency spending priorities; approval of agency budget requests; and assignment of duties and top-level personnel by divisions within the agency. In the absence of boards, such decisions are often made by agency administrators and not the governor, which provides an indi-cation of state administrative agency policy making. The arrangement has led some observers to depict the states as "government by boards and commissions."

Public administration experts have opposed executive branch boards with this kind of authority, and some states have sought to transform certain key boards from policy to advisory status. In fact, this has happened recently in the states of California, Massachusetts, Delaware, and others. The experts argue that boards or multiheaded administration interfere with effective and centrally directed policy implementation by dispersing authority and responsibility and make popular accountability through an elected executive difficult at best.

While their phasing out is encouraged by management professionals, administrative boards are in reality defended by technicians and admin-istrators in the substantive, policy, or agency field affected; this is true regardless of what they say at distant conferences. And these technicians and administrators are commonly tied to, are members of, or are supported by interest groups that are represented on the boards in the first place. This gives a clue as to why the boards are still so prevalent in view of a considerable body of expert and pro-fessional opinion opposing them, and it should additionally give us an indication of the likelihood of substitute mechanisms such as advisory committees being established to give interest groups a voice in the administration in the event the boards were abolished or downgraded. For some reason public administration studies have rarely acknow-ledged the permanence of interest group influence on state executive agencies, whether through boards or by other means, preferring to concentrate on more general principles or to avoid the issue entirely; this is especially true of the "little Hoover Commission" investigations of the 1950s and 1960s.

Almost invariably interest groups are represented on state admin-istrative boards, and in almost always they occupy a majority if not all of the seats. This pattern was discussed to some extent in Chapter 5, and many states, apparently unaware of or unconcerned with the broader currents of thought on the matter, have even backed up the arrangement with legislation, thus giving it stronger institu-tional support. That is, by law interest group representatives must be appointed to most or all the seats on the boards that run the state bureaucracies. The states' rationale for this has been that it is those most directly involved in a particular agency's policy field who know the most about it and who have the most to contribute. "The experts know best" is the feeling—in this case extending to interest groups which are clearly not viewed by the public as such (that is, as interest groups, such as the state medical society). The state is the victor, the argument goes, for it gets expensive talent free or virtually so (usually the board members serve without compensation, although expenses are covered; their payoff is more in terms of policy and politics). The political implications of interest group representation in state administration will become clearer in the following paragraphs.

The interest groups found on state administrative agency boards are rarely the ones listed in introductory political science texts— such as the chamber of commerce or the AFL-CIO (both of which incidentally are specifially organized at the state level). Instead, they are more specialized political groups, representing narrower interests or those with the greatest economic or other stakes in a given agency's policies. It will be recalled from the discussion above that state bureaucracies are organized along lines of policy area, usually one bureaucracy for each policy area (highway department, for example), and this is the way most interest groups are structured, which makes for close ties. In the business sector, it is generally the specialized interest groups—representing highway contractors (state road builders' association), developers (state home-builders' association), or merchants (state retail merchants' council), for example—that have the greatest clout in particular state policy fields and that are represented on particular state administrative boards, not the more broadly based ones like the chamber. (State chambers of commerce, in fact, often steer clear of the specifics of administrative policy, preferring to deal with broad "fiscal" and related policies, where they cannot be pinned down.) In labor, it is likely to be the Teamsters, the United Mine Workers, or a particular segment of the AFL-CIO such as the Building and Construction Trades and not organized labor in general. In the professions, it is likely to be organized doctors or organized dentists, in other words, specialized professional groups. The same is true in the agricultural area where particular crop or cattle groups will be named, or when general farm organizations are involved a <u>specific</u> one of these such as the state Farm Bureau or the state Grange is likely to be named.

To illustrate, state highway bureaucracies are commonly aligned with interest groups, which may be represented on their administrative boards. Together, the agencies and supporting interests lobby for policy decisions that are favorable to highways—in other words, expanded outlays and protected funds. At least until recently it has not been an overstatement to say that the two plus their supporters in state legislatures and Congress have <u>made</u> most state and national highway policy decisions. In fact, the <u>only</u> transportation interest group to oppose the "roads lobby" in the states has been organized railroads, and you can be sure that trainmen are rarely if ever

represented on the state highway boards.[32] Roads interest groups
include state highway users' conferences which are mostly industry
(oil, rubber, car) funded, organized truckers, organized automobile
manufacturers, organized oil companies, organized rubber firms,
organized roads contractors, organized farmers, and others dependent
on large highway outlays in state capitals.[33]

Similarly, state health boards are frequently composed of representatives of affected interest groups especially organized doctors
and pharmacists, but perhaps others such as organized nursing homes,
organized podiatrists, and organized hospitals—in short, those with
the most concrete interests in state health policy. The groups represented are likely to be those with the greatest dependency on administrative subsidies, particular priorities in allocation of funds, or
other agency-determined spending policies. The interest groups and
agency administrators jointly make the decisions, but they explain to
outsiders that the policies are chiefly of benefit to those other than
themselves; most of them have "clients" other than their immediate
members in whose name they prefer to act, and sometimes the "client"
is the public at large or some "legitimate" portion of it such as the
poor, working families, welfare recipients or "patients." Rarely if
ever will they name themselves—or the interst groups and bureaucracies—as the chief beneficiaries,[34] although they may be the real beneficiaries.

There are other forces of decentralization in state executives. That
many administrative agency board members and key top-level agency
officials are appointed for fixed terms, frequently overlapping that of
the governor, certainly has this effect. When the governor does not
do the appointing, which is not uncommon, the effect is even more
marked. It is also true that governors are sometimes restricted on
whom they can name, if indeed they have the authority, and these
restrictions may include professional, occupational, interest group,
or geographical stipulations. In some states—perhaps by law—physi-
cians must be appointed to the boards that run state health departments
(maybe a majority), as in Ohio; "affected" interests appointed to state
highway agency boards (many states); wood product interest groups
to forestry department boards; and agricultural interest groups (state
Farm Bureau or Grange) to state natural resources boards as in
Maryland. In addition, the civil service serves as a constraint on
gubernatorial appointment power in many states, and this can curtail
his political options.

State administrative agencies also commonly have direct ties to
the leadership in state legislative bodies and to legislative committees
with power over their programs and appropriations. The former
practice builds on a long tradition in state government, preceding
the development of the executive or gubernatorially prepared budget,
while the latter pattern is only beginning to emerge in most of the
states. The agency-legislative link is furthered along at the national

level, and the reason it has developed more slowly in the states has
to do with legislative organization; in the states, power is more centralized, the committee structure less formalized, and the committees
do not have as stable a membership. The direct agency-legislative
tie of course, regardless of the specifics, makes central executive
direction harder to attain, and Professor Wright's research, cited
above, suggests that state agencies may have closer relationships
with the legislature than the governor.

Furthermore, a key institution that shapes many states' administrative processes is a special board in the executive that makes
far-reaching financial, program, administrative, and policy decisions.[35]
This represents a carry-over from the collegial executive concept
that was part of the country's first state constitutions, and the arrangement remains a potent force in many states today.[36] These panels
normally include administration and legislative members, with their
authority extending to major capital expenditures, to the acquisition
of large tracts and properties by the state and to other key matters,
and they may be called "controlling boards," "public works boards,"
or other names. Almost certainly they are more important in the
states' executive decision-making process than is commonly supposed,
and it is clear that they serve to curtail gubernatorial power. In practice, particular administrative agencies may prove the decisive influence over their actions in areas affecting the agencies. Whether a
state planning and zoning agency would have this influence cannot be
known, but it is by no means a certainty since other agencies have
long traditions and have built close political ties in and out of the
administration; yet we can see by this the kind of pressures planning
programs would be subjected to in the state executive.

It is also true that state administrations contain a number of
independent elected officials, most of whom head their own executive
agencies; also included, but in a minority of states, are entire boards
or commissions in selected functional areas (the entire Tax Commission
is elected in Arizona and the full Highway Commission in Mississippi).
Additionally, the typical state administration contains a large number
of departments and agencies, perhaps as many as 50 to 100 or more,
and this resembles the situation in Washington prior to reorganizations
of the 1930s and the two Hoover Commissions. Independently elected
executive officials are not subject to much direct gubernatorial control,
and the governor cannot effectively supervise 50 to 100 agencies even
if he had the authority (which he often does not). The result is the
same in either case: a deconcentration of power in the executive.

At the same time, the governor is not without any power over the
bureaucracy, and even where it is limited or less than it might be, it
still exists and should not be underrated. The governor sponsors
legislation affecting state agencies, submits policy proposals, reports
reorganization plans affecting the administration to the state legislature, addresses the legislature and the public on matters of concern

to state agencies, usually prepares the state budget (executive budget), may have discretion over the allocation of appropriated funds, serves as a chief conduct for officials in local governments with business with state agencies (and the same at the federal level as noted), and has the constitutional authority to "execute the laws."

In addition, many governors are pressing to widen their appointment powers, and a number have been liberally using their executive reorganization authority to streamline their administrations and effect greater central direction; in all, 13 governors have the authority to reorganize by executive order, which, although usually requiring legislative confirmation, takes this power out of the legislature where it has traditionally been. And collectively, governors are lobbying in Washington to tailor federal legislation and administrative regulations toward expanding gubernatorial influence in the states, specifically through the National Governors' Conference.[37]

Also all states now have central clearinghouses to coordinate a wide range of federal assistance and other projects, a procedure stemming from recent national legislation and an Office of Management and Budget regulation (Circular A-95). Operating close to the chief executive, the state clearinghouses review and comment on proposed development projects, taking into account their consistency with overall state objectives, planning, and programming, and they are designed in part to strengthen the governor's control over the free-wheeling state bureaucracies. While some agencies have resisted its centralizing features and regard it as an infringement on their professional prerogatives, the process is viewed cautiously as a success by the Council of State Governments. With expanded state planning and an adopted state master plan, it could presumably be even more successful.

Of course, governors have political resources at their command, which can be helpful in bargaining with state agencies, and the party comes to mind in this respect. In some states, the governor's party has considerable patronage in key state agencies such as the highway and public works departments, and this can be tapped to improve the executive's position in the administration. Furthermore, the party provides the governor access to political leadership at the local level in all parts of the state, which may provide a ready base of support for high-priority gubernatorial programs. The governor is also popularly selected, and this can prove effective especially when he reminds agencies of the fact. And finally, governors like bureaucracies have links to interest groups, and the groups can serve gubernatorial ends just as they do those of administrative agencies. Governor Gilligan of Ohio recently mobilized a number of health groups to get support for additional Medicaid payments in the administration and the legislature, and DiSalle operated much the same before him. So have recent Pennsylvania governors such as Shapp, Scranton, and Leader, Maryland's governor Mandel, and many others.

Planning is just beginning to develop administratively in the states, and it is obvious from this section that it will have to have more than the governor's support to survive and get much done. It would appear that its political tasks would be the most important ones, and viewing the appropriate administrative structure and similar questions outside this frame will almost certainly set it back. It is clear that it will have to have ties to the governor as the literature now stresses, but it is equally clear that it will have to have legislative and interest group ties as well. Also, planning will be operating in a highly competitive state environment, and this will become especially noticeable if it tries to take on land-use control powers or other functions which impact on the programs of existing state agencies. Specifically, there is likely to be a good deal of tension between the state planning agency and the environmental/natural resources bureaucracies, that is, if the planning agency does anything other than "plan."

Courts

The courts represent the third branch of state government, and most states—over two-thirds of them—elect their judges. In a minority of states, the judiciary is appointed by the legislature, the governor, or the governor subject to a later popular vote (the most modern and professionally preferred plan). Direct gubernatorial judicial appointments are normally subject to legislative approval or limited to names supplied by a specially constituted panel. The organization of state courts was presented in Chapter 8, and we shall not go over it again, and the links of the courts to planning and land use were also covered.

Political Parties

Some states have competitive two-party systems and some do not. The incidence of one-party arrangements is especially high in the South (Democratic) and in some New England and midwestern states (Republican). In all, one study classifies seven states in the one-party Democratic column (Louisiana, Alabama, Mississippi, South Carolina, Texas, Georgia, Arkansas), no states as purely "one-party Republican," and five states as "modified one-party Republican" (North Dakota, Kansas, New Hampshire, South Dakota, and Vermont); ten states are in the "modified one-party Democratic" camp (North Carolina, Virginia, Florida, Tennessee, Maryland, Oklahoma, Missouri, Kentucky, West Virginia, New Mexico), and the remainder, or 28 states, had two-party systems. The classification system is based only on state offices and not the U. S. Senate, House of

Representatives, or votes for president, and it was done for the years 1956-70.[38]

One of the strongest correlates of party competition is the degree of urbanization, and the more the urbanization the greater the competition between the parties, but also income levels, percentage of the labor force in manufacturing and agriculture, and portion of the population that is of foreign stock. In brief, the higher the income, the greater the proportion of manufacturing and the lower that of agricultural workers, and the more the incidence of foreign stock in the population, the greater the interparty competition. Also party cohesion (in the legislature) is importantly linked with party competition, and it is high (both parties) in the states where the parties are the most competitive and low in one-party (lowest) and modified one-party states.

But what is the meaning of all this? What does it mean for public policy, perhaps planning policy? We do not know the answer for sure, but research provides some indication. It has been shown, for example, that high levels of interparty competition are significantly related to high levels of social welfare spending, although the extent to which these spending levels can be traced to party competition as opposed to other (possibly more basic) factors such as urbanization (social welfare outlays also rise with an increase in urbanization) is unclear.[39] It does seem that competition causes politicians to scramble to raise expenditures, as a means of pleasing special publics in the electorates, and if so, it is possible that greater party competition could mean more outlays for planning and land-use programs. Still land use is principally a regulatory area, and its success or failure can be less easily measured in appropriations levels than would be possible in education or welfare. The parties are generally not the chief variable involved in regulatory programs but interest groups, which are treated next.

Interest Groups

This book is about interest groups, and there is no real need for a special section on the subject. But suffice it to say that interest groups are found in all areas of state government, permeating the structure and informal processes, and this includes the executive, the governor, bureaucracies, legislatures and their committees, the courts, and any place where policy is made, proposed, or discussed. Interest groups will be represented in any important decision made by anyone in the state, and there is no way of keeping them out; nor would it be desirable to do so.

In planning and land use, the ones to watch are organized builders and developers (state builders' associations), organized local governments (state leagues of cities and associations of counties and town-ships), and organized state government interests (such as the National Governors' Conference, Council of State Planning Agencies, Council of State Governments, and National Legislative Conference), which, although operating nationally, have plenty of influence on particular states' policies.

The organized local governments are especially important since it is local governments that now have the planning and land-use powers and that are going to resist any real state programs in these areas. Their power in state capitals is typically great, and reapportionment of the state legislatures may have strengthened it (shifted powers to the cities, urban counties, and suburban local governments, which are best represented in the statewide lobbies).

One statistical study in Georgia found the Georgia Municipal Association to be one of the strongest sources of influence over state policy, and this was true both before and after reapportionment; the results can be seen in Table 4. The figures are divided into "before" and "after" reapportionment, and while the local governments got pretty much what they wanted out of the state legislature before reapportionment (with the exceptions of the years 1964 and 1965 in the House, when the record was not all that bad, and 1961 in the Senate), they did even better afterward. They did better, in other words, under conditions most like the present. This success rate for what the author calls "city" legislation probably means failure for state zoning, at least in many states and if it infringes too much on local powers. Certainly it spells defeat for comprehensive state zoning in the average state. Interesting, is it not? Now that the cities and suburbs have the power in state legislatures, no change affecting them is possible. Much evidence suggests moreover that Georgia is not all that unique, less so than Vermont it seems.

IMPLICATIONS FOR STATE PLANNING

It is not easy to assess the meaning of all this for state planning, not in the aggregate. It is clear that it is going to take more than the support of the governors, whether we are talking about what we propose in this book or what Congress is working on. It is going to take more than the support of the state legislatures, for they are clearly influenced by interest groups, the parties, governors, and others and in reality are not policy initiators but "arbiters" as a recent study concludes; they are especially influenced by the city lobby, which cannot be expected to support strong state land-use controls (only advisory "planning"). The courts likewise react to stimulants from others, especially in land-use aggrieved interests, although their role is crucial in this sense (they set precedents for the future by reacting to present stimuli).

TABLE 4

Outcome of Georgia Municipal Association
Supported and Opposed Bills and Resolutions

A. Before Reapportionment

Year	Supported Bills and Resolutions Introduced	Passed	Failed	Year	Opposed Bills and Resolutions Introduced	Passed	Failed
	Senate				Senate		
1960	3[a]	5[a]	0	1960	0	0	0
1961	0	8	0	1961	1	0	1
1962	0	5	0	1962	1	1	0
Totals	3	18	0	Totals	2	1	1
	House				House		
1960	2[a]	5[a]	0	1960	0	0	0
1961	10	8	2	1961	1	0	1
1962	6	5	1	1962	2	0	3
1963	12	7	5	1963	2	0	2
1964	8	4	4	1964	1	0	1
1965	11	6	5	1965	0	0	0
Totals	49	35	17	Totals	6	0	7

B. After Reapportionment

Senate

Year	Senate			Senate		
1963	0	7	0	0	0	0
1964	0	3	1	0	0	0
1965	2	8	1	0	0	0
1966	14	14	0	4	1	3
1967	14	13	1	3	0	3
Totals	30	45	3	7	1	6

House

Year	House			House		
1966	32	28	4	12[b]	0	13[b]
1967	41	34	7	8[b]	0	8[b]
Totals	73	62	11	20[b]	0	21[b]

[a] Excluding failures, the difference between bills introduced and passed is due to the fact that some passed bills were introduced in the other chamber. Such differences appear frequently in the table.

[b] In 1966 a total of 16 opposed bills and resolutions was introduced. All 16 failed, but for 3 of them the chamber of introduction could not be traced. The three are here recorded as introduced in the House, where most other bills were introduced. They are also recorded as having failed in the House.

Source: Brett W. Hawkins, "Consequences of Reapportionment in Georgia," in Richard I. Hofferbert and Ira Sharkansky (eds.), State and Urban Politics (Boston: Little, Brown, 1971), Table 4, p. 294. Reprinted with permission.

It is our judgment that state zoning, if it is to succeed, will have
to be based on present patterns in state government, most notably a
kind of decentralized administration dominated and thoroughly political
decision-making process. This means that the programs will have to
be specialized and "fragmented." This is not all that bad, and in any
event it reflects the realities of American state politics. What it means
for Congress is that it will have to offer special inducements to the
states to do special things, such as grants for state flood plain controls,
state wetlands management, state-induced regional planning, and
revision of state zoning, planning, and subdivision enabling legislation;
this follows the pattern already set in the 1972 coastal zone management act. It means as well that powerful interest groups such as
builders, environmentalists, and others will have to back the state
planning agency (they can fight over the specifics) and perhaps gain
direct representation on state planning boards for state planning to
have any real meaning.

It also suggests that we can have comprehensive "planning"—
not zoning, but planning. The other state bureaucracies and local
governments are not too upset with central planning (they may not like
it, but they are not too upset) as long as it remains innocuous and
does not get into controls, or at least comprehensive controls such as
statewide zoning. There is no other way to do it. The states' political
systems are established, and they have been in operation for years.
They are not going to change, no matter what the outside force, given
present probabilities.

The only alternative to this is the creation of some very powerful
interest that has much to gain by direct and comprehensive statewide
land-use controls, and frankly we cannot see that interest anywhere
on the horizon. Probably the closest to it is developers, especially
the big ones, but most reformers do not like to work with them; so
this may rule it out. Besides, developers are split, and many prefer
the present system of local controls, however undesirable, since it
is a known evil. The cities cannot be counted on in this respect, and
in fact they will oppose it, vigorously in many cases. The federal
government will simply have to build on these conditions; it cannot
circumvent them, not with all the reorganization and "centralizing"
inducements it can provide.[40] We can make progress, and the states
can do more than they are doing at present. But what they will do
will have to fall within a frame that already exists and is compatible
with it. This will mean slower progress, but it will be progress non-
theless.

The courts can help too, and this means mostly the state courts.
They can begin to see the "general welfare" more in regional and
less in local terms, and they will need help from the state legislatures
and governors—but whether they can get it is uncertain. Can the legislatures as a political matter afford to antagonize the localities and
the suburbs, particularly after reapportionment? It is, after all, the

suburbs that have gained most in the bodies and that are the most fearful of state interference in the land-use area. The answer is unclear.

It will take at least a central city-minority group-developer-landowner alliance to loosen the suburban grip in the statehouses insofar as planning and zoning are concerned. The governors have always had a (more) popular base and thus are faced with the same pressures as legislatures now are (local, suburban), but still governors may have more freedom than the legislatures and may on occasion be able to override suburban or other local constituencies. The courts are probably the best bet in getting broader criteria introduced into local zoning and land-use decision making, acting alone, that is, but they will not be acting in the interests of property owners as much as a new "public interest."

NOTES

1. The State of the States in 1974: Responsive Government for the Seventies (Washington, D. C.: National Governors' Conference, 1974), p. 4.

2. Robert H. Weber and Ralph J. Marcelli (eds.), The Book of the States, 1972-73 (Lexington, Ky.: Council of State Governments, 1972).

3. For a study of state education politics and decision making and especially the influence of the bureaucracy on school policy, see Stephen K. Bailey and others, Schoolmen and Politics (Syracuse: Syracuse University Press, 1962). The relative power of the education lobby in state politics is assessed in Harmon Zeigler and Michael Baer, Lobbying (Belmont, Calif.: Wadsworth, 1969), pp. 32-33.

4. See R. Joseph Novogrod and others, Casebook in Public Administration (New York: Holt, Rinehart and Winston, 1969), Chap. 2.

5. See, for example, Richard G. RuBino, A Quest for Integrated and Balanced Transportation Systems in State Government (Tallahassee, Fla.: Florida State University, 1971).

6. James L. Martin and Vincent T. Smith, The Intergovernmental Cooperation Act of 1968: Federal and State Implementation (Washington, D. C.: Council of State Governments, 1971). See also B. Douglas Harman, "Areawide Review of Federal Grant Applications: Implications for Urban Management," Urban Data Service Reports, International City Management Association, 4 no. 2, (February 1972), 23 pp.

7. Block grants have since been approved in a few other areas including manpower. For a discussion of the different types of grants, see Michael D. Reagan, The New Federalism (New York: Oxford University Press, 1972) and Arthur W. Macmahon, Administering Federalism in a Democracy (New York: Oxford University Press, 1972).

228   THE STATES AND LAND-USE CONTROLS

8. Vincent J. Moore, "Politics, Planning, and Power in New York State: The Path from Theory to Reality," in Journal of the American Institute of Planners 37, no. 2 (March 1971): pp. 66-77.

9. Fred Bosselman and David Callies, The Quiet Revolution in Land-Use Control (Washington, D. C.: Government Printing Office, 1972), pp. 164-186.

10. For general information on the subject, see chapters by Bernard J. Frieden and John Myer in Samuel H. Beer and Richard E. Barringer (eds.), The State and the Poor (Cambridge, Mass.: Winthrop, 1970), pp. 107-163.

11. John N. Kolesar, "The States and Urban Planning and Development," in Alan K. Campbell (ed.), The States and the Urban Crisis (Englewood Cliffs, N. J.: Prentice-Hall, 1970), pp. 116-119.

12. Elizabeth H. Haskell and others, Managing the Environment: Nine States Look for Answers (Washington, D. C.: Woodrow Wilson International Center for Scholars, Smithsonian Institution, 1971), pp. 162-204.

13. See Morton Grodzins, The American System: A New View of Government in the United States (Chicago: Rand McNally, 1966). For a discussion of others who adhere to this view, see Richard H. Leach, American Federalism (New York: W. W. Norton & Co., 1970), Chap. 1.

14. See Thomas R. Dye, "A Comparison of Constituency Influences in the Upper and Lower Chambers of a State Legislature," Western Political Quarterly XIV (1961): 473-480.

15. Malcolm E. Jewell and Samuel C. Patterson, The Legislative Process in the United States, 2nd ed. (New York: Random House, 1973).

16. Douglass Cater, Power in Washington (New York: Random House, 1964).

17. Thomas R. Dye, "State Legislative Politics," in Herbert Jacob and Kenneth N. Vines (eds.), Politics in the American States (Boston: Little, Brown, 1965), p. 199.

18. Ibid, 2nd ed. (1971), pp. 163-209.

19. V. O. Key, Jr., American State Politics (New York: Knopf, 1956); Duane Lockard, New England State Politics (Chicago: Henry Regnery, 1959); Allan P. Sindler, Huey Long's Louisiana: State Politics, 1920-52 (Baltimore: Johns Hopkins Press, 1956); and John H. Fenton, Midwest Politics (New York: Holt, 1966).

20. See Ira Sharkansky, Spending in the American States (Chicago: Rand McNally, 1969).

21. Ira Sharkansky, Regionalism in American Politics (Indianapolis: Bobbs-Merrill, 1969). See also his Public Administration 2nd ed. (Chicago: Markham, 1972), pp. 298-304.

22. See Summary, Twenty-Seventh Annual Meeting of the Southern Legislative Conference, Hot Springs, Arkansas, July 17-20, 1973 (Atlanta: Council of State Governments Southern Office, 1973).

23. The Citizens Conference report is John Burns, The Sometime Governments: A Critical Study of the 50 American Legislatures (New York: Bantam Books, 1971).

24. Joseph A. Schlesinger, "The Politics of the Executive," in Jacob and Vines (eds.), op. cit., 2nd ed. (1971), p. 232.

25. Ira Sharkansky, "Agency Requests, Gubernatorial Support, and Budget Success in State Legislatures," American Political Science Review 62 (December 1968): 1220-1231.

26. Wayne L. Francis, Legislative Issues in the Fifty States (Chicago: Rand McNally, 1967), pp. 76-77.

27. Wallace the "populist" is portrayed in Thomas R. Dye and L. Harmon Zeigler, The Irony of Democracy, 2nd ed. (Belmont, Calif.: Wadsworth/Duxbury, 1972), pp. 151-154.

28. Robert B. Highsaw, "The Southern Governor—Challenge to the Strong Executive Theme?" Public Administration Review XIX (Winter 1959): 7-11.

29. Research generally assumes that the governor or the legislature controls the bureaucracy, and the questions are phrased only this way. See Deil S. Wright, "Executive Leadership in State Administration," Midwest Journal of Political Science 11 (February 1967): 1-26.

30. Richard E. Neustadt, Presidential Power (New York: Wiley, 1960).

31. Theodore J. Lowi, The End of Liberalism (New York: Norton, 1969). Lowi also describes the process (interest group liberalism) as "corporatism" and "syndicalism" and calls for a reassertion of public authority in its place. The argument is similar to Walter Lippmann's in The Public Philosophy (New York: New American Library, 1955).

32. See Andrew Hacker, "Pressure Politics in Pennsylvania: The Truckers vs. The Railroads," in Alan F. Westin (ed.), The Uses of Power (New York: Harcourt Brace Jovanovich, 1962), pp. 323-376.

33. Helen Leavitt, Superhighway—Superhoax (Garden City, N.Y.: Doubleday, 1970).

34. This is a tactic that Schumpeter properly associates with "politicians," but it is also used by administrators. See Joseph A. Schumpeter, Capitalism, Socialism, and Democracy 3rd ed. (New York: Harper, 1950), p. 268.

35. Ira Sharkansky, "State Administrators in the Political Process," in Jacob and Vines (eds.), op. cit., 2nd ed. (1971), pp. 248-252.

36. Alan P. Grimes, American Political Thought, rev. ed. (New York: Holt, Rinehart and Winston, 1960), pp. 103-108.

37. The governors, for example, call for the creation of a single Transportation Trust Fund at the national level (highway, mass transit, airport) and urge the billions of dollars in it to be sent directly to the governor since he is "best able to determine the transportation needs and priorities of his state. . . ." Policy Positions 1973-74 (Washington, D. C.: National Governors' Conference), p. 74.

38. Austin Ranney, "Parties in State Politics," in Jacob and Vines (eds.), op. cit., 2nd ed. (1971), p. 87.

39. Ira Sharkansky and Richard I. Hofferbert, "Dimensions of State Politics, Economics, and Public Policy," American Political Science Review 63 (1969): 867-879.

40. The reorganization condition to federal grants is discussed in Henry S. Reuss, Revenue-Sharing: Crutch or Catalyst for State and Local Governments (New York: Praeger Publishers, 1970). Congressman Reuss (D-Wisc.) backs the idea.

10

**CONCLUSIONS:
WHERE WE GO
FROM HERE**

The book has an important message, and we shall restate it here as clearly as we can. Let us summarize what has come out of each chapter first. Chapter 1 gives an introduction to the state planning system. Chapter 2 demonstrates that state planning has deep roots in the American tradition and that it is not new. This is so in spite of the fact that contemporary politicians are attempting to cast it in an "innovative" light. We saw that planning at this level could be traced back beyond the founding fathers, to the colonial legislatures, and more recently to the New Deal era. Important legislation in the earlier period set a pattern to be later resurrected.

State planning in the 1930s was limited in terms that we understand today, but it was a start in the current age. With a short-lived emphasis on economic development after the war, we appear to be now returning to more comprehensive planning the states, and the future is generally bright in this regard. Yet the state record in planning is mixed, and the state legislatures have been particularly disinclined to provide the kind of broad-based enabling authorizations to local planning and governing bodies that are needed to widen local planning and land-use perspectives.

Chapter 3 introduced us to the general concepts and lexicon of state planning and related the field to proposed national land-use policy. We found that the latter policy has been significantly based on direct state planning and land-use control, especially zoning for "critical areas." The chapter then turned to Hawaii, sometimes cited as a model for stronger state land-use powers in the mainland states. The chapter gave little encouragement to this tendency and showed how Hawaii differs in key and significant respects from most of the other states and how its patterns of land-use control and ownership are at variance with those in the other states. Hawaii, in other words, is atypical, and what we discovered there cannot be used widely as a model elsewhere.

Yet much can be learned from the Hawaii experience, as much what not to do as what to do. Hawaii's four-zone plan on the other hand, does hold promise for other states, and the conservation, agriculture, and rural zones are particularly applicable here. The state has made considerable substantive progress in its planning and land-use program, but its administrative apparatus lags somewhat behind. In actual practice, we found local control to be the dominant pattern in this state for most zoning categories, notwithstanding the strong legal and formal role of the state in planning and zoning there, and this suggests that Hawaii's practice may not differ greatly in reality from that in most other states.

Vermont represents a different story, and Chapter 4 indicates that it may be a better model. It is the only other state and the only state on the mainland that has a statewide system of planning and zoning in effect, and this is obviously its importance. We discovered Vermont's program to be working fairly well, in the sense that it has been enacted and that the state has been able to determine development where otherwise it would not have been controlled by any government authority or would have been controlled by local government. Vermont's history and tradition are also somewhat more like those of other states than Hawaii's, although there is no strong municipal or "town" lobby there to interfere with the state effort. One professional assessment of the state's land-use law is that it is "progressing well," and this is our judgment too.

On the plus side, Vermont's planning program is law, and this is not true anywhere else at either the state or local level in this country since planning is typically advisory; relations between the state and localities are generally good; the state's zoning is flexible, "modern," and "positive"; the state is actually enforcing its land-use law, and this may give it an advantage over Hawaii, which is a little weak in this regard; and there is considerable citizen involvement in its administration. Still there are some problems, and two experts who have studied the situation closely report that the Vermont plan is cutting into the supply of low- and moderate-income housing, and this cannot be favorable. Land-use and planning developments in a few other states including Oregon and Florida are also covered in this chapter, and some progress is apparently being made there.

Chapter 5 is on specialized state zoning and covers strip mining, power plant siting, flood plain, coastal zone, wetlands, and other forms of comparable zoning and land-use regulation powers. In sum, more and more states are getting into each of these areas as time goes on, and the future holds much more of the same in store. The Maryland case study at the end of the chapter shows the importance of local governments and local interests in shaping state legislation, state administration, and proposed land-use bills, and suggests that states with similar political structures may encounter real difficulties from the local government lobby in seeking statewide zoning and planning authority. Some suggestions on tactics are proposed in this chapter, and this includes most notably working local governments well into the administration of any program enacted; while this means less independent state influence, it may mean a state program, and its absence may mean none. The California experience with Proposition 20 on coastal zoning suggests this conclusion.

The broader lesson may be that states should avoid comprehensive planning and land-use controls, even for "critical areas" (which could turn out as comprehensive zoning and which are commonly viewed this way by local governments), and concentrate on specialized forms of state zoning covering wetlands, coastal areas power plants, flood plains, and the like. This is based on the political realities in the states and not necessarily an idealized conception. This will also require a change in the federal approach so far, which is based on more comprehensive controls for the states.

We also suggested a strategy in Chapter 6 for the states in regard to regional planning. It is the states that set the ground rules and that have the police powers. They are, as the Advisory Commission on Intergovernmental Relations has called them, the "strategic middlemen" in the effort to establish meaningful regionalism and effective "confederalism" in the states.[1] It is the states that can promote metropolitan, regional, rural, and interstate centralizations, and their actions in the case of the Twin Cities Metropolitan Council (Minnesota), the New Jersey Hackensack Meadowlands Development Commission, the San Francisco Bay Conservation and Development Commission, the Tahoe Regional Planning Agency (interstate), and Indianapolis' metro government suggest that they are capable of important moves in this direction; in some cases, the action has come over local government oppostion. Our only suggestion is that more regional agencies including substate districts be given operating programs such as sewers, airports, water supply, and mass transit, providing them a broader perspective and likely more efficient and economical operations. Operating assignments will also strengthen the regional agencies in the political sense.

Perhaps the states have been most derelict in providing workable enabling legislation to localities in such areas as planning, zoning, subdivision controls, and housing, and the greatest good can probably be done here. Chapter 7 shows how state enabling legislation in these fields is fragmented, out-of-date, overly detailed, and negative; how it lacks in consideration of regional factors and needs and in providing housing for all income groups; and how it is negligent in taking public facilities' needs and their provision into account. We propose key revisions in this area, and this will require sweeping and courageous actions on the part of the states. Many local governments will resist the changes and will lobby against them, and this will not make the task any easier.

Our approach requires the establishment of no new agency, no new professional staff, no research bureau—only some serious thought by state legislators and administrators including planners and by university people as to how enabling authorizations can be rewritten and gotten through state legislatures. We provide no model statute, although the one from the American Law Institute might serve as a guide. It is especially crucial that the community and neighborhood focus gives way to metropolitan, regional, statewide, interstate, and even national considerations—and this by law. The legal changes will be the beginning, but as the chapter shows, this will have to be followed by political and administrative changes, which are equally important if not more so. We have suggested steps that the federal government can take in promoting these changes.

Chapter 8 takes a close look at the role of the courts in state and local zoning and planning matters, especially the state judiciary. We found that the federal courts have generally deferred to state tribunals on planning/zoning questions, and it is the state bodies that set the tone here. The federal judiciary has upheld zoning and its constitutionality, and this has been its major contribution; it has also set the "presumption of validity" test which state courts follow. State courts have typically looked more favorably on wider (in terms of area) exercises and delegations of land-use powers, which has to be a plus. In general, they have sustained wide-ranging zoning and land regulation powers at both the state and local levels.

It is worth noting that the battles in the last few years and likely in the future are not apt to be between "public" and "private" (property) rights as much as between two sets of public rights, often "local" versus "regional" and "minority" versus "suburban." The courts have generally thrown out land-use decisions only when they have conflicted with some other public rights and only rarely when only property rights are involved. In all, broad authorizations to state and local agencies in the planning and land-use field are almost certain to be upheld in the courts, and this includes the use of the police power and government regulation for aesthetic purposes, the most far-reaching of this authority.

Chapter 9 points out that planning does not take place in a vacuum and that it is part of a broader political system. We attempted to see how it related to this system, how it was affected by the system, and how it affected it. All of the key functions of the states were found to be related to planning in some important way, and this included education, transportation, health and welfare, law enforcement and public protection, housing and development, natural resources, labor and industrial relations, and public utility regulation. The chapter described centralization in state legislatures, decentralization in state executives, the effects of legislative and administrative actions and policies on planning, the ties of courts to planning, political party organization in the states and the probable effects of different patterns of party competition on planning and land-use policy, and the interest and influence of pressure groups in state planning.

We concluded in Chapter 9 that any change in planning policy will have to consider present patterns in state government, especially a marked tendency toward decentralization in the executive branch and a thoroughly political decision-making process in general. This means that greater emphasis should be put by federal and state planners on specialized zoning and land-use control programs in the states and the use of government powers at these levels to encourage such programs. The governors of the states may play a particularly strong part in the effort, and almost certainly the courts will. The critical need is to interject wider points of view and broader interests into the whole planning and land-use control process at both the state and local levels. If we can do this, state planning will be successful; if not, we can expect more of the same. We might also say that the sooner we get comprehensive planning in the states the better. What we have to say about zoning definitely does not apply to planning, as planning is possible in the states.

So where do we go from here? The courses have been set in this book. We shall testify on legislation related to the subject in the states and in Congress, and we hope others will do the same. We need more money for state planning; there is no question about this. But the real need is deeper than that. We need good decisions, decisions that take the kind of thought and consideration that state legislators are somewhat unaccustomed to—and that is the kind that may encounter interest group opposition and attract only limited support from affected interests. This is so because it is mostly the allocation of power that has to be changed. Power has to be shifted from communities to metropolitan areas, and from metropolitan areas to the states; short of this, the decisions exercised at the local or metropolitan levels have to consider broader interests and viewpoints. The housing needs of the poor in cities are important as input in suburban land-use decisions, but they are rarely if ever raised. The transportation needs of state residents are important in the suburbs, and yet no organized group speaks for these needs in most areas. The planning needs of the metropolitan area as a whole must be considered in suburban decisions, and yet they usually are not. Pollution control programs cannot stop at local boundaries, or even state ones, and new instruments are required to deal with such problems across these borders.

We do not say that we have the answer, but we know how to get a start in the right direction. Changes in state zoning and planning enabling legislation are the most important changes that can be effected in the coming years, and these may be the hardest to achieve since key groups are dependent on present assignments. But it is worth the try, and the alternative is direct central control, possibly direct federal zoning. Most people and state and local officials do not want this, it seems to us, but inaction on the enabling legislation front will virtually guarantee it. This is the way we view it from our vantage point.

NOTE

1. Advisory Commission on Intergovernmental Relations, Regional Decision Making: New Strategies for Substate Districts (Washington, D.C.: Government Printing Office, 1973), p. 14.

239

Maryland Municipal League, 116, 123
Maryland-National Capital Park and Planning Commission, 39, 110, 145, 147, 150, 155
McCall, Tom, 21, 70, 95
McFarland, J. Horace, 42
McMahon, Arthur W., 76, 113
metropolitan government, 139-140, 150, 233
metropolitan planning, 12
Mississippi Forestry Association, 62
Missouri Farm Bureau Federation, 62
Model Land Development Code, 58, 59, 91, 97, 145, 234
Moore, Vincent, 36
Muskie, Edmund S., 209

Nader's Raiders, 102
National Association for the Advancement of Colored People, 188
National Association of Counties, 14
National Association of Regional Councils, 14
National Cattlemen's Association, 62
National Capital Planning Commission, 165
National Commission on Urban Problems, 45, 47, 113, 162
National Environmental Policy Act of 1969, 139, 165
National Governors' Conference, 14, 27, 54, 109, 205, 220, 223; southern branch of, 213
National Industrial Recovery Act, 24, 160
national land-use policy, 56-60, 101, 111, 125
National League of Cities, 14, 27
National Legislative Conference, 14, 130, 205, 223

National Planning Board, 24
Nebraska Farm Bureau Federation, 62
Neustadt, Richard, 83
Nevada Tahoe Regional Agency, 149
New Mexico Cattlegrowers' Association, 62
New York State Conference of Mayors, 47
North Carolina Forestry Association, 62
Northwest Michigan Economic Development District, 142-143
Northwest Ordinance of 1787, 22

Office of Management and Budget, U.S., 12, 220
official map, defined, 153
Oklahoma Cattlemen's Association, 62
Olmsted, Frederick Law, 42, 43, 45
Oregon land-use controls, 95-96, 107, 168-169

Petaluma plan, 189, 195, 196
political parties, 6, 14, 26, 56, 70, 137, 221-222; influence in courts, 179; and Vermont controls, 80-81;
political system: and systems analysis, 1-16
Polynesian law, 60
Plato, 120

Ramapo plan, 85, 166-167, 194-195
Ranney, David, 46
Reagan, Michael D., 90
Reagan, Ronald, 214
regionalism in state politics, 213
regional planning, 12, 15-16, 44, 143-147
Regional Planning Council, Baltimore, 39, 112
revenue sharing, 12
Rockefeller Brothers, 56
Rockefeller, Nelson, 13

Roosevelt, Franklin, 24

Saloman, Thomas P., 00, 01, 03, 91
San Francisco Bay Conservation
  and Development Commission,
  38, 145, 150, 233
Schlesinger, Joseph A., 83
Scranton, William, 220
Seattle Metro, 140-141, 150
Shapp, Milton J., 220
Sharkansky, Ira, 1, 3, 9, 213
Sher, William, 109
Siegen, Bernard H., 69, 169, 187
Sierra Club, 13, 56
Skinner, B.F., 49
social Darwinism, and planning,
  17, 23, 160
South Dakota Stockgrowers' Association, 62
Southeast Michigan Council of
  Governments, 142-143
Southern Legislative Conference,
  213
Standard City Planning Enabling
  Act, 44, 155
Standard State Zoning Enabling
  Act, 41, 155, 160
state administrative boards and
  commissions, 215-219
state coastal zone regulations,
  104-106
state controlling boards, 219
state critical areas controls, 108,
  109-125, 207
state flood plain controls, 103-104
state legislative committees, 114-
  115, 211-212
state planning agency, 7-10
state planning boards, 24
state power plant siting, 102-103
state public service commissions,
  102, 103, 210-211
state spending patterns, 202
state strip mining control, 101-102
state subdivision controls, 107

state wetlands controls, 106-107
subdivision controls, defined, 153;
  in local governments, 155; in
  states, 107
substate districting, 12, 14, 39, 141-
  143, 150
Sundquist, James L., 141

Taft, Robert A., 26
Tahoe Regional Planning Agency,
  149, 233
Texas Association of Soil and Water
  Conservation Districts, 62
Texas Forestry Association, 62
Texas Sheep and Goat Association,
  62
transferable development rights, 172
Transportation Department, U.S., 12
Twin Cities Metropolitan Council,
  145, 146, 150, 233

Urban Development Corporation,
  New York, 207
Urban Land Institute, 87
urban renewal, 185
U.S. Advisory Committee on City
  Planning and Zoning, 44
U.S. Civil Rights Commission, 188
U.S. Conference of Mayors, 14, 27
Utah League of Cities and Towns,
  47

Veiller, Lawrence, 42
Vermont:
  Environmental Board, 83, 87, 90,
    91;
  and governmental power, 88-93;
  and housing, 93;
  interest groups in, 81-82;
  International Paper Co., 82;
  Landowners' Steering Committee,
    82, 93;
  land-use controls, 78-95;
  parties, in, 80-81;
  and planning, 83-84, 85-87, 89-

90, 91-103;
population density, 95;
and zoning, 83
Vermont Citizens' League, 82
Vermont League of Cities and
Towns, 82, 114
Vermont Natural Resources
Council, 82
Vermont Watchman, 93

Walker, Jack, 95
Walker, Robert, 45
Wallace, George, 214
Washington Post, 36, 111
Whyte, William H., 104
Wyoming Association of Conserva-
tion Districts, 62

Zeigler, Harmon, 121
zoning: Charlevoix County, Mich.,

62, 169, 170;
defined, 153;
and density bonus plan, 162, 166;
Euclid decision, 179, 183-184,
186, 187, 195, 198;
history of, 41, 43;
and housing, 68-69, 162;
in Houston, 170;
and innovative techniques, 174-175;
large lot, 197
Model Land Development Code,
58, 59;
negative nature of, 159-160;
and Ogle County, Ill., 62;
and Polynesian law, 60;
and public facilities, 162-165,
166-167;
Standard State Zoning Enabling
Act, 48, 155, 161;
state property and institutions, 107

R. ROBERT LINOWES practices law in the Maryland suburbs of
metropolitan Washington and in the District of Columbia. He has
served as zoning attorney for some of the largest developments on
the east coast as well as for municipalities and citizens' groups. His
firm, Linowes and Blocher, has represented the developers of a number of major office-shopping-residential complexes.

Mr. Linowes is coauthor of another title in the Praeger Special
Studies series, The Politics of Land Use, published in 1973, and he
has been an innovator in developing new land-use concepts contributing
to orderly development. Mr. Linowes served in the county attorney's
office in Montgomery County and currently is advising the government
of the District of Columbia on inner-city redevelopment.

Mr. Linowes has an L. L. B. from Columbia University and is a
member of the American, Maryland, District of Columbia, and Montgomery County Bar Associations and the American Society of Planning
Officials.

DON T. ALLENSWORTH has been Visiting Lecturer at the University of Pennsylvania, where he was affiliated with the faculty of the
Fels Institute of Local and State Government. He serves as an expert
witness for citizens' groups and developers on planning and zoning
matters, and has been a consultant to city planning commissions.

Dr. Allensworth is the author of The Political Realities of Urban
Planning, published in 1975 as part of the Praeger Special Studies
series, and coauthor of The Politics of Land Use, also in the Praeger
Special Studies series and published in 1973. He is author of Public
Administration, a college text published in 1973, and of three books
in the U. S. Government in Action series: Essentials, a basic text
on American national government; Public Policy and Change, a text
on contemporary political issues; and Policy and Structure, a text
on American government and public policy. He is also coauthor of
The Politics of States and Urban Communities, published in 1971.

THE POLITICAL REALITIES OF URBAN PLANNING
Don T. Allensworth

THE POLITICS OF LAND USE: Planning, Zoning,
and the Private Developer
R. Robert Linowes and
Don T. Allensworth

LAND USE AND THE GOVERNMENT PROCESS:
The San Francisco Bay Area Experience
edited by Edward Ellis
Smith and Durward S.
Riggs

LAND BANKING IN THE CONTROL OF URBAN
DEVELOPMENT
Harvey L. Flechner

COMMUNITY DEVELOPMENT STRATEGIES:
Case Studies of Major Model Cities
Goerge J. Washnis

NONGROWTH PLANNING STRATEGIES: The
Developing Power of Towns, Cities, and Regions
Earl Finkler and David
L. Peterson; introduction
by William J. Toner